The Flaming Sword in Serbia and Elsewhere

by

M. A. Stobart

Double 9
BOOKS

The Flaming Sword in Serbia and Elsewhere
by M. A. Stobart

ISBN: 978-93-61421-31-0

Published by

DOUBLE 9 BOOKS

2/13-B, Ansari Road
Daryaganj, New Delhi – 110002
info@double9books.com
www.double9books.com
Tel. 011-40042856

ABOUT THE AUTHOR

M. A. Stobart was a British nurse, author, and suffragist, full name Millicent Annie Stobart. She was well-known for her humanitarian efforts and her autobiographical writings. She was born on September 12, 1870. Stobart first received her nursing training in the London Hospital, where she fell in love with helping people. She served as a volunteer nurse with the Scottish Women's Hospitals for Foreign Service during World War I. Dr. Elsie Inglis established this organisation to offer medical support to soldiers. Throughout her service, Stobart worked tirelessly to care for injured soldiers and civilians in a number of locales, including Serbia. Her memoir, "The Flaming Sword in Serbia and Elsewhere," was published in 1916 and was based on her experiences during the war. Her personal story of her time working as a nurse in Serbia is told in detail in the book, which also sheds light on the effects of the conflict on the area. Apart from her profession as a nurse and writer, Stobart actively participated in the suffrage campaign, championing the cause of women's equality and rights. She took part in suffragette actions such as hunger strikes and protests and was a member of the Women's Social and Political Union (WSPU).

CONTENTS

PART III

PREFACE

I have written this book in the first person, because it would be an affectation to write in the neuter person about these things which I have felt and seen.

But if the book has interest, this should lie, not only in the personal experiences, but in the effect which these have had upon the beliefs of a modern woman who is probably representative of other women of her century.

I believe that humankind is at the parting of the ways. One way leads to evolution—along spiritual lines—the other to devolution—along lines of materialism; and the sign-post to devolution is militarism. For militarism is a movement of retrogression, which will bring civilisation to a standstill—in a *cul-de-sac*.

And I believe that militarism can only be destroyed with the help of Woman. In countries where Woman has least sway, militarism is most dominant. Militarism is maleness run riot.

Man's dislike of militarism is prompted by sentiment, or by a sense of expediency. It is not due to instinct; therefore it is not forceful. The charge of human life has not been given by Nature to Man. Therefore, to Man, the preservation of life is of less importance than many other things. Nature herself sets an example of recklessness with males; she creates, in the insect world, millions of useless male lives for one that is to serve the purpose of maleness. It is said that the proportion of male may-flies to female is six thousand to one. Nature behaves similarly—though with more moderation—with male human babies. More males than females are born, but fewer males survive. Is war perhaps another extravagant device of Nature; or is society, which encourages war, blindly copying Nature for the same end?

On the other hand, Woman's dislike of militarism is an instinct.

Life—for Woman—is not a seed which can be sown broadcast, to take root, or to perish, according to chance. For Woman, life is an individual charge; therefore, for Woman, the preservation of life is of more importance than many other things.

By God and by Man, the care of life is given to Woman, before and after birth. With all her being, Woman—primitive Woman—has defended that life as an individual concrete life; and with all her being, Woman—modern Woman—must now, in an enlarged sphere, defend the abstract life of humankind.

Therefore, it is good that Woman shall put aside her qualms, and go forth and see for herself the dangers that threaten life.

Therefore it is good that Woman shall record, as Woman, and not as neuter, the things which she has felt, and seen, during an experience of militarism at first hand.

PART I

CHAPTER I

To go through the horrors of war, and keep one's reason—that is hell. Those who have seen the fiery Moloch, licking up his human sacrifices, will harbour no illusions; they will know that the devouring deity of War is an idol, and no true God. The vision is salutary; it purges the mind from false values, and gives courage for the exorcism of abominations still practised by a world which has no knowledge of the God of Life. The abominations which are now practised in Europe, by twentieth century man, are no less abominable than those practised of old in the Valley of Hinnom. The heathen passed their sons and daughters through the fire, to propitiate their deity; the Lord God condemned the practice. We Christians pass our sons and daughters through the fire of bloody wars, to propitiate our deities of patriotism and nationalism. Would the Lord God not also condemn our practice? But we, alas! have no Josiah to act for the Lord God (2 Kings xxiii.). The heathen wept at the destruction of Baal, but the worship of the pure God prevailed. No one believes that his god is false, till it has been destroyed. Therefore, we must destroy militarism, in and through this war, and future generations will justify the deed.

I am neither a doctor nor a nurse, but I have occupied myself within the sphere of war for the following reasons.

After four years spent on the free veldt of the South African Transvaal, I returned to London (in 1907) with my mind cleared of many prejudices. The political situation into which I found myself plunged, was interesting. Both men and women were yawning themselves awake; the former after a long sleep, the latter for the first time in history. The men had been awakened by the premonitory echo of German cannons, and were, in lounge suits, beginning to look to their national defences. Women probably did not know what awakened them, but the same cannons were responsible.

For self-defence is the first law of sub-conscious nature; and the success of Prussian cannons would mean the annihilation of woman as the custodian of human life.

It was natural that woman's first cry should be for the political vote: influence without power is a chimera. But it was also natural that at a moment when national defence was the rallying shibboleth for men, the political claims of women should be by men disregarded. Political power without national responsibility would be unwisdom and injustice.

But was woman incapable of taking a responsible share in national defence?

I believed that prejudice alone stood in woman's way. Prejudice, however, is not eliminated by calling it prejudice. Practical demonstration that prejudice is prejudice, will alone dissipate the phantom.

But what form should woman's share in national defence assume? In these days of the supremacy of mechanical over physical force, woman's ability as a fighting factor could have been shown. But there were three reasons against experimenting in this direction.

Firstly, it would have been difficult to obtain opportunities for the necessary proof of capacity.

Secondly, woman could not fight better than man, even if she could fight as well, and, as an argument for the desirability of giving woman a share in national responsibility, it would be unwise to present her as a performer of less capacity than man. The expediency of woman's participation in national defence could best be proved by showing that there was a sphere of work in which she could be at least as capable as man.

Thirdly, and of primary importance, if the entrance of women into the political arena is an evolutionary movement—forwards and not backwards—woman must not encumber herself with legacies of male traditions likely to compromise her freedom of evolvement *along the line of life.*

If the Woman's Movement has, as I believe, value in the scheme of creation, it must tend to the furtherance of life, and not of death.

Now, militarism means supremacy of the principle that to produce death is, on occasions—many occasions—more useful than to preserve life. Militarism has, in one country at least, reached a climax, and I believe it is because we women feel in our souls that life has a meaning, and a value, which are in danger of being lost in militarism, that we are at this moment instinctively asking for a share in controlling those human lives for which Nature has made us specially responsible. "Intellect," says Bergson, "is characterised by a natural inability to comprehend life." Woman may be less heavily handicapped in an attempt to understand it?

It may well have been the echo of German cannons which aroused woman to self-consciousness.

Demonstration, therefore, of the capacity of woman to take a useful share in national defence must be given in a sphere of work in which preservation, and not destruction of life, is the objective. Such work was the care of the sick and wounded.

In a former book, *War and Women*, an account has been given of the founding of the "Women's Convoy Corps," as the practical result of these ideas. The work which was accomplished by members of this Corps, in Bulgaria, during the first Balkan War, 1912-13, afforded the first demonstration of the principle that women could efficiently work in hospitals of war, not only as nurses—that had already been proved in the Crimean War—but as doctors, orderlies, administrators, in every department of responsibility, and thus set men free for the fighting line.

I had hoped that, as far as I was concerned, it would never be necessary again to undertake a form of work which is to me distasteful. But when the German War broke out in August, 1914, I found to my disappointment, that the demonstration of 1912-13 needed corroboration. For I had one day the privilege of a conversation with an important official of the British Red Cross Society, and, to my surprise, he repeated the stale old story that women surgeons were not strong enough to operate in hospitals of war, and that women could not endure the hardships and privations incidental to campaigns.

I reminded him of the women at Kirk Kilisse. "Ah!" he replied, "that was exceptional." I saw at once that he, and those of whom he was representative, must be shown that it was not exceptional. But where there is no will to be convinced, the only convincing argument is the deed. Action is a universal language which all can understand.

I must, therefore, once more enter the arena; for my previous experience of war had corroborated my belief that the co-operation of woman in warfare, is essential for the future abolition of war; essential, that is, for the retrieval of civilisation. For these reasons I must not shirk.

CHAPTER II

I had gone to Bulgaria with open mind, prepared to judge for myself whether it was true that war calls forth valuable human qualities which would otherwise lie dormant, and whether it was true that the purifying influence of war is so great, that it compensates the human race for the disadvantages of war. My mind had been open for impressions of so-called glories of war.

But the glories which came under my notice in Bulgaria, were butchered human beings, devastated villages, a general callousness about the value of human life, that was for me a revelation. This time I should go out with no illusions about these martial glories.

But how should I go? To my satisfaction I found that the Bulgarian "first step" had led to an easy staircase, and when I offered the services of a Woman's Unit to the Belgian Red Cross, I was at once invited to establish a hospital in Brussels.

The St. John Ambulance Association, at the instigation of Lady Perrott, and the Women's Imperial Service League (which, with Lady Muir Mackenzie as Vice-Chairman, had been organised with the view of helping to equip women's hospital units), together with many other generous friends, provided money and equipment, and a Woman's Unit was assembled.

I went to Brussels in advance of the unit, to make arrangements, and was given, as hospital premises, the fine buildings of the University.

The day after arrival, I had begun the improvisation of lecture and class-rooms into wards, when, that same day, the work was interrupted by the entry of the Germans, who took possession of the Belgian Capital. During three days and nights the triumphant army, faultlessly equipped, paraded through the streets. For some hours I watched it from the second floor window of a restaurant in the Boulevard des Jardins Botaniques, together with my husband, who was to act as Hon. Treasurer, and the Vicar of the Hampstead Garden Suburb, who was to act as Chaplain to our unit. And my mind at once filled with presage of the tough job which the Allies had undertaken.

The picture upon which we looked was indeed remarkable. Belgium had been "safeguarded" from aggression, by treaties with the most civilised nations of the world. But here now were the legitimate inhabitants of the capital of Belgium standing in their thousands, gazing helplessly, in dumb bewilderment, whilst the army of one of these "most civilised" Governments streamed triumphantly, as conquerors, through their streets. And in all those streets, the only sounds were the clamping feet of the marching infantry, the clattering hoofs of the horses of the proud Uhlans and Hussars, and the rumbling of the wagons carrying murderous guns.

The people stood silent, with frozen hearts, beholding, as fossils might, the scenes in which they could no longer move.

For them, earth, air, sky, the whole world outside that never-ending procession, seemed expunged. No one noticed whether rain fell, or the sun shone, whilst that piteous pageant of triumphant enmity, passed, in ceaseless cinema, before their eyes.

All idea of establishing a hospital for the Allies had to be abandoned. The Croix Rouge was taken over by the Germans, and hospitals would be commandeered for German soldiers. My one desire was to get in touch with my unit; for they might, I thought, in response to the cable sent by the Belgian Red Cross, on the night of our arrival, be already on their way to join me, and might be in difficulties, surrounded by the Germans. Whatever personal risk might be incurred, I must leave Brussels.

The Consuls advised me to remain: they said I should not be able to obtain a passport from the German General. When I remonstrated, they shrugged their shoulders and said, "Well, go and ask him yourself!" I went, and obtained an officially stamped passport for myself and my two companions, who gallantly, and against my wishes, insisted on accompanying me, and sharing the risks of passing through the enemy's lines.

But, notwithstanding our stamped passport, we were, at Hasselt, arrested as spies, and at Tongres we were condemned to be shot within twenty-four hours. The story of our escape and eventual imprisonment, at Aachen, has been told elsewhere, but one remark of the German Devil-Major Commandant at Tongres, is so illuminative of the spirit of militarism that it bears repetition.

The Major said, "You are spies"; he fetched a big book from a shelf, opened it, and pointing on a certain page, he continued, "and the fate of spies is to be shot within twenty-four hours. Now you know your fate." I answered cheerily, as though it were quite a common occurrence to hear little fates like that, "but, mein Herr Major, I am sure you would not wish to do such an injustice. Won't you at least look at our papers, and see that what we have told you is true; we were engaged in hospital work when," etc. He then replied, and his voice rasped and barked like that of a mad dog, "You are English, and, whether you are right or wrong, *this is a war of annihilation.*"

I shall always be grateful for that phrase, for I recognised in it an epitome of the spirit of militarism, carried, as the Prussian arch-representatives of war carry it, to its logical extreme. For, according to modern militarism, war aims at annihilation of the enemy, and the enemy includes not only the combatants—these are the least offensive element—but the non-combatants, the men who represent the rival commerce, the women who represent the rival culture, and the men and women who represent codes of honour and humanity which are the beacons of the rival civilisation—at one and all of these, is aimed the blow which is delivered through the medium of the proxies in the field.

We three non-combatants—namely (a) a minister of the Holy Church, (b) a university man, who had officiated as judge in Burma, and (c) a woman engaged in hospital work, were now condemned to death, not because we represented a military danger, but because we represented, although in humble degree, those qualities of the rival nation, which had brought that nation to the front of civilisation. War aims at the annihilation, not of that which is bad, but of that which is best.

The Devil-Major, as we called him, then made us follow him upstairs, to the top floor, to a room in which we were to spend the night—the last night? He ordered me to be separated from the others, in another room, but I was responsible for the position of my companions, and without my influence—as a woman—death for them was certain, and I resisted the separation successfully. The Major then drove us into a room that was bare, except for verminous straw upon the floor. He refused to give us food, though we had not eaten since the day before, but water in tin cans was brought to us to drink, and we were told to lie down on the dirty straw.

The Devil-Major then warned the guards that if we moved, or talked to each other, they were to shoot us, then he left us for the night.

Sleep was impossible, owing to the ceaseless chiming of half-a-dozen church clocks, which seemed purposely to have clustered within a few hundred yards of us. The bells were all hopelessly out of tune, the tuners being presumably at the front; and every quarter of an hour all the bells of all the clocks, played different tunes, which lasted almost till the next quarter's chime was due. The discord was a nightmare for sensitive ears, but the harsh jangle of these bells, as they tumbled over each other, brutally callous to the jarring sounds, and to the irrelevancy of the melodies they played, seemed in keeping with the discordance—illustrated by our position—between the ideal of life, designed by God the Spirit, and the botching of that design, by murderous man.

Was our position, I wondered, another of the glories of war? These glories, exhibited at that time in Belgium, were, as I noticed, all of one stamp—devastation, murder of women and children, rapine, every form of demoniacal torture. All these glories are visualised, and not exaggerated, in the cartoons of Raemaekers.

But we three escaped by miracles, and returned safely to England.

CHAPTER III

I found that my unit had not yet left London, and I was able in a short time, with them, to accept an invitation from the Belgian Red Cross to go to Antwerp. We went out under the auspices of the St. John Ambulance Association, and established our hospital in the big Summer Concert Hall, in the Rue de l'Harmonie. Here once again the glories of war were manifested.

After three weeks' work upon the maimed and shattered remnants of manhood that were hourly brought to us from the trenches, the German bombardment of the city began. For eighteen hours our hospital unit was under shell fire, and I had the opportunity of seeing women—untrained to such scenes—during the nerve-racking strain of a continuous bombardment. They took no notice of the shells, which whizzed over our heads, without ceasing, at the rate of four a minute, and dropped with the bang of a thousand thunderclaps, burning, shattering, destroying everything around us.

The story of how these women rescued their wounded, carried them without excitement, as calmly as though they were in a Hyde Park parade, on stretchers, and when stretchers failed, upon their backs, from the glass-roofed hospital, down steep steps, to underground cellars, has also been told elsewhere.

We saved our wounded, but in the picture of the murderous shells, dropping at random, here, there, and everywhere; of the beautiful city of Antwerp in flames, its peaceful citizens, its women and children, with little bundles of household treasures in their arms, fleeing terror-stricken from their homes into the unknown: in all this it was difficult to see glory, except the glory triumphant of the enemy's superior make of guns—superior machinery.

Photo, Vandyk, C.
H.R.H. PRINCE ALEXANDER OF SERBIA

We lost, of course, all our hospital material, but once again, thanks to the Women's Imperial Service League and to the St. John Ambulance Association, now in conjunction with the British Red Cross Society, who also assisted us; thanks also again to friends and sympathisers, we were enabled to collect fresh equipment, and as, alas! hospitals could no longer be worked in Belgium, we offered our services to the French Red Cross, and were invited to establish our hospital in Cherbourg.

At this port, every day, arrived boat-loads of wounded from the northern battlefields. Their uniforms indistinguishable with blood, maimed, blinded, shattered in mind and body, these human derelicts were lifted from the dark ship's-hold, on stretchers, to the quay, and thence were transported to hospitals for amputations, a weary convalescence, or perhaps death. It was again a little difficult to recognise the glory of it all. And then came Serbia.

We had been working for four months at Cherbourg, when I read one day that an epidemic of typhus had broken out in Serbia; that the hospitals were overcrowded with sick and wounded; that one-third of the Serbian doctors had died, either of typhus, or at the front, and that nursing and medical help were badly needed. I knew from the moment when I read that report, that I should go, but I confess that I tried, at the beginning, to persuade myself that my first duty was to the Cherbourg hospital. I dreaded the effort of going to London, of facing the endless red tape, snubs, opposition, the collecting of money, and a unit, difficulties of all sorts with which I was now familiar. One of my plays was going to be acted at the theatre in Cherbourg, at a charity matinée, and I wanted to see it. Also, after a winter of continuous rain, the sun had begun its spring conjuring tricks, and one morning before breakfast, as I was walking in the woods, I noticed that through the damp earth, and the dead beech leaves, myriads of violets, ferns and primroses were showing their green leaf-buds. I felt a momentary twinge of joy; and that decided me. This would be a pleasant place in Spring; many women would be glad to do my work.

The wounded were no longer coming south in such numbers as at first, owing probably to the dangers of the sea voyage; the hospital was in thorough order, and the administration could be left in capable hands. The call had come, and I could no more ignore it, than the tides can ignore the tugging of the moon.

I went to London (in February, 1915) to see if I was right in my surmise as to the need for help in Serbia, and I was at once asked by the Serbian Relief Fund, to organise and to direct a hospital unit, also to raise a portion of the funds. We were to go to Serbia as soon as Admiralty transport could be procured. This involved considerable delay, and it was not till April 1st that we set sail from Liverpool for Salonica.

CHAPTER IV

The unit numbered forty-five, and comprised seven women doctors—Mrs. King-May Atkinson, M.B., Ch.B., Miss Beatrice Coxon, D.R.C.P.S.R., Miss Helen B. Hanson, M.D., B.S., D.P.H., Miss Mabel Eliza King-May, M.B., Ch.B., Miss Edith Maude Marsden, M.B., Ch.B., Miss Catherine Payne, M.B., Miss Isobel Tate, M.D., N.U.I.—eighteen trained nurses, together with cooks, orderlies, chauffeurs, and interpreters. The principle that women could successfully conduct a war hospital in all its various departments, had now been amply proved, and had been conceded even by the sceptical. The original demonstration had already borne ample fruit. Units of Scottish women were doing excellent work in France, and also in Serbia, and even in London, women doctors had now been given staff rank in military hospitals. The principle was firmly established, and I thought, therefore, that no harm would now be done by accepting the services of a few men orderlies and chauffeurs.

Amongst the applications for the post of orderly, were some Rhodes scholars; and an interesting reversal of traditional procedure occurred. At the last moment, the scholars asked to be excused, because, owing to the additional risks of typhus involved in the expedition to Serbia, they must first obtain permission to run the risk, from their relatives in America, and for this, they said, there would not now be time. Our women, on the other hand, braved their relatives, knowing that a woman's worst foes, where her work is concerned, are often those of her own household.

Determined, however, to dodge the typhus if possible, I proposed to the Serbian Relief Fund that our hospital should be housed—both staff and patients—entirely in tents. It was only a question of raising more money; and this was obtained through friends and sympathetic audiences.

Typhus infection is carried by lice, and these would naturally be more difficult to eliminate within already infected houses than in tents in the open air. Also by the use of tents we should render ourselves mobile, and be more likely to be of service in emergency; this was later amply proved.

The Committee of the Serbian Relief Fund agreed to the proposal, and sixty tents, mostly double-lined, were specially made to order, by Messrs. Edgington of Kingsway, for wards, staff, X-ray, kitchens, dispensary, lavatories, baths, sleeping, etc., etc., with camp beds and outfit.

Lady Grogan and Mrs. Carrington Wilde, who were giving up their lives to Serbian Relief Fund work, did wonders for our unit, and in every way helped to make things easy for us. Mr. B. Christian, chairman, also gave wholehearted support, and the Women's Imperial Service League, with Lady Muir Mackenzie, Lady Cowdray, Mrs. Carr Ellison, Lady Mond, Mrs. Ronald McNeill, and their indefatigable secretary, Mrs. McGregor, were of invaluable service.

The Admiralty transport, for which during six precious weeks we had waited impatiently, was an old two thousand ton boat, of the Royal Khedivial Mail Line, only accustomed to carrying passengers from one port to another, short distances on the Mediterranean coast, and she could only give us nineteen places. It was arranged, therefore, for the remainder of the unit to follow overland, and to arrive, if possible, simultaneously at Salonica.

The captain of our boat received twenty-four hours' notice of the fact that he was to carry to Salonica a couple of hundred members of various hospital units. His chief steward, to whom would have been entrusted the purchase of food stores, was laid up with a broken leg, and the captain had been obliged himself to go from house to house, in Liverpool, to find a crew. We were lucky, therefore, to get any food or any crew at all, and still more lucky in the captain, who, by his courtesy, and concern for our welfare, compensated for little deficiencies in the ménu. Besides, one was thankful to be on the way to work, after so much delay.

But after having waited six weeks for the boat, I nearly lost it at the last moment. The cabby who drove me and two others from the station at Liverpool, to the dock, was a fool, and couldn't find the dock in which the *Saidieh* was berthed, and for half an hour, in the rain, our four-wheeler crawled up and down, and in and out of a tangled maze of nine miles of docks. The horse, the cab, and the cabby were all extraordinarily old, and when we were at the point farthest from possibility of help, they all three collapsed. We patched up the horse and cab, but had more difficulty with the cabby. He couldn't see why we were so fastidious about sailing in one boat rather than in another, and time after time he drove, with triumphant flourish of whip, through the dock gates, and stopped in front of an old coal barge, and was much hurt by our refusal to get on board. But all this worked a miracle, for when at last we hit upon the right dock, a short time before the departure of the *Saidieh*, I was, for the first time in my life, thankful to find myself on board a steamer.

No places had been reserved for our party, but after a general scramble with the members of portions of six other hospital units, mostly women, voyaging with us, we all settled down comfortably to sea-sickness and submarines. The rough weather provided us with the former, but saved us from the latter. Submarines were supposed to be waiting for us off the Scilly Isles, and at first we were afraid that the *Saidieh* would be sunk; but later we were afraid she wouldn't.

The units, which kept to themselves in a remarkable way, were a source of much abstract interest to each other, and to me. It was particularly satisfactory to notice the unstinting way in which the principle of women's work in all departments, responsible as well as irresponsible, of a war hospital, was—as represented on this ship—now acknowledged. The woman administrator, the woman surgeon, the woman orderly, in addition, of course, to the woman nurse, who had been the first to win her position in war work.

I should like incidentally to suggest that uniform for women employed in public work, should be as compulsory always, as it is for men. Occasional hobble skirts, and low-cut blouses, reminiscent of the indecorums of the Society puppet, struck a peculiarly jarring note amongst a boat-load of people prepared for life-and-death realities, on a mission of humanity.

Of all these doctors, nurses, orderlies, administrators, chauffeurs, interpreters, how many would return? One should be taken and the other left? Laughing, singing, acting, reading, playing cards, flirting, quarrelling— how many were doing these things for the last time? Towards what fate were each and all being borne? Were we, as adjuncts of the Serbian Army, sailing to life or death, to victory or defeat?

How quickly all grew accustomed to, and ignored, the grandeur of moon, stars, planets, the wonders of a firmament new to most, because generally hidden by chimney-tops and smoke, and, conscious only of a little shrunken circle, grew absorbed in trifles. The vastness, the peace, the tumult, the joy of Nature, all unseen; the main interests, hair washing, gossip, fancy dress, bridge parties, quality of cigars, and food. Nobility of character curiously hidden, but ready to spring forth when pressed by the button of emergency.

A little excitement at first, from rumours of submarines, then boat drill, a sense of adventure, half enjoyable, half unpleasant, followed by the comfortable assurance that danger is passed, and enjoyment now legitimate, for those who are not kept low by sea-sickness. New friends and sudden confidences, as suddenly regretted; the inevitable Mrs. Jarley's waxworks, badly acted, but applauded; vulgar songs, mistaken for humour; real talent shy in coming forward, false coin in evidence; pride in attention from the captain; the small ambitions, to be top dog at games, to win a reputation as bridge player, to become sunburnt: all pursued with the same vigour with which work will later be attacked.

Danger from above, from below, from all around, but none so harmful as the tongue of a jealous comrade.

The story of one voyage is the story of all voyages. It is the story of mankind caricatured at close quarters, reflected on a distorting mirror.

The ship's first officer was a Greek; he was keenly on the side of the Allies. He hoped shortly to enlist, and he told me that it was his firm conviction that if Greece did not join the Allies immediately the people would revolt against the King.

The third officer, also a Greek, was a rabid pro-German. His presence on board seemed particularly undesirable; but the wonder was that there were not more undesirables on the ship, for anyone could have entered it at Liverpool.

Rough weather continued till we reached Gibraltar, on April 8th, and, after one fine day, resumed sway till the 11th, when we sailed past the Greek coast.

We reached Salonica on April 15th, the various units full of eagerness to learn their respective destinations.

We were met by the Serbian Consul, Monsieur Vintrovitch, and by the English Consul-General, Mr. Wratislaw, also by Mr. Chichester, who has since, alas, succumbed to typhoid.

There was disappointment amongst members of our unit, when they learned that we were to establish our hospital at Kragujevatz. They would have preferred Belgrade, as being nearer to the supposed front. Fronts, however, are movable, and as Kragujevatz was the military headquarters, we were, I knew, much more likely to get the work we wanted, if we were immediately under the official army eye; I was, therefore, more than content to go to Kragujevatz.

We spent that night on board, at the kind invitation of the captain, as there was a scrimmage for rooms in the hotels. We then had comfortable time next day in which to find quarters. The portion of the unit travelling *via* Marseilles arrived, excellently timed, by Messageries boat, on Saturday, the 17th. We spent the next few days struggling with, or trying to find, quay officials, and getting the stores and equipment unloaded, and placed in railway trucks. It was difficult to hit upon a working day at the dock, for we were now in one of those happy lands in which eight days out of every seven, are holidays. Friday was a fast day—no work; Saturday was a feast day—no work; Sunday was Sunday—no work; Monday came after Sunday, Saturday and Friday—therefore no work, a day of recovery was necessary after so many holidays. One had to be awake all night, to discover an odd moment when a little work was likely to be smuggled into the day's routine of happy idleness.

STOBART UNIT AND CONVALESCENTS OUTSIDE THEIR HOSPITAL
AT ANTWERP. (Concert Hall of Société de l'Harmonie)
Mrs. Stobart showing medals presented by grateful patients.
Dr. F. Stoney on her right; Dr. Ramsey left; Dr. Joan Watts,
Dr. Emily Morris, Dr. Rose Turner and Dr. Helen Hanson
behind. Miss S. Macnaughtan in front, centre

Photo. Dover Street Studios
STOBART HOSPITAL—SERBIAN RELIEF FUND UNIT No. 3
Mrs. St. Clair Stobart in centre second row, with (from
left to right) Doctors King-May, Payne, Marsden,
Atkinson, Tate and Coxon. Dr. Hanson absent

But by the evening of Monday, the 19th, everything—tents, equipment, stores, etc.—was on the trucks and ready to travel with us. And I, with eleven members, as advance party, left Salonica at 8 a.m. for Kragujevatz. We had all duly, the night before, performed the rite of smearing our bodies with paraffin, as a supposed precaution against the typhus lice. But it is probably a mistake to think that paraffin kills lice. Paraffin is a good cleanser, and lice, which flourish in dirt, respect their enemy, but are not killed by it.

The railway journey was interesting, especially to those amongst us who had never before been away from England.

We were amused to see real live storks nesting on the chimney-tops. So the German nursery tale, that babies are brought into the world by storks, down the bedroom chimney, must be true. German fables will probably in future teach that babies are brought through the barrels of rifles, double barrels being a provision of Providence for the safe arrival of twins, which will be much needed for the repopulation of the country.

We reached Skoplye at 9 p.m. Sir Ralph Paget kindly came to the train to greet us, and whilst we had some very light refreshments at the station, he stayed and talked with us. Lady Paget was then, we were thankful to hear, recovering from the attack of typhus which she had contracted during her hospital work at Skoplye.

The country through which we passed, was magnificent; mountains, rivers, gorges, and picturesque houses—one-storied, of sun-dried brick—with clear air, warm sunshine, and blossoming fruit trees. Occasionally a ruined village, or a new bridge replacing one that had lately been destroyed by Bulgarian raids, or newly dug graves of those killed in the last raid, were reminders that man, with his murderous works, would see to it that enjoyment of Nature's works should not enter for long into our programme.

We reached Nish at 7.30 next morning, April 21st. At the station we were met by Dr. Karanovitch, Chief Surgeon of the Army; Dr. Grouitch, Permanent Under-Secretary for Foreign Affairs; Mr. Blakeney, British Vice-Consul; Professor Todorovitch, Secretary to the Chief Surgeon; Mr. Petcham, Official of Foreign Affairs; and Dr. Soubotitch, President of the Red Cross Society.

All were most courteous and hospitable, and during the one and a half hour's halt they took us to breakfast at the Red Cross Hospital, and later accompanied us to the station to speed us on our last stage of the journey to Kragujevatz.

We left Nish at 10 a.m., and reached Kragujevatz at 7 p.m. The scenery was superb, and we were sorry when the journey came to an end. At the station, we were met by Colonel Dr. Guentchitch, the head of the Army Medical Service. He had most thoughtfully arranged sleeping quarters for the staff in the empty wards of a hospital; but it seemed wiser, and less trouble to all concerned, for us to stay for the night in our train, in a siding.

On arrival, the Colonel drove me and the Treasurer and two of our doctors to see a proposed site for our camp hospital—the racecourse, then disused, above the town. Excellent—nothing more suitable was likely to be found. The unit was then invited to dine at the officers' club mess. Here we met Colonel Harrison, British Military Attaché, and also Colonel Hunter, who was in charge of the Royal Army Medical Corps mission. The French and Russian attachés were also there.

It was homely to meet once more the genus military attaché; it was indeed difficult to imagine conducting a hospital without them. For at Kirk Kilisse, when we arrived in a starving condition, the British attaché had found us food, and the Italian attaché, whom, in the dark, I had mistaken for some one else, had sportingly acted up to the character of the some one else, and had provided us with straw for mattresses.

Though some folks find Serbian cooking too rich, the dishes have a distinctive and pleasing character of their own, and the dinner, after two days of cold meals, was much enjoyed. It was delightful to find that the Serbian officers, both medical and military, were cultured men of quick and sympathetic intelligence. I knew at once that I should like them. Most of them spoke German, a few talked French, but all could converse fluently in either one or the other language, in addition, of course, to their own. One is always reminded abroad that all other nations are better educated than we are. We are still so insular, and are still, with the pride of ignorance, proud of our defect. We have not yet reached the stage of realising that we can never take a leading part in the councils of Europe, till we can converse, without interpreters, with the leading minds of Europe.

Next day Colonel Guentchitch took us to see alternative camp sites, but nothing half as suitable as the racecourse was available, and upon this we decided.

By the evening of Thursday, April 22nd, we had unpacked, and pitched some small ridge tents in which to spend the night, refusing the kind offer of sleeping accommodation in the town, though we again accepted the officers' hospitality for the evening meal.

The next day was spent in pitching the camp, and the authorities were pleased, and surprised, because we refused all offers of help in putting up the tents. We had gone to Serbia to help the Serbians, and not to be a nuisance. Foreign units which arrive and expect to have everything done for them, are more bother than they are worth.

The remainder of the unit, with Dr. King-May, arrived from Salonica, and under the supervision of Dr. Marsden and Miss Benjamin (head orderly) a small town of tents, gleaming white in the brilliant sunshine, soon appeared in the local geography.

One long wide street of tents for the staff, then a large interval of open grass space, and another avenue of ward tents, with a connecting base line of tents for offices, kitchens, X-ray, and dispensary.

CHAPTER V

The camp was finely situated. We were surrounded on all sides by hills, not ordinary dead hills, these were alive with picturesque villages, half-hidden amongst orchards of plum and apple trees. On the far side of the white, one-storied town of Kragujevatz, the hills to the east, and south, seemed to be in poetic partnership with the clouds, and all day long, with infinite variety, reflected rainbow colours and storm effects—an endless source of joy.

At night, when the tents were lighted by small lanterns, and nothing else was visible but the stars, the camp looked like a fairy city.

The cuckoo had evidently not been present during Babel building, for all day long, and sometimes at night, he cuckooed in broad English—a message from our English spring. But the climax of surprises came when we found ourselves kept awake by the singing of the nightingales. Was this the Serbia of which such grim accounts had reached us?

We were ready to open our hospital either for the wounded, or for typhus patients, and we gave the authorities their choice. Colonel Guentchitch promptly decided that he would rather not start a new typhus centre; he wished us to take wounded. We began with fifty, and these were in a few days increased to one hundred and thirty.

And at once I realised, that the impression which even now largely prevails in Western Europe as to the bellicose character of the Serbian nation, is wrong.

The average Serbian peasant-soldier is not the truculent, fierce, fighting-loving savage so often represented. He does not love fighting, but he loves, with all the enthusiasm of a poetic nature, his family, his home, his hectares of land, and his country. He has fought much in the past, but in defence of these possessions which he prizes. No one can accuse the Serbian soldier of cowardice, yet his dislike of fighting, and his love of home, were so marked, that it was easy to distinguish, by his brisk walk, and cheerful countenance, or by his slow gait, and depressed attitude, whether a drab-dressed soldier, with knapsack, walking along the road, was going *Kod kutche* (home) or—his ten days' leave at an end—was going once more *y commando* (to the front).

Our wounded were the most charming patients imaginable, and it was always a joy to go into the wards and have a talk with them. They were alertly intelligent, with a delightful sense of humour, and a total absence of vulgarity or coarseness. They were all so chivalrous, courteous and delicate in their behaviour to the nurses, and to us women generally, and so full of affection and gratitude for the help given to them, that it was difficult to realise that these were not officers, but peasants, with little knowledge of the world outside their own national history.

With this every Serbian peasant is familiar, because it is handed down from generation to generation, in ballads and heroic legends, by the bards or guslars.

Our patients were all wonderfully cheerful and happy, and the convalescents enjoyed their meals in a tent which had been given by the men working on a ranch in British Columbia. *Popara* (a national dish—a sort of porridge of bread and lard), and eggs, bread, and *pekmez* (plum jam), and tea or coffee for breakfast; a rich stew of meat and vegetables, or a roast, and pudding or pastry for dinner; and again, meat, and stew, or soup, and pudding for supper. On Fridays, however, the soldiers always refused meat.

Colonel Nicolaivitch (now Serbian Military Attaché in London) told me the other day that, on one of his visits to our Kragujevatz camp, he had been talking in one of the wards, with a man who was sitting up in bed with a bandaged head. He was much enjoying his dinner, and the Colonel said, "I expect you would like to stay in this hospital half a year?" "No," replied the man promptly, "a whole year."

The men are not accustomed to play games, except with cards. A card game called "Jeanne d'Arc" was the favourite. But they loved "Kuglana": this was a game like skittles, played with nine pins and a large wooden ball, which was swung between two tall posts. It was made for us at the arsenal, and gave our convalescents much joy and recreation.

I was a little surprised at the matter-of-fact way in which the men all accepted women doctors, and surgical operations by women. Indeed, they highly approved, because women were, they said, more gentle, and yet as effective as men doctors.

I was also surprised that at first, in April, when the weather was cold, they did not fear the tents and the open-air life. But the ward-tents, being double-lined, were as warm as could be wished at night, or when it rained; and in sunny weather, when the sides were lifted, gave an open-air treatment which was at once appreciated.

Camp hours were:—

Reveillé at 5.30 a.m.

Breakfast at 6 (the sun was very hot in the middle of the day and it was better to get the heaviest part of the work done in the cooler hours).

Lunch at 11.30.

Tea at 4.

Supper at 6.30 (as the town was out of bounds it seemed wise to avoid the possibility of dull evenings by going early to bed).

Lights out at 9.

Much attention was attracted by our novel form of hospital, and all day long, visitors, official and otherwise, flocked to see all the arrangements. These seemed to be highly approved.

The kitchen department was under the supervision of Miss M. Stanley; dispensary under Miss Wolseley; laundry, Miss Johnstone; linen, Mrs. Dearmer. The X-ray Department was managed by Dr. Tate and Mr. Agar. The Secretary was Miss McGlade, and the Hon. Treasurer, John Greenhalgh.

The sanitation was in the hands of Miss B. Kerr, and was a subject of interested and invariably of favourable criticism. And it required some system to cope successfully with open-air sanitation, on a fixed spot, for more than two hundred people. Colonel Hunter, sometimes twice a day, brought visitors to whom he was anxious to show certain features in the scheme of which he specially approved. He told me that we were useful to him as object-lessons, and he cabled home in favourable terms to the War Office, concerning our hospital work, and also, later, concerning the dispensary scheme, with which he was well pleased.

It soon, indeed, came to be considered quite the correct thing for visitors to Kragujevatz to come up and visit the camp, and the only relief from the monotony of showing people round, was the variety of language which had to be employed. Sometimes, simultaneously, a Serbian, who, in addition to his own language, only spoke German, another who only spoke French, another who could only talk Serbian, and perhaps an Englishman who could only talk English—these must all be entertained together. It was like the juggler's feat with balls in the air.

Almost everybody of note in Serbia visited us at one time or another, and our visitors' book, now, alas! in the hands of the Germans, was an interesting record.

His Royal Highness the Crown Prince (Alexander) honoured us with a visit as soon as he learnt that he would be able to converse in French or German. He speaks good English, but has presumably not had the same opportunities of practice in this language. But in the visitors' book, which he took back to the palace for the purpose, he wrote a page and a half, in excellent English, describing his impression of the work of the hospital, and expressing his gratitude for the help given to his brave soldiers.

A fine fellow this Prince: straightforward, unostentatious, full of sympathy and quick intelligence; in every way worthy of a throne. He looked at every detail of the camp with critical interest, then as he walked, in the scorching sun, from the hospital quarters to the tents reserved for the staff, he asked, as he looked around, "Have you no sun-shelters?" We had none, and he immediately turned to a member of his staff, and told him to see that "ladniaks," or arbours, made of young trees, and dead branches, were at once arranged for us.

Accordingly, in a few days, a procession of wagons arrived, carrying a whole forest of young trees for props, and dead branches for roof and sides; and arbours were erected, and much comfort to us all was the result.

On the evening of the Prince's visit, the convalescent soldiers celebrated the event by giving us an impromptu entertainment after supper. Dressed in their light-coloured pyjamas, scarlet bed-jackets, and big mushroom-shaped straw hats, they formed, outside our mess tent, a picturesque group, silhouetted against the white tents which were aglow with fairy lamps, and looked like inflated stars.

The Serbian national instrument is the gusla, a one-stringed banjo, played with a bow; the sound is like the plaintive buzzing of a bumble bee, when, round and round a room, it blindly seeks an exit.

Accompanying himself upon the gusla, one soldier after the other sang, or rather chanted, in mournful monotone, the old poetic legends in which the tragic history of their country has been transmitted from one generation to another; or they sang together, in parts; or they recited stirring tragedies— always tragedies—of which Serbian history is composed.

It is wise to allow plenty of time for a Serbian concert, as no self-respecting guslar cares to deal with less than half-a-dozen centuries of his national history at one sitting. One guslar, at this concert, caused us some embarrassment. He wouldn't leave off "guslaring." We tried every inducement. He paid no heed; and I saw, with despair, that he meant to carry his country safely into freedom from Turkish tyranny, and that meant another 500 years. The moon came and went; but moons might come, and moons might go, he went on for ever. Finally, in desperation, we all clapped vigorously. Good! He stopped, placed his gusla on the ground, and joined heartily in the clapping—but for a moment only. We weren't quick enough, and before we could take away his instrument, he had picked it up and begun again, and we were back again at the year 1389.

Every Serbian peasant is a poet, and one of these soldiers recited a portion of a fine dramatic poem which he had just written and presented to me. The poem began as an epic of Serbian history, past and present, and ended in a pæan of gratitude to the Stobart Hospital.

Tragedy, always dominant in Serbian history, gives a sad dignity to Serbian music, and, in contrast, the songs sung by the unit, as interludes in the Serbian concert, seemed commonplace.

The fitful moon had now set; the soldiers sat on benches placed one behind the other, and in the darkness, their faces were almost invisible. But here and there a lighted cigarette illumined the war-worn face, and showed the result of hardships and suffering. We did not then know that the future was to bring a fate more terrible still.

But no entertainment in Serbia can be reckoned a success, if it does not end in a spontaneous burst of kolo dancing. Two men, with arms linked, will suddenly begin dancing a slow shuffling step. Another man will, as suddenly, produce, as though from the skies, a gusla, or a violin, or a flute, and will start playing, and will play over, and over, and over again, a dozen bars of the same melancholy tune. This has a remarkable effect. Immediately, everybody within sound of the music will, one after the other, join in, in pied piper style, and, linking arms, form a circle round the proud musician.

There are many varieties of steps, both quick and slow, and the dance can be extremely graceful in effect. But whether it is well or badly danced, the kolo is always dignified, with total absence of rowdyism, vulgarity, or sensuousness.

The kolo and the gusla are to Serbia, what the reel and the bagpipes are to Scotland. The kolo, like Serbian music and Serbian literature, reflects the spirit of their tragic history; even when the steps grow quicker with increased excitement, the feet are scarcely lifted from the ground; the movements are never movements of joy; the high kick, the leap, the spring, indicative of a light heart, are always absent.

On this evening, after an hour of the concert, the men suddenly broke into kolo. To their intense delight, Maika (mother), their name for the Directress, boldly joined the circle. "Dobro (well done), Maika! dobro! dobro!" they all shouted in chorus. Nurses, doctors, and orderlies all promptly followed suit, and as a finale to a successful evening, the various national anthems of the Allies were sung, and "lights out" bell rang the "Amen."

CHAPTER VI

One of our most frequent and most welcome visitors was Colonel Dr. Lazaravitch Guentchitch, Head of the Serbian Army Medical Service. He had held this post also during the wars of 1912-13-14. He was brimful of quick and generous sympathy and insight; efficient and businesslike, with a delightful sense of humour and absence of red tape, it was always a real pleasure to talk with him. Taken one with another, indeed, the Serbian officials whom I had the privilege to meet were—unlike most officials in other countries—human.

Our most frequent visitor was Major Dr. Protitch, Director of the Shumadia Military Hospital. He was our official inspector, and was responsible for the evacuation of the convalescent wounded. He came always officially, once a day, during all the six months of our work at Kragujevatz, and he never came once too often.

Nothing that could be done for our comfort, or to show the sympathy and generosity of the officials, was forgotten by him. One morning, soon after the establishment of the camp, I saw a man carrying a spade, and another wheeling a barrow filled with earth, coming towards my tent. When they were in front of it, they stopped. I wondered what they were going to do, and I tried to remember the Serbian words for "What's your business?" when Major Protitch came up. He smiled, and told me that he had heard me say that I was fond of flowers, and that at home, in England, I had a garden of my own. He was therefore going to plant a little garden in front of my tent, and in front of one of every two tents, all up the line, to remind us of our homeland. Barrow loads of earth were accordingly deposited, and were then planted with violas, carnations, cinerarias, and many varieties of gay flowers. The gardens were in shape and size suspiciously like graves: they were, alas! as shown by later events, symbolic of the graves of many Serbian hopes.

One day Major Protitch invited me and our Treasurer to his Slava feast. Slava is the anniversary of the day on which the ancestors of the family were converted to Christianity. We were to be present at the inauguration ceremony in celebration of his patron saint day. Madame Protitch was in deep mourning, and for that reason there were to be no other guests.

At 9 a.m. the Major and his wife, their small son of five years old, and the priest, and verger, were waiting for us, round a table, in a wood, outside the little shooting box club-house, which the Major and his wife had improvised as summer quarters, at the southern end of our racecourse. After we had wished them "Sretna Slava" (happy feast day) and shaken hands, the priest led the way into the house, and we all followed. A tiny room was arranged, in excellent taste, as living and bedroom. On a small table in the middle of the room, were two large cakes, a long, fat, brown, unlighted candle, a crucifix, and a saucer of water. In the latter was a sprig of a faded flower called boziliac.

The priest, who had long hair, and wore a blue embroidered robe, said a short prayer, and the verger, a Serbian peasant in ordinary dress, without a collar—probably because the weather was hot—said the response. Then the big candle was lighted by the little son, who was nervous, and received surreptitious help from his father. Then came more prayers by the priest, and responses by the verger, who seemed to play quite as important a part as the priest; the family only crossed themselves vigorously at intervals.

Next, the priest immersed the crucifix in the water in the saucer, and with the wet crucifix sprinkled the Major, and the boy, and various objects on the table and about the room. He did not sprinkle the wife, she was scrupulously omitted from all the proceedings. The priest then made the sign of the cross on both the cakes; took one cake and held it upside down, and without severing it, made two cross cuts, and poured a little red wine into the cuts. When this had soaked in, he turned it right side up again. Then he and the two honoured males, together held the cake again, and turned it slowly round and round in their hands, the wife still looking on.

The priest then took the cake and held it sideways, almost, but not quite severed, to show the cross cuts; he held it thus for the father and son to kiss, removed it, and gave it to them again to kiss, and once again for the third time; the cake had then done its duty, and was replaced on the table.

Then came more prayers, the congregation standing. After this the priest shook hands with Major Protitch, and the boy, and the religious ceremony, in which the wife had had no share, was over. She was only servitor, and now she handed first to the priest, the other cake, made by herself, of corn, and nuts, and sugar. He helped himself with a spoon to a small portion; the cake was then handed to me. I found it delicious, and should have liked more; and then to the others. Madame Protitch then handed round other cakes, and cognac, and the priest bade us farewell, and departed. After that we were given orange, sliced, and spiced, and water, and Turkish coffee. And then we talked, in German. Our hosts told us that a cake of corn, and nuts, is always made, at funerals, for the dead, and as the patron saint is dead, he gets the benefit on his name day. But there is one unfortunate patron saint, who is an archangel, and therefore he is not dead, and because he is not dead, he is not entitled to this cake. Who'd be an archangel? But this means, of course, that the people who have this star turn, for their patron saint, cannot have this fascinating corn and nut-cake on their Slava day—all distinctly discouraging to the worship of archangels.

I asked Madame Protitch how she liked being left out of all the blessings. She was surprised at my surprise, and I remembered having read that, in Serbia, the formula used by a man on introducing his wife used to be: "This is my wife, God forgive me." And in describing his children, a father would say: "I have three sons and—God forgive me—three daughters."

The extreme modesty on the part of the husband concerning his wife, may be due to the fact that a wife was considered to be the property of the man, and it is, of course, unbecoming to boast of one's possessions. One should minimise their value as far as possible. Mothers, who are not regarded as property, are always spoken of, and treated by men with extreme respect.

That was, however, not an appropriate moment for feminist propaganda—it's extraordinary how few moments ever are appropriate for this. I therefore contented myself with saying that in England we were beginning to have different ideas about the relative position of women, and of men. I should have liked to add that the world is on its way to the discovery that the highest interests of men, and of women are identical, and that it is only the lowest interests of men, that clash with the highest interests of women.

But in some ways the Serbians are ahead of other European nations in their respect for women. Major Protitch told me that the Government were intending to give recognition to the peasant women who, by working on the farms during the prolonged absence of their men folk, at the front, had saved the country from famine. Our Government might well take a hint in this respect. Who could say that there was no woman's movement in Serbia? It is a woman's movement, moved by men.

Another frequent visitor was the British Military Attaché, Colonel Harrison. He dined with us almost every night during four months—a compliment to the cooking—and until he was invalided home—not as a result of the cooking. He was a good friend to Serbia. He had the preceding autumn been one of the factors, behind the scenes, partially responsible for the sudden turn in the fortunes of the Serbian Army. An interesting book might be written if the true origins of great events were traced and revealed. We should have to re-learn many pages of history.

It was largely due to the agitation of Colonel Harrison, who cabled continuously for ammunition to be sent, that the tables had been turned on the Austrians. The latter were expecting the usual feeble volleys, from the depleted Serbian cannons, but instead, on a certain occasion, a fierce cannonade, with live ammunition, suddenly thundered from the guns, and the Austrians were so surprised and dismayed that they fled, and Serbia was—temporarily—saved.

But we had the satisfaction of seeing for ourselves that ammunition was now being made in large quantities, for Kragujevatz was the home of a large and excellently appointed arsenal. The director, who stood about six feet four—a magnificently fine fellow—showed me round the arsenal one day, and gave me various souvenirs, and then he paid a return visit to our camp. As a memento of this, he presented me with a beautiful big bell, cast from cannons taken from the Austrians; it was inscribed, and will always be a precious possession. During six months in our camp on the racecourse of Kragujevatz, this bell, with loud but musical voice, summoned the unit from and to their beds, and to their meals and prayers; later it journeyed over the mountains of Montenegro and Albania, hidden in a sack. Its voice was then hushed, for on the mountains there were no beds, few meals, and prayers were spontaneous; and now it hangs in an English home as gong, calling us to meals; but it also serves as muezzin, calling to that form of prayer which is the only effective prayer—determination—on Serbia's behalf.

Another visitor was Sir Thomas Lipton. He and his yacht had brought hospital units to Serbia, and he was now touring to see the country. The officials, when he was expected at Kragujevatz, asked me if I would meet him at the station, at 5.17 a.m. He and I had recently lunched as co-guests of Sir Ralph Paget, at Nish, and afterwards Sir Thomas had shortened a tedious night railway journey by telling amusing stories of his life's experiences. Also, at a reception given by Lady Cowdray to our unit before we left for Serbia, he had been present, and had said kind words to and about us. He was thus an old friend. I always rose at 4.30, to set things going, and to make sure of the joy of seeing the sun rise—getting up at four, therefore, to meet him, was no hardship.

The sunrise rewarded me as usual. A blaze of crimson over the eastern hills, followed by a glare of yellow, melting into rainbow colours. I met the train, and Sir Thomas and his suite breakfasted with us. I hope we gave him porridge, but I've forgotten. But we showed him the camp; then he lunched at the officers' mess, inspected the arsenal in the afternoon, and came back to us for tea and supper.

In the evening, in his honour, we gave a little supper party, which included Colonels Guentchitch and Popovitch, and Captain Yovan Yovannovitch, of the Intelligence Department, Mr. Robinson of *The Times*, and Mr. Stanley Naylor of *The Daily Chronicle*. Sir Thomas seemed to like the cheery, homely atmosphere of the corporate supper-table, at which all members of our unit—doctors, nurses, orderlies, chauffeurs, interpreters, myself and guests—messed, as always, together. He made one of his happy speeches, and response was made. After supper we gave an open-air concert, on the grass space between the hospital and the staff tents. The night was warm and lovely; the moon was bright, and all Kragujevatz, invited or not invited, considered it the correct thing to come to the concert.

The Crown Prince had kindly lent us his band, and, in addition to excellent music by them, the programme included part songs by a company of theological students, who were now working in hospitals in Kragujevatz (in lieu of military service), also songs and recitations by other people.

Our own convalescent soldiers were too shy to perform, but in their bright-coloured dressing-gowns, or with blankets pinned round them, they formed a patch of picturesqueness amongst the audience. But they were not too shy to join in the final impromptu kolo dance. As usual, at the right moment, the guslar and the kolo-starter dropped from the skies, and for a few minutes all Kragujevatz were linked arm in arm, in happy abandonment of care and sorrow, in the magic kolo circle. But the happiness was of short duration. Has there ever been a time during the last five hundred years when Serbia could rejoice with a light heart? Will the time ever come when Serbian swords can be beaten into ploughshares, and their bayonets into pruning hooks?

Even amongst our comparatively cheerful patients, during this temporary lull in the fighting, tragedies were occurring in the usual humdrum fashion. One man who was badly wounded, and unable to leave his bed, received a letter from home, telling him that his wife, two children, and a brother, had just died of typhus, and that two other children, and his mother, all members of the same zadruga (family community) were dangerously ill with the same disease.

A few hundred yards beyond our camp, four thousand newly dug graves, containing typhus victims, testified to the virulence of this one disease in this one town. With curious ingenuity, the typhus fiend stepped in to carry on the destruction of human life, during the interlude when the fighting fiend was in abeyance. Is it a wonder that the Serbian peasant forgets to see the hand of God in all his suffering? For many centuries the hand of the Turk has been too plainly the direct cause of his tragedies. There has been no desire to seek for further causes. Even those of us who have made it our business to search diligently for God, have not always found Him; but perhaps we are like the players in "hunt the thimble" game, we cannot find God, because He is in too conspicuous a place—in our own hearts.

But for centuries, the salvation of the Serbian peasant has been working itself out on larger lines than those of a narrow theology; the struggle of his nation has been for that which is the basis of Christian faith—for Freedom. For the outer frills, the rituals of that faith, the Serbian peasant has had no time. With us, in England, this situation is reversed. We have had plenty of time to attend to the frills, and have perhaps lost sight of that which is the basis of our common faith.

It is undoubtedly true that in Serbia, religion, if by religion is meant theological doctrine, and adherence to ritual, has little hold upon the people. But during centuries of oppression, religious teaching has been necessarily confined to the monks, and they, to avoid persecution, have been obliged to seclude themselves amongst the mountains. And so it has come about, as usual, that the praying men have been content with prayer, and the men of action with action. Neither of them has perceived that a combination of prayer, and action, is necessary for the fulfilment of divine destiny.

CHAPTER VII

Amongst the Serbian soldiers many primitive notions still prevailed. One day, after one of the big thunder-storms which were frequent during the spring and summer months, I asked the men in one of the wards, what was their idea of the origin of thunder? "God must have something to do in Heaven," replied one man. "We work on earth and He must work above, so He makes thunder and lightning. He mustn't sit up there and do nothing."

"No, no," answered another; "it is not God that makes thunder, it's St. Ilyia; it's he who works the thunder and lightning."

I asked who was St. Ilyia? Didn't I know St. Ilyia? He was a workman, paid by the day, to work on the land. One evening late, as he was on his way home, he met a devil. The devil reminded him that he, the devil, had been best man at his, Ilyia's, wedding. "And I now congratulate you," the devil added mockingly, "that your wife has run away with another man." Ilyia was furious, but said nothing, and walked on. Soon he met another devil. This one reminded him that he had been first witness at his wedding, and he, too, added mockingly, "I congratulate you that your wife has run away with another man." Ilyia was still more furious, but he walked on. Soon he met a third devil. This devil reminded him that he had been godfather to his, Ilyia's, child, and he also added mockingly, "I congratulate you that your wife has run away with another man."

Mad with anger, Ilyia rushed home determined to kill the guilty pair. He went into his bedroom, and saw a man and woman in the bed. He did not stop to look, but he killed them both. They were his father and mother. For a punishment, God made him serve as ferryman, to carry people across the river in his own village. He must give to each passenger a melon seed. One day there came a passenger—a devil—in such a hurry he wouldn't take the seed. "Why won't you take it? But you must," urged Ilyia. "No," replied the devil, "I am in a hurry to spoil a wedding, and I have no time to wait." Immediately, in answer, Ilyia killed the devil, and threw his body into the water. God, however, pardoned Ilyia, and took him to heaven as His servant, but he must work the thunder and lightning. So he kept killing all the devils with his lightning. But one deformed devil always managed to hide away, and one day this poor devil managed to get to God, and asked Him why He allowed all the devils to be killed. It is the devils, he argued, who bring the wars which cause deformities, and the devils who cause all sickness and poverty, and as it is only the sick and the poor who pray to God—why get rid of them?

The argument seemed to appeal to God, for He replied, Very well, He would at any rate not let him, the deformed devil, be killed by Ilyia.

But Ilyia still tries to kill him, and whenever it thunders and lightens, that is Ilyia trying to kill the deformed devil.

There were several points in this story, upon which I should have liked enlightenment; but when I began asking questions, I was told, simply, that it was so, and that it always had been. How, then, could I doubt? And I assured them that I did not doubt.

Then another man said that there had been a thunderstorm last night, because Italy was now going to join in the fighting; the thunder and lightning was a sign that another land was going to shed its blood. I had thought of that myself, and was glad that they voiced my thought. Much more interesting and reasonable to believe in concrete causes.

During the night, whilst the thunder-storms had been immediately overhead, many of the wounded left their beds, and stood and prayed to God not to let them be killed—presumably by Ilyia, as deformed devils.

It was not strange that a relationship between politics and weather in Serbia should be assumed, for violence was the keynote of both. When the sun shone, its heat was fierce, it scorched the body through thick clothes; when rain fell, it poured in waterspouts, as though the skies had burst a dam. The wind blew tornadoes, and with the brutality of a gigantic peg-top, whirled everything within reach, into space, at the rate of eighty miles an hour. Thunder and lightning had the force of up-to-date artillery, and the mud was—Balkan.

One Sunday afternoon, I was standing with our chaplain, outside the tent in which, in two minutes' time, he was to conduct the evening service.

We were choosing the hymns, but we were suddenly interrupted by a whirlwind of dust, which nearly blinded us, and before we could close our books, and with a suddenness which is, as a rule, only permitted on the stage, a tornado, rushing at the rate of eighty miles an hour, hurled itself point-blank at our camp, and though everybody immediately rushed to tighten tent ropes, within fifteen seconds, fifteen tents were blown flat upon the ground, and chairs, tables, hairbrushes, garments of all sorts, a menagerie of camp equipment, and personal effects, were flying over the plain, beyond possibility of recovery. There was no church service that evening.

After a day or two of rain, skirts became a folly and indecency. I was at first shy, as a guest in a foreign country, of casting the recognised symbol of feminine respectability. But my work required me to be constantly on the tramp, around the extensive camp, and one day, when my skirt had become soaked, and bedraggled, and I could no longer walk in it, I took it off. I found that with my long boots and a longish tunic coat, over breeches which matched the coat, the effect was respectable, and was approved by the rest of the unit, who soon followed the example on wet days. But it was a little bit of a shock to me when, on that first morning of audacity, a car drove up to the camp, and out stepped the representatives of three nations—viz., Sir Ralph Paget (British Commissioner), Dr. Grouitch (Serbian Foreign Secretary), and Mr. Strong, who was on a mission to report for Mr. Rockefeller on the condition of Serbian hospitals. But they didn't seem as shocked as might have been expected; and I became more than ever confirmed in the belief that even if skirts are retained by women for decorative purposes, they will have to be abandoned by workers. The question of women's work is largely a question of clothes.

But the Serbian soldiers would never sympathise with us in our abhorrence of mud. "No, no, mud was 'Dobro, dobro' (good, good), because mud meant rain for crops; also mud had saved them from the Austrians who, in November last, had not been able to advance their big guns further, on account of the mud. Yes, mud was 'Dobro, dobro.'"

There never was in any language a word so omnipotent, so deep-reaching as this word "Dobro." Of what use to worry with phrase books, grammars and dictionaries; why trouble to learn a difficult language, written in arbitrary characters, when one simple word could open all the gates of understanding! With "Dobro" on the tip of the tongue—every tongue—Serbian and English tongues alike, how could there be "confusion of tongues"? The heritage of Babel could be flouted. Diagnosis by doctors, nursing, treatment, orders, warnings, instructions from and to one and all, within and without the camp; interchange of ideas; even proposals and acceptance or refusal of marriage; all could be understood by means of the blessed word "Dobro" and its negative "Ne-dobro," spoken with appropriate variations of accent.

THE GERMAN ARMY ENTERING BRUSSELS AUGUST, 1914
(Pontoons passing the German Staff in the Boulevard des Jardins Botaniques, in front of the Gare du Nord)

**STOBART HOSPITAL AT CHÂTEAU TOURLAVILLE
NEAR CHERBOURG
Showing Recreation Tent given by workers
on a Ranch in British Columbia**

Is it a wonder that good understanding prevailed between Serbians and English? Misunderstandings arise from words. In Serbia there only was one word—"Dobro"; and I'm longing for the day—"Der Tag"—when we can go back to Serbia and find that all is indeed once more "Dobro, dobro."

When we first arrived in Serbia, we were much interested in the sight of many thousands of Austrian prisoners of war, working in every department of life, and living in apparent freedom. Those who were officers were often employed in hospitals. In Dr. Protitch's hospital, one of the prisoners had been Professor of Mathematics, at the University of Prague. His work now was to count the dirty linen, and he did it very badly. I suppose even the Professor's mathematics couldn't make ninety nightshirts that came back from the wash, equal to one hundred that went out.

We had no commissioned officers in our hospital, but forty Austrian so-called prisoners helped us in the rough work of the camp, as trench diggers, stretcher bearers and ward orderlies, etc. These men were working in a camp hospital controlled by women; they were working for the enemies of their country, yet they were quite unguarded, and slept at night, in tents, like the rest of us. But after the first wonder had evaporated, thoughts of the possible mischief they might do, never entered our minds. It showed the artificiality of war. These men—forty thousand or more—were told that by the rules of the game, they were prisoners, and therefore must keep off Tom Tiddler's ground, and they obeyed the rules with scarcely any supervision.

There were Serbian Austrians, and Austrian Austrians. The latter spoke only German, and were less to be trusted politically than the former, who talked only Serbian. The Serbian Austrians were to all intents Serbians, and dreaded nothing so much as the prospect of being retaken by the Austrians—their former masters.

The main distinction between the two is that of religion, Croats or Serbian Austrians are Catholics, whereas the others belong to the Greek Church. But all alike were excellent workers, and very happy in their work. Both they and we grieved terribly when later, owing to political causes, all our Catholic prisoners were removed from their positions of freedom, and happy work in our hospital, and were sent, under strict escort, to dig tunnels on the railway to Roumania, or to other work in which supervision was feasible.

Amongst these orderlies working for us, was a funny old man called Jan. He had a wife and children somewhere in Serbia, and he developed a chronic habit of coming to ask for leave to go and see them. On one occasion when he came to say good-bye to "Maika" (mother), I noticed that he was hugging two bottles, which were carefully wrapped in paper. I asked him what he was carrying, and he answered proudly, "Medicine for my little ones." "Dear! dear! are they ill?" I asked with some concern; "I am sorry." "Oh! no. They're not ill. I am only taking them the medicine as a treat." He had apparently explained his idea to our dispenser, and she had given him something harmless to satisfy his fatherly instinct of giving joy. A side-light on the scarcity of medicines.

Our hospital received several visits from German and Austrian aeroplanes. Kragujevatz was one of their main objectives, on account of the arsenal and the Crown Prince.

We, and the town authorities were unprepared for the first Taube arrival. The day after Sir Thomas Lipton's visit, I went to bed with typhoid. I had been in bed a week, when one morning, as I lay in my tent awake, looking out at the camp, I heard a sound—familiar from memories of Antwerp. In the air above, a whirring of machinery, then a noise like a chariot of fire cleaving the air, followed by a crash, as though all the glass-houses of the earth were smashed. Typhoid or no typhoid, I jumped out of bed to see what had happened, and to take any measures possible for the safety of the unit, and I saw clouds of smoke and débris rising from the town.

The unit, who were then getting up, rushed from their tents in their pyjamas, and watched with interest whilst three biplanes, two German and one Austrian, dropped bombs in quick succession on the town, evidently in futile effort to destroy the arsenal and the Crown Prince's house.

Suddenly we heard a still louder crash close to us, and we saw that one hundred and fifty yards away, a bomb had fallen just outside our camp, to the east—close to the wireless station. Another whirr through the air, and a second crash, and a bomb fell near the wireless on the other side, a few yards from the last. Some of the shrapnel fell upon our tents, but no harm was done to us. Our four guards, stationed at the four corners of our camp, to keep off undesirable visitors, bravely fired their pop-guns at the machine hawks, but that was all the attention the Taubes received, and they sailed triumphantly away into the blue. I then went back to bed to go on with my typhoid. I ought to have died, but I don't do the things that I ought.

I realised the damage that might be wrought if further Taubes chose to mistake us for a military camp, and hurl their bombs upon our patients, and I immediately organised a scheme for the quick evacuation of the hospital on any future occasion, and sent the new rules to the mess tent and to all the wards. Five people had been killed and eighteen wounded as a result of this first attack.

One woman had been on her way to market at Kragujevatz, but when she heard the bombs, she was frightened, and turned to go home, without fulfilling her purpose. She was on her way back, and was just outside our camp, when the bomb near the wireless station fell, and she was hit. Two of our doctors, and some nurses who had run to look at the big hole made by the bomb, and to pick up relics, found her staggering by the hole—bleeding profusely in one arm. The doctors took her into hospital, and found that she had shrapnel in the lung, as well as a shattered arm. Moral: had she continued her work, and not turned back, she would not have been hit.

A few minutes later another woman was brought to us with a smashed leg. She had with her a tiny baby three months old. It had not been hurt, but it was a miserable specimen. The mother, by some curious freak of Nature, disliked the child, and had neglected it. We hoped the mother's misfortune might be the baby's opportunity of life, and Ginger, the red-haired nurse in whose charge it was given, made for it a cradle out of an old packing case, and devoted herself to the baby heart and soul. (The same nurse, who at Antwerp during the bombardment, had carried her soldier patients on her back, down steep cellar stairs, to a place of safety. Later, when our Kragujevatz hospital was evacuated, and those members of the staff who had not gone with me to the front, were on their way to the coast, she was shot accidently. The bullet entered both lungs; she became dangerously ill, and could not be moved from Mitrovitza; two of our doctors, Iles and Macmillan, Nurse Bainbridge, and the Rev. J. Rogers, stayed to look after her. They were all made prisoners, but all—including Ginger, who recovered by a miracle—returned safely to England in February.)

But even Ginger's devotion could not save the poor mite of a baby who had been too long neglected. It died, and Ginger cried her eyes out. The mother remained indifferent, and talked of nothing but her own leg, and her elder child at home.

We had not long to wait before we had an opportunity of a dress rehearsal of the scheme of evacuating the hospital. I received one morning early, a telephone message saying that enemy aeroplanes were on their way towards us. We waited till we saw them in the distance; then, owing to the admirable way in which instructions were carried out, the hospital was cleared of patients and of staff, within a quarter of an hour of sighting the first aeroplane. Our motor ambulances with stretchers and ox-wagons, and the two carts which had been generously presented to the unit by Messrs. Derry and Toms, and which were always now—when not in use— in readiness, conveyed the wounded soldier patients, also the women and children patients, from the wards to a safe distance along the western road; nurses and orderlies went with them, and brought the patients all back when the aeroplanes departed. Only the doctors and I and a few members of the staff remained to look after the camp. We felt a fine sense of security, knowing that our patients were out of harm's way.

Bombs were as usual dropped upon the town, also upon the new barracks—a building close to the camp which had been given by the authorities to us for a winter hospital. Here we kept some of our newly arrived stores and tents, etc., and these were damaged, and some of the staff had narrow escapes. Another bomb fell in the camp, but buried itself in the soft ground, and did not explode. But, certainly in future, tents should be green or khaki, not white. Our camp must have been an easy target.

We had one or two other similar alarms, but no great harm was done, and no serious harm was done to the town. A few shop windows were broken, and pavements destroyed, and the ground around the arsenal was ploughed up, but the arsenal itself remained uninjured.

The town was not caught napping twice, but after the first surprise visit, it arranged a welcome of anti-aircraft guns. On the first two or three occasions, however, these were ineffective. But one day Kragujevatz had its revenge. A Taube arrived, as other Taubes had arrived, full of confidence and bombs. The guns at once fired at her from all directions, and we watched the woolly clouds puffing behind, in front, and all round the biplane. Suddenly we saw a burst of flame in the middle of the machine; we all shouted with excitement, and we watched the Taube turn upside down, and fall to earth like a torn umbrella. It had fallen at the entrance to the town; and an officer dashed up in his car and asked some of us if we should like to see it at close quarters. By the time we arrived, the townspeople had surrounded the wreckage, but I photographed as much as could be seen. I had the misfortune to see also the two aviators, German and Austrian officers, who were smashed to pulp.

CHAPTER VIII

All this time, we were taking elaborate precautions with our patients against typhus. An admission tent was set apart; every man, on entrance, was placed on a mackintosh sheet, he was stripped, his clothes were at once wrapped in the sheet, labelled, and taken to the disinfector; the man was bathed in an adjoining portion of the tent, shaved, and rubbed with paraffin, wrapped in blankets, and sent to the ward tents; there clean shirts and pyjamas and nurses awaited him.

The doctors who received the patients, and the nurses or staff members who undressed and washed the newcomers, and I—when I was present at the reception—all wore a quaint-looking combination garment made of white batiste, which fastened tightly round the neck, the trouser feet, and the wrists. Long boots, rubber gloves, and an oilskin bathing cap completed the fancy dress. This anti-lice armour, together with other methods, successfully kept at bay the lice which carry typhus infection.

And against typhoid every possible sanitary precaution was taken, and water and milk were, of course, scrupulously boiled. The camp was said to be a model in outdoor sanitation, not only by the local authorities, who sent up men to take plans of the arrangements, but by Colonel Hunter and other British and American experts who inspected it. But, in spite of all our precautions, though we happily kept our patients free from typhus, and from typhoid, an epidemic of typhoid broke out amongst the staff. The only theory which seemed to offer a satisfactory explanation was that the typhoid germ might have entered by means of uncooked salad, though this had been properly washed in water which had been boiled.

On June 1st, our young Narednik (Sergeant-Major) appointed to keep the Serbian records of the hospital, and to look after the Austrian prisoners, was taken ill with typhus. He must have contracted this in the town, as no further case occurred. He was removed to a hospital in Kragujevatz, and another excellent young Narednik came.

On the same day, one of our nurses, and I, also became ill with fever, and it was naturally feared at first, that typhus had, after all, forced an entrance. But our complaint was, in Serbian phraseology, *typhus abdominalis*, and not *typhus exemptimaticus*—in other words, typhoid or enteric, and not typhus.

This was perhaps a less serious disease, but it was disappointing enough, because every member of the unit, before leaving England only two months before, had been inoculated against typhoid.

At first, therefore, we hoped that we should only have one or two accidental cases, and that the attacks would be slight. But this was unhappily not to be. One after the other, seventeen women members of the unit were laid low, and three, including Mrs. Dearmer, died; no men, and none of the patients, were attacked.

It was a nightmare to hear every day, as I lay ill with my own attack, that another and still another victim had been laid low. But I shall never forget the sympathy and kindness of our Serbian official friends. Many of them, including Colonels Guentchitch and Popovitch, also Dr. Antitch, the fever expert, came twice daily, and Major Protitch always twice a day; they brought me flowers and ice—a rare luxury, as Kragujevatz possessed no ice machine—and sat and talked with me, and in every conceivable way, showed the truest friendship. Had they thought the green cheese in the moon good for me, they would have gone—on chivalrous quest—in search of it. But, thanks to the care of our own doctors, and nurses, and my own electric constitution, I was only ill for a short time, and was soon playing the old game of showing visitors round the camp.

Photo. Topical
MRS. ST. CLAIR STOBART
Talking to Serbian peasant patients at the Roadside Tent
Dispensary at Kragujevatz. Doctors and Nurses on the left

THE TRAIN OF WHICH I WAS COMMANDER, AND SOME OF THE FLYING FIELD HOSPITAL UNIT
With Field Kitchen, Motor Ambulances, Wagons, Oxen, Horses and Soldiers, leaving Kragujevatz for the front

The first to be shown round was Prince Alexis Kara Georgevitch. I had had the pleasure of meeting him, and the Princess, at tea in their London house, shortly before leaving for Serbia.

I was extremely thankful—if I had to be ill—that I had chosen a time whilst military events in Serbia were still quiescent. For it had always been understood, from the time shortly after our arrival, when confidence in the organisation and the mobility of the hospital had been established in the minds of the medical-military authorities, that if military activities should be renewed, a portion of the unit was to be detached to accompany the Serbian Army, as a flying field hospital, to the front. Colonel Guentchitch wrote a letter to this effect, and the prospect of this work kept up the spirits of those who wanted active military work. And it was fortunate for all of us, in the light of subsequent events, that our epidemic timed itself thus opportunely.

But, after my recovery, came Mrs. Dearmer's turn. From the first I had misgivings about her; I felt that she had not the physique to withstand this type of illness. It was partly on this account that I had been unwilling to accept her services when first offered.

The circumstances of her offer could scarcely have been more dramatic. Just before we went to Serbia, the Church League for Woman Suffrage had, although we were not a suffrage unit, organised a farewell service for us, with Dr. Dearmer as minister. They also generously collected more than £500 towards our equipment fund. Before the service began, Dr. Dearmer asked me to come into the vestry and discuss some details of the service. He then told me that he had, only an hour or two ago, been invited to go to Serbia as chaplain to the British units, and he asked me if he might make his headquarters with our unit. I gladly agreed. Presently, in his address, he referred to the fact that he now was also going to Serbia. I did not know that his wife was in the church, or that she had not known of his appointment. But as I walked down the aisle, at the conclusion of the service, Mrs. Dearmer, with tears on her face, came up to me. "This is the first I have heard of my husband going to Serbia; Mrs. Stobart, you *must* take me with you—as an orderly. My sons are both at the front, and now my husband is going, I must go too."

I'm afraid I was brutal. I pointed at her earrings and pretty chiffons. "This kind of thing isn't suitable," I said.

"I will leave them all behind, and wear—well, your uniform!" as she looked bravely at my dull grey clothes.

"But you would have to obey discipline, and as an orderly do all sorts of things disagreeable to you."

"Oh! I should love discipline, and I wouldn't care what I did; anything would be better than"—and tears would not be restrained—"being in that house alone."

"But," I remonstrated, "you are not strong enough, you would never——"

She interrupted. "I never have anything the matter with me, and if a doctor passes me? Besides, my husband will be there, and if I am not suitable, you can send me away with him. You'll have no responsibility for my health."

And—in the end—she came, and was a huge success.

The positions of responsibility were already filled, and, not knowing at first what work she could do, I asked her to help in the linen tent. I soon found that she had method and organising power, and I gave her the control, thankful to be able conscientiously to put her in a position of some responsibility. Her work was to keep, sort, and distribute all linen, blankets, and soldiers' clothes. Also to see that each soldier, when he left the hospital, received his own bundle of clothes after it had been disinfected. Not such an easy job as perhaps it sounds. Curious work, too, for a woman who was an artist, successful in drama, drawing, and romance. But none of her various rôles in life were better played than her rôle of orderly in a Serbian camp hospital. She never asserted herself as Mrs. Dearmer, but kept scrupulously to her new part; in a word, she played the game. I had only known her slightly, and I had feared difficulties from the artistic temperament. But she adapted this to the work in hand, and everything that she had promised, in the aisle of St. Martin's Church, was fulfilled to the letter. My instinct about her suitability had only been right in regard to her physique.

I could not see much of her, as I never allowed myself the privilege of individual friendships, but as I passed to and fro about the camp, I loved to meet her, and to hear her humorous accounts of various little troubles. I would often stop her and ask hopefully, "Any grievances to-day?" just to have the fun of a chat with her. I grew to love her, and looked forward to the time, when in happier days in England, I could hope to count her amongst my real friends.

But this was not to be. Like all of us, she had been doubly inoculated against typhoid, but she took the fever badly. Her husband was at Salonica, and we warned him of her illness by telegram, and advised his immediate return. I went to the station to meet him with Dr. Marsden, who was attending Mrs. Dearmer and, by that time, to our intense relief, we were able to give him the good news that she was better. For a time I believed that, even as regarded her physique, she was going to prove right, and I wrong.

CHAPTER IX

Meantime, Nurse Ferriss, also ill with typhoid, became worse, and, to the great sorrow of all the camp, on Sunday, July 4th, heart weakness proved fatal, and she died. She, almost alone of all the nurses, had not been content with the "Dobro" dumb show language, but had troubled to learn Serbian, and had made excellent progress. She was engaged to be married, as soon as her work in Serbia was ended. How little we guessed that it was not an earthly marriage which would await her at the end of her camp life.

During the afternoon of her death, a violent thunderstorm, with torrential rain, fell upon us—the worst of many storms we had experienced. The heavens seemed to corroborate our sense of tragedy. The whole sky became black like night, and over the eastern hills, messages were flashed in hieroglyphics of zig-zag lightning, up and down the blackness. In the west, blood-red clouds spread themselves crudely over a dark grey sky; and on the northern side, in curious opportuneness, a rainbow—in the mythology of our Scandinavian ancestors, the bridge which led heroes, fallen in battle, to their heavenly Valhalla—shone, as an inspiration of the Life beyond.

I was glad of the fierceness of the storm, because it distracted the attention of the Unit; they were obliged to watch carefully their tautened tent ropes, if they did not want to see their tents whirled across the plain. Tent ropes are awkward customers when rain and wind are combined, for until you get used to such conundrums, it is difficult to see how you can simultaneously obey the rule—to loosen them during rain, and tighten them during wind.

Nurse Ferriss had died in a large ward tent in which other nurses, her friends, were also lying ill. From them it was necessary to keep the news that she was dead. We told them that we had moved her to a quieter tent. Quite true. On the funeral day, at the time when most of the members of the Unit were collecting, to join the procession, a member of another unit, who chanced to be staying with us for a couple of nights, thoughtfully suggested that he should keep the ears and eyes of the patients occupied, by singing and playing to them on his banjo. For ten minutes before I started, as chief mourner, I sat on Nurse Ferriss's empty bed and listened, with outward ears, to nonsense about a cat that wouldn't come home at night, and a needle in a hay stack that wouldn't let itself be found. Then, when the time came for the procession to start, I said I was busy, and left the banjo party sitting up in their beds, shouting with laughter at the latest caprices of the cat.

I then marched with our Unit, to the little chapel attached to Major Protitch's hospital, for here our dead was lying.

The Kragujevatz authorities, to show their sympathy, had decided to give a public military funeral, and though I think that funerals and marriages are occasions which should be sacred to the chief mourners, it was impossible not to appreciate this testimony of a very real public sympathy. Colonels Guentchitch, and Popovitch, and Major Protitch, and Colonel Harrison went with us to the chapel. There were already assembled the British, French, Italian and Russian Attachés, medical and military officials, and representatives of the Crown Prince and of the town, members of other units, and friends of the hospital, etc. The brass band of the Crown Prince played funeral music as the coffin was brought from the chapel, and placed for a few minutes on trestles whilst Dr. Dearmer said a short prayer. Then appeared a hearse-carriage, drawn by a pair of terribly lean bay horses. More music whilst the coffin and many beautiful wreaths were placed in the carriage; and the procession started, to slow music—the same melancholy bars played over and over again—for the cathedral.

First walked a Serbian soldier carrying a cross, on which was written the name of the dead, also a wreath, with flaring pink ribbons; then Dr. Dearmer, carrying his Prayer Book in one hand, and a brown, lighted candle—given him by a Serbian official—in the other. Candles play an important part in Serbian death ceremonies. Next I followed as chief mourner, and our British Military Attaché, who kindly offered to stay by me, Dr. Coxon, who had attended Nurse Ferriss, then the other doctors, and Captain Yovannovitch, the Unit, officers, representatives of the town and general sympathisers.

This was the first walk that I had taken since my illness. The sun was scorching—at three in the afternoon—and the walk, at snail's pace, on the rough cobbled streets, seemed interminable. But the streets were lined with townsfolk, and I felt it was necessary to look stoical. I thought how it might easily have been myself, instead of poor Ferriss, inside that ugly nailed-down box. But I would have changed places if I could. Then I thought of Ferriss's mother, and of her *fiancé*; perhaps they were writing to her at this moment, planning all kinds of future happiness; and there she was, lying, just in front of me, in a Serbian coffin, indifferent to it all.

Now that she was dead, she was saluted by passing officers and soldiers. I wondered if she wasn't a *little* pleased at the posthumous honour, and whether it would always be necessary to reserve honours for women till after they are dead.

I looked at Dr. Dearmer, walking steadily, his candle still alight, ahead of me, and the thought flashed across my mind—how awful if—but she, Mrs. Dearmer, was better now. It was impossible that she should die.

When we arrived at the cathedral, half-a-dozen great brutal bells, hanging by themselves, in a frame in the churchyard, began to flop clumsily, and, as we entered the cathedral gates, they suddenly, all together, higgledy-piggledy, on different notes, broke into a deafening jangle, proclaiming in fiendish discord, "Here's the end of all things; you can't understand life; you can't understand death; there is no time, or rhyme, or reason anywhere; it's just a jumble, and the end is death."

The brass band, with its attempt at tune, persisted bravely for a minute or two, and the disharmony was complete; it reminded me of the bells during that "last night" at Tongres.

Permission to hold an English service in the Serbian Church, had been specially obtained from the Archbishop at Belgrade. Never before in the history of the Church, has the Anglican ritual been performed in the Church of the Greek orthodox faith. I hoped this was significant of a future when political alliances would mean unity, not only in worldly, but in spiritual policy. It testified, however, to a considerable breadth of view on the part of the Serbian Archbishop, and of the local chief priest at Kragujevatz.

At the end of the service the representative of the Crown Prince came up to me and expressed—in French—in graceful phrases the gracious sympathy of his Royal Master. And the procession formed once more, and started for the cemetery. Here a temporary resting-place had been provided; the town had the generous intention of erecting, when the war was ended, a permanent memorial to the British nurses, and doctors who had given their lives for Serbia; and this intention will, I am sure, one day be fulfilled. The final prayers were spoken; all was over; and we returned to camp.

We found Mrs. Dearmer not so well; temperature 105°. But one of the nurses, thinking to cheer me, told me that one of the patients—a consumptive tubercular soldier—had died. This should be a great relief, she said, as now we had had our three deaths (including the baby) and according to superstition we needn't have any more. Besides, Mrs. Dearmer was better again. "Ah, yes; she's all right now," said one of her nurses to me; "she has sneezed three times, and no invalid ever sneezes unless getting better." I mentioned this to Dr. Dearmer, and he reminded me that the child whom Elisha cured had also sneezed.

But on July 9th, after various ups and downs, Mrs. Dearmer grew seriously worse. Oxygen and other available expedients were tried without success. Our doctors, also Major Protitch, myself, and Dr. Inglis (chief of the Scottish Women's Hospital Unit in Kragujevatz), who was throughout most kind and helpful, sat up all that night, outside the double-lined ridge tent; I, tramping backwards and forwards, glad to be occupied, arranging for the continuous supply of oxygen bags from the arsenal, which was kindly supplying us. While there's life, there's hope; and all the next day Mrs. Dearmer was still with us. But when night came, we knew it must be her last. Another long vigil—now without hope. We sat outside her tent, speaking only rarely, and in whispers, when something needed to be done, or fetched. At one time the sky threatened a thunderstorm, but this passed. All Nature was hushed, waiting—with us. She had loved the wind, and several times, as she lay ill, she had told me what a joy it was to her to feel the air blowing through the tent; she couldn't have borne, she said, to have been ill within closed walls. But to-night there was no wind; it, too, was waiting, hushed.

The camp was asleep; and silence was only broken by the croaking of bull-frogs in a mud pond, half a mile away. There was no moon, and dark clouds hid the stars. For those who kept watch, the whole world was in darkness, except that at intervals, almost as regular as pulse-beats, flashes of summer lightning illumined the inside of the death tent; the camp bed, with its still and silent occupant; the figure bending low, and whispering in prayer, snatches of "Our Father," his hand in hers—companions since boy and girlhood, now to part for ever? Oh, no! Their sons were at the front (one of them has now joined his mother). Could they, I wondered, feel that this was happening?

I sat a little apart from the other watchers, and prayed—not now that she should live—life seemed too small a thing to pray for, but that our souls should be illumined to see the meaning of death. Another flash of lightning, and I saw that there is no such thing as death. Death is a misunderstanding of the mind. The body does not die, for the body has never lived; the body is matter, and inert. Life is a force, and forces do not die. The body is the habitation of the life-force, but the quitting by the life-force of the body, is not death. Nothing has died, since nothing has ceased to live. The life-force cannot die, or it would not be a life-force. The body cannot die—it has never lived; yes, yes—death is a misnomer. The word death, together with the sister words, sunrise and sunset, all perpetuate ancient ignorance. The sun does not rise, the sun does not set, and—the body does not die. Why then talk of death as though it were an ending? It is a transference of life-force from the seen to the unseen. As soon as matter begins to disintegrate, the life-force passes on—that's all. I understood.

In the early morning, as a gust of wind swept through the tent—her tent—the life-force passed; in our stupid, misleading, blundering language, Mrs. Dearmer—mother, wife, poet, artist, dramatist, and last, but not least, camp orderly—was dead. But I knew that the life-force had carried with it all that was real; it had taken to the Beyond Land the idea, the logos, the norm, the soul, of which the body that was left, was only a graven image.

Again a public funeral, but this time—a graceful compliment by Dr. Dearmer—the service was to be conducted by the priests of the Greek Church, officiating in their own cathedral. A chapel in which to lay her, with altar, was improvised in the doctors' reading tent, and was filled with wreaths and crosses of beautiful flowers, sent by friends and sympathisers.

The military attachés, medical and military officials, public representatives, members of other units, and general sympathisers, assembled at the chapel tent at 5 p.m. Four priests, with long hair and gorgeously embroidered robes, three of blue and one of red, said preliminary prayers round the altar. Strange that when men symbolise religion they adopt the garb of women?

The Crown Prince's band played whilst the coffin was lifted to a hearse-carriage—generally reserved for dead officers—and the procession, in the same order as before, moved slowly across the racecourse to the road, and on to the cathedral. Alternately with the music of the band, a choir of men and women from Kragujevatz, sang beautiful funeral anthems. We had persuaded Dr. Dearmer to evade the procession and the cathedral service, and, with Dr. Marsden, to join us at the grave-side.

Again the same frenzied clanging of discordant bells greeted our arrival at the cathedral; but inside God's house, harmony and reverence reigned.

The coffin was placed on trestles in the centre of the nave; the mourners, as before, standing at a little distance all around. In Greek churches it is the custom always to stand, at all services; there are no chairs, no kneeling cushions, no compromises with comfort.

The service lasted an hour; the heat was terrific, and I was thankful we were not mid-Victorian women, or we should have had sensational fainting scenes. These would have spoilt the service, which was extremely beautiful; more sympathetic and compassionate than the cold, callous, burial prayers of our English ritual, with its theories of dust and ashes.

The priests stood in line behind the coffin, facing the altar, and chanted their prayers in the old Slavonic language, common to Serbia, Bulgaria and Russia, and the trained choir of men and women in the gallery behind, sang exquisite responses. The music—a great surprise—was enchanting; it produced that atmosphere of faith and divine love, of which the best music is a revelation, and bad music the negation. Better no music than bad music in churches.

Again the representative of the Crown Prince expressed to me his condolences; and, as we emerged from the cathedral into the material world once more, the bells jangled forth their discordant message, in shocking disharmony with the brass band. But I didn't mind them now, their message had no terrors for me; I was fortified, and knew I could hold up. We marched slowly forward, now to face the worst part of the ceremony. For outside the graveyard Dr. Dearmer was awaiting us. It was a dreadful moment as we drew near, and the band announced to him that *she* was there, coming to meet him for the last time. I tried to interest myself in the fine view of distant hills, showing purple against the field of ripening Indian corn, near which he stood awaiting us; but I saw only one figure; I thought my heart would burst. He joined us, and we entered the cemetery, and moved to the grave-side. The coffin, before being lowered, was placed inside a wooden case, to lessen—at Dr. Dearmer's request—the harsh sound of clods of earth upon the metal. The final prayers were spoken by the Rev. J. Little, chauffeur of one of our ambulance cars; dust to dust; ashes to ashes; all was over; the last terrible moment came; we turned, and left her lying in her Serbian grave alone.

CHAPTER X

That was the last typhoid tragedy within our camp. Nurse V. Bury died later, as the result of typhoid, in England in her own home. She had, with others of our staff patients, convalesced under the kind and hospitable care of Mr. James Berry, B.S., F.R.C.S., and of Mrs. F. May Dickinson Berry, M.D., B.S., in their fine hospital amongst the mountains at Vrnjatchka Banja. Mr. and Mrs. Berry had given us much pleasure by staying with us in our camp on several occasions, and I always regretted that I was unable to give myself both pleasure and instruction by visiting their hospital, but I made it a rule never to leave the camp except on business, and I refused all invitations, even to teas in Kragujevatz. It seemed wise to make visiting prohibitive for the unit, because of typhus and for other reasons, (except for the doctors, who could take care of themselves), and I thought it fair that I should share the penalty. Also, we were never safe from risk of Taubes, and I was responsible for the safety of the camp.

It was not until a day in September that the last typhoid tent could be dismantled. On this happy day, a woman, an orderly from another unit, arrived without warning in our camp, and asked leave to spend a few days with us. She had a high temperature, and went at once to bed, and we found that she had acted cuckoo, and had deliberately come to lay her typhoid egg in our camp; this, at the moment when we had hoped at last to clear ourselves of the epidemic, was troublesome. After some weeks of illness, which she said she enjoyed more than any other experience in Serbia, she recovered.

The original engagement for members of our unit was for three months, but at the end of that time, the Crown Prince and the medical-military authorities requested us and some other British units to remain, and, with the exception of some members who were invalided home, the members of our unit almost unanimously agreed to continue for a further period.

We all much regretted that Dr. Hanson was obliged to return to her work in London. The L.C.C. would not spare her valuable services any longer. She had been with me at Antwerp, and also at Cherbourg, and when she left I much missed her enthusiasm and cheery, genial company. She returned to London *via* Russia, and the night before she left, Colonel

Guentchitch kindly gave a farewell dinner in her honour. I was also invited, and I sat next to the Colonel. I was innocently happy till, at the end of dinner, the Colonel suddenly rose and made a speech, in Serbian, in praise of Dr. Hanson and our hospital. Applause followed, then came dead silence. Was anyone going to translate the speech for us? Apparently not, so I signalled and grimaced to Dr. Hanson to reply, but she naïvely pretended that she hadn't understood a word of the speech. Somebody must say something, in some language. Much taken aback, I jumped up, hesitated for a moment about the language, and then chose French. But, as the Colonel's points had been made in one language, I had digested them in a second, and replied to them in a third, the points must have been very robust if they survived.

PART II

CHAPTER XI

But during all these months, since the establishment of our camp hospital, we had been occupied not only with military work—wounded soldiers—but also with civilian work. We had started with one hundred and thirty wounded within the first few days; but I had at once realised that as the typhus epidemic was diminishing, there would, in all probability, not be enough work to absorb all our energies, unless military activities were resumed.

But it is never of much consequence whether this, that, or the other thing happens; it is the way in which you treat what happens, that is important. If you have an ideal, everything will work together for good. It doesn't so much matter what you do, so long as you do something. Something, even if it is not the ideal, may lead to the ideal, whereas inaction leads to nothing. The one and only fatal disaster is to do nothing.

In a country which had suffered as Serbia had suffered, during years of continuous warfare, there must be need for help of some kind, the only question was, in what direction?

The inspiration came the fifth day after our arrival at Kragujevatz. I was talking with Major Protitch; he was describing the conditions of the country, and he mentioned that one-third of the Serbian doctors had died, either of typhus, or at the front, and that the remainder were all occupied, either with military work, in the hospitals in the towns, or with administrative work, or at the front; with the result that no medical aid was available for the peasants in the country districts.

I realised in a moment what that meant. The country was going through a serious epidemic of typhus, in addition to diphtheria, typhoid, and other diseases; and in the villages, and small towns, there were no doctors to prescribe for the patients, or to check the spread of the infection. Typhus victims, in ox-wagons, still passed our camp all day long on their way to join the four thousand already buried in the typhus graveyard, a short distance beyond our hospital.

It was market day at Kragujevatz (Friday, April 30th), and as I said good-bye to the Serbian doctor, on the edge of our encampment, near the road, I stood and watched the streams of peasants on their way to the market; women in Scotch plaid skirts, with coloured or black kerchiefs on their heads, and children, and old men, all driving pigs and sheep, or carrying geese and poultry slung on sticks, head downwards, over their shoulders, or leading oxen which were drawing wagons filled with barrels of rakiya—the native whisky. And at once an idea came. It was straightway discussed with our doctors, who approved, and promised co-operation, and it was at once carried into effect. Unless we seize time as it passes, it is apt to pass us by. We immediately pitched a bell tent at the outer edge of the hospital encampment, on the roadside, improvised a notice board from an old packing case, and, with the help of an interpreter, wrote, in Serbian, words to the effect, that if folks would bring their own bottles, medicine and medical advice would be given gratis. A doctor, a nurse, and an interpreter took charge of the tent dispensary, and we waited with eager curiosity to see what happened. The result was that within a few weeks 12,000 people, men, women, and children, came to this roadside dispensary, either in ox-wagons or walking from distances of fifty, sixty, even seventy miles—ill with typhus, diphtheria, typhoid, smallpox, tuberculosis, and every conceivable and inconceivable form of disease.

Besides medicine and general treatment and injections of serum, advice was given as to hygiene, sanitation, the need for fresh air and cleanliness, etc. Diphtheria, especially amongst the children, was rampant. Whole families were being exterminated. One day a man brought to the dispensary his little girl, who was suffering from diphtheria, and he asked us to inject her with the serum, of which he had heard from other peasants. He told us that another child had just died, at home, of the same sickness; he had been afraid to bring her, but he had now brought this child to be treated, as it could only die once. The serum was injected, and next day the child was so much better that the following day both the father and the mother arrived, in their ox-wagon, bringing with them their six remaining children, who were all ill with the same disease. They were, of course, all treated with the serum, and this little family was thus saved from being blotted out.

The after-effects of neglected typhus are often worse than the original disease; and amongst ignorant peasants, without doctors, every case of typhus is a neglected case. One day a man brought his little girl (Rositza by name) in an ox-wagon from a distance of thirty miles. The child was suffering from a loathsome-looking leg, the result of neglect after typhus. The two bones of the leg were as bare of flesh as though a dog had gnawed them clean; and the foot was a gangrenous mass of black pulp. Above the knee were huge holes and horrible sores. The child's mother was dead; the father was going to the front next day, and he begged us to take Rositza into our hospital that he might go with a less heavy heart. He quite understood, when he was told, that the only hope for the child's life was amputation of the leg, and his eyes filled with tears of gratitude when we told him that there was no reason why, under our care, her life should not be spared. The leg, half way up to the thigh, was amputated; Rositza, an intelligent and charming child of about twelve years of age, recovered rapidly, and was soon, on crutches, hopping around, mothering other children who occupied our children's ward tents.

For though we were primarily a military hospital, the military authorities waived the usual rule as to the exclusion of civilian patients, and we put up tents respectively for civilian men, for women, and for children, in order to deal with cases which could not be peremptorily treated at the dispensary. Our doctors entered whole-heartedly into the scheme and took it in turns to be on duty by the roadside.

This dispensary work brought clearly to light the fact that war is responsible for maiming and killing not only the fighting portion of the population; it also maims and kills, by slow torture, the women and children who are responsible for the life, health, and vigour of future generations.

Roughly speaking, one-half of the peasants who came to be treated for various diseases, and probably one-half of those who did not come, were suffering from advanced forms of tuberculosis, the result largely of neglect during the last few years of warfare.

The small tent soon had to be exchanged for a larger one; this was curtained into three compartments, one for diagnosis, one with a bed for more private examination by the doctor, and one for the dispenser and dresser.

From the first day the dispensary was besieged, especially on feast-days and fast-days, and most days in Serbia belong to one or the other category, and then sometimes one hundred and eighty patients arrived from near and far; they sat on the grass in the shade of some trees by the roadside, or they stood in a long queue, all waiting their turn to be seen by the doctor. Some cunning ones arrived in their ox-wagons during the night, or at dawn, in order to get their names first on the list. A policeman from the town kept the rota, and saw that turns were fairly kept.

One of the first arrivals was a girl, who had walked for four hours, to ask for medicine for her two brothers and for her mother, who were all ill with typhus. There was no one but herself to tend them, and she had been obliged to leave them alone during her absence. She would not stay to rest, but started back on her four hours' return tramp, her face beaming with happiness as she carried off the precious medicine. Who would tend her, and the others, if she contracted the disease?

Another day six women arrived in a wagon drawn by two cows, from a village forty miles distant. They were all seriously ill with diphtheria, but after the serum injection they climbed back into their straw lairs for the return journey, as happy as queens.

One man walked sixty miles to come to us, and sixty miles back to his home, to bring his daughter, who was suffering from swollen glands, which needed an operation. The girl had no mother, and the father, who was going to the front in a few days, rejoiced greatly at being able to leave her in safe hands.

Interesting side-lights were sometimes thrown on the beliefs and superstitions of the people. A woman came complaining of pains in her chest. They were not from indigestion, and none of the usual questions by the interpreter brought any enlightenment. But after much roundabout talk it was discovered that the woman had lately lost her father and two brothers, the former from typhus, and the latter at the front. And, in the customary demonstration of her grief, she had beaten her chest violently; the force of the triple grief had been too much for the poor chest, and it felt hurt.

For those who came from long distances, refreshments were provided, and Miss Anna Beach, one of our orderlies, arranged a stove and tables near the dispensary, and stood all day in the hot sun, or the rain, serving tea, and coffee, and bread, and plum jam—all much appreciated, especially by the children. Mr. Beck distributed refugee garments to those who were in need, and made himself otherwise useful at the dispensary.

The people had a great prejudice against going to hospitals. A man, who brought his twelve-year-old boy, suffering from confluent smallpox, wept bitterly when he was told he must take him to the hospital in the town. On another day, a woman brought her daughter, who was at death's door with diphtheria; and when our doctors said that the girl must stay with us in hospital, as she was too weak to bear the jolting of the wagon on the return journey, the woman replied, astonished, "Hospital! Why, she is much too ill to go to a hospital!" The girl was taken away, and probably died in the cart on the way home.

But the people soon regarded our hospital in a different light, probably because of the tents, and also because the doctors were women, the nurses were devoted, and the atmosphere was homely. Our difficulty soon was, indeed, in preventing them from coming. One woman travelled for twenty-four hours, bringing with her in her ox-wagon four of her children—the eldest eight years old—all ill with malaria; she had confidently expected that they would all be allowed to come into the hospital.

Indeed, it became the fashion for people, even of other classes than the peasants, to come to the dispensary, especially on feast days. Then, after a time, a spirit of emulation seized the patients, and, as the best available means of distinction from other patients, was a surgical operation, they all clamoured for operations, irrespective of requirements. The doctors often gave offence by refusing to concede this much-wanted luxury.

One woman, who had been cured of a dislocated shoulder, still demanded an operation. When she was told that this was not necessary, and that no operation would be performed, she was angry, and retorted, "Very well, I shall cure myself." The doctor asked her how she would do this, and she replied triumphantly, "I shall hold a live frog in my hand as soon as I get home." Another woman, very ill with diphtheria, came to the dispensary buoyed by the hope of tracheotomy. She was delighted when we took her into the hospital and told her that there was a possibility that her wish might be gratified. The only trouble was that she had a tiny baby at home; but she had been brought to us by her old mother, so we sent grannie back for the baby. It was a sickly child, and we took care of it in the baby ward. The mother was disappointed of her tracheotomy, but when she recovered and saw her baby again, her joy and surprise on seeing that it had grown fat and rosy, almost compensated her for her own disappointment.

Children loved being in the hospital, and when they were there, it was difficult to get rid of them, especially when they lived great distances away. Return transport was not easy to arrange, if the parents were not in a hurry to arrange it. "Ah!" said one small girl reproachfully to her mother, who at last came to fetch her, "*you* never give me sheets like this!"

WITH SOME OF OUR SERBIAN SOLDIERS OF
THE FIRST SERBIAN ENGLISH FIELD HOSPITAL

photo by Monsieur Bettich
WITH COL. TERZITCH COMMANDING OUR SCHUMADIA
DIVISION (NOW SERBIAN MINISTER OF WAR)
Superintending the repitching of his tent near Piro

Another child, a boy of about ten years old, who had something the matter with his knee, had spent a fortnight in the hospital, in the ward tent reserved for small boys. Life during that fortnight had been full of joys, and when he was cured, he left with tearful eyes. One day, about a week later, the doctor on duty in the dispensary, saw a woman coming towards the tent. She was leading by the hand, a boy of about ten years old, who was limping extravagantly. The doctor recognised him at once, and shrewdly guessed the truth. The boy had worried so much to be allowed to come back, that the mother had tried the hoax of lameness, in the vain hope of deceiving the doctor.

But it was not only the children who were difficult to move. One old man firmly refused to go; he said that his daughter's children were very troublesome at home, and food wasn't too plentiful there, and he was happier where he was. But as he knew that sooner or later the evil day must come, he providently secreted under his pillow a little stock of boiled eggs, saved from his breakfasts, to take with him when the day came. He was so long in departing that he had a plentiful supply of rotten eggs to throw at the children.

The peasants had delightful remedies of their own. One day we found a mouse's nest, and a woman who heard us talking about it, asked us eagerly what we had done with the young mice? When she heard that they had been killed, and thrown away, she was very shocked. Of course, they ought to have been kept to put in the ear for ear-ache. It was stupid of us not to have thought of that!

The X-ray department, under Dr. Tate and Mr. Agar, was also much in demand. Indeed, great was the confidence shown by both women and men in the skill of our women doctors. Some well-to-do people came all the way from Belgrade to consult them. The women said it was so much pleasanter to discuss health conditions with one of their own sex. I chanced one day to ask a young well-dressed girl of about twenty-four, who was waiting for her turn, what was the matter with her, and she confided to me that she had been married for three years, and had now become infected, through her husband, with a terrible disease. She would not, she said, consult a man doctor, but she had tried many remedies, remedies from old women and remedies out of books, and now at last she was hopeful. But, if nothing could be found to cure her she was going to shoot herself, with a revolver which she had bought for the purpose.

We were thankful to be able to help so many, but it was sad to think of the many more who needed help in their homes. Every day we had illustrations of this need for visiting the people in their homes. One man came in a wagon with his little boy; both father and son were very ill with diphtheria, and whilst the doctor was injecting the father with the serum, the child died in the wagon. The doctor scolded the father, and told him that he should have brought the boy sooner; but the poor fellow answered that he had only just returned from the front, and could not come before. He added that another child had just died at home, because there had been no one to bring her.

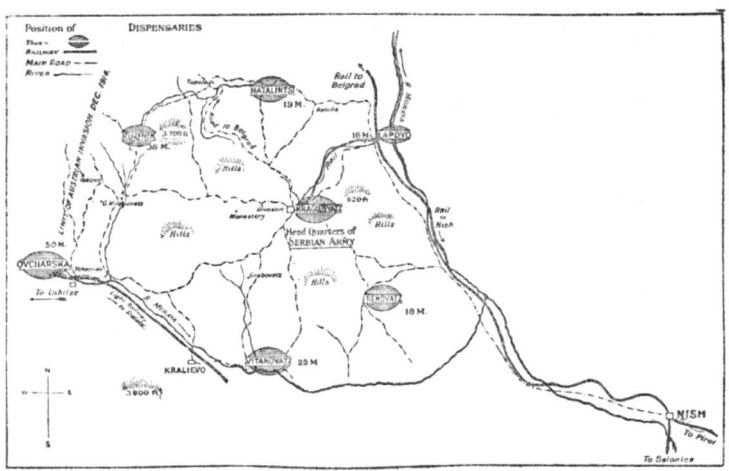

STOBART DISPENSARIES AROUND KRAGUJEVATZ, SERBIA.

CHAPTER XII

It was clear that if there was this urgent need for help amongst the peasants in our district, there would be an equally urgent need in other districts. Therefore, as soon as the success of the Kragujevatz dispensary was assured, and Colonel Guentchitch and the local authorities had expressed approval, I determined to extend the work and to establish a series of roadside tent dispensaries, within an average radius of thirty miles around Kragujevatz, in the Schumadia district, the heart of Old Serbia. Accordingly, on May 9th, I cabled home to Mr. Christian, the Chairman of the Serbian Relief Fund, explaining the scheme, and asked his Committee to send out, without delay, material, equipment, and personnel for additional dispensaries. "I should like twelve," I said, "but I must have six." Colonel Harrison also cabled to his wife, asking her to collect money for our purpose; she responded nobly, and in the North of England held meetings which brought in several thousand pounds.

Each dispensary was to comprise one woman doctor, two nurses, one cook, one interpreter, and one chauffeur, the latter to drive the motor ambulance which would convey to the mother hospital at Kragujevatz, patients who needed operations or prolonged treatment. Tents were to be used as long as weather permitted, partly to avoid infectious buildings, partly to escape the difficulty of finding suitable houses, and also in order that the dispensary could be placed wherever it would be most likely to be useful—along the roadside, and probably where cross roads met.

The scheme received the hearty approval of Sir Ralph Paget, who was acting as British Commissioner for Serbia, and of Colonel Hunter, Chief of the Royal Army Medical Mission in Serbia. The latter told me that he had mentioned the dispensary scheme, and also the hospital work, in despatches to the Foreign Office, and had asked that all facilities should be granted us. I felt confident, therefore, that the scheme would be supported.

The Serbian Relief Fund rose to the occasion, and the Chairman cabled approval and agreed to send material and personnel for six additional dispensaries. Dr. King-May kindly agreed to go to London and help to make arrangements for the medical requirements. She left Kragujevatz on May 20th, and returned on July 23rd. But there was no need to wait till the latter date to start the new work. Time was of life-and-death importance to the peasants. The first consignment of stores and tents came on July 13th, and as Dr. Iles, who had cabled from India acceptance of service, had arrived on June 29th, we established a dispensary at Natalintzi, about thirty-five kilometres from Kragujevatz, on July 14th.

The site had been selected on June 29th by Major Protitch, and the District Prefect, Dr. Hanson, and myself.

We had intended to go to Natalintzi on the 28th, but the Prefect remembered that this was a fast day, in commemoration of the Battle of Kossovo, and that he must attend cathedral service. At Kossovo, in 1389, more than five hundred years ago, the Serbians had, upon the field of blackbirds, lost their independence to the Turks. I little guessed that I should, before long, be riding over that plain of Kossovo, with the Serbian Army, whilst it once more fought for independence.

June 28th (15th in the Serbian calendar) was also the anniversary of the murder of the Archduke Ferdinand and his wife.

A motor drive on a Serbian road is always an interesting adventure, owing chiefly to the mud, which is, literally, in places feet deep, and of a substance peculiar to the Balkans, owing partially also to the neglect of road-mending during many years of warfare. But the motor will now probably arouse a new conscience about roads. Any road has been good enough for the ox-wagon, and we shall see in the near future whether the ox-wagon is the cause of the continuance of bad roads, or whether the bad roads are the cause of the ox-wagon. Perhaps the Germans will make themselves useful during their temporary visit to Serbia, and will remove the question from the vicious circle in which it now rotates. It is possible that the cloven hoof of the ox has an advantage over horse hoofs and motors by its power of gripping that glutinous and skiddy substance euphemistically termed mud.

During our drive to Natalintzi we saw something of the beauty of the Serbian country. Mountains girt with maple, beech, and oak forests; valleys fertile with ripening grain—wheat and oats, and endless fields of the dignified kukurus (Indian corn or maize), its tall, green, large-leaved stalks hugging the half hidden yellow cobs. And orchards, and orchards, and always orchards of purple plums.

Maize, vines, and plums are the mainstay of national food and drink. The people make bread, and porridge from the maize, and rakiya, as well as wine, from the grapes. Rakiya—with, of course, a different flavour—is also brewed from plums.

The universal plum also provides huge quantities of jam, known as pekmez.

We were surprised to find how much land had, in the continued absence of the menfolk, been cultivated by the women.

Our route to Natalintzi lay through the village of Topola, the village which fired the first shot in 1804, during the rebellion of the Serbs, under Kara George (Black George), against the tyranny of the Turkish janissaries, three years before the Battle of Ivankovatz, the turning-point in the destiny of Serbia.

A sharp curve in the road brought us in view of a surprise range of hills. Upon an isolated kopje, which commanded the whole land, an exquisite church of white marble shone, against a brilliant sky of blue, silver in the sunlight, which was elsewhere clouded. The marble had been quarried partly in Serbia and partly in Italy, and the church, of best Byzantine architecture, had been built by order of King Peter. The King had also built, not far from the church, a fine hospital and a school. He had as yet no palace for himself; he had first built houses for God, for the sick, and for the children; his own house he had left till last. But it will be built some day. He was living meanwhile with the Topola priest, sharing an unpretentious, one-storied house, opposite the church.

We wrote our names in the King's visitors' book, and then spent a quarter of an hour inside the church. For many months our eyes had dwelt chiefly upon maimed and diseased bodies—desecrated shrines of the human spirit. Here, at last, was a shrine of the Greater Spirit, conceived and perfected with a true sense of religion—the noblest of the arts.

The proportions of the church were beautiful, and a happy effect of ethereal atmosphere was produced by some windows of blue glass. But I wondered if we should not some day look back with curiosity on the custom of churches. We enclose a small space, within walls of marble, brick, or stone, and think that we entrap God. We are not far from the days of Moses and of the mercy seat for God's special use in the Jewish Ark of the Covenant, and we are, I'm afraid, very far from realisation of the vision of St. John, of the New Jerusalem, churchless, because the worship of God should be universal. The absence of cheap, ugly chairs and pews, interfering with the architectural lines, gives the interior of Greek churches an æsthetic advantage over Protestant churches, though the compulsion to stand is, for most people, probably a grievance. Man adopts more and more the crumpled, sitting posture, as though he were not happy at getting away from the ape attitude. But we had no time to spare for thought and sentiment; there never is time for such essentials of civilisation in these barbaric, anti-Christian days; and we were soon again on the high road, all thoughts centred on how we were going to persuade the car to leave a deep mud-hole, into which it had sunk, in the middle of the road. It ended in the visual way—ignominiously, with oxen.

We had one narrow escape. We were deep in another mud-hole, when some peasants who had stopped to help us, remarked casually that a few hundred yards ahead of us, there was a bridge over a flooded stream, and that there was a big hole in the centre of the bridge. The warning was opportune, for the bridge was so narrow that there was barely room to pass, and the hole could not be avoided; only by emptying the car of passengers, and by the exercise of much care and skill was the bridge safely crossed. If we had come upon it unawares, a disaster must have occurred.

But we arrived safely at Natalintzi. The village consisted of a picturesque street of one-storied houses, lined on both sides with acacia trees. We drove first to the café; here we met the Prefect, and then we all drank Turkish coffee, sitting round small tables on the pavement under the trees.

Major Protitch and our Kragujevatz Prefect explained to the Natalintzi Prefect our intention of establishing a roadside dispensary. The idea was warmly welcomed, and stories were told us of the appalling need for medical help among the peasants. Meantime the inhabitants of the village crowded round us, and listened with delightful *naïveté* to our conversation. They followed us as we moved to see the site proposed—around the school. But this site was not large enough. The priest then joined us, and we went to the church. This was at the end of the street, and a little way back. Around it was a large enclosed grass space, with fine shady trees; an excellent site, for churchyards in Serbia are never graveyards, and we promptly accepted it. The dispensary tent would stand near the road, and tents for doctor and staff on the other side of the church. The priest kindly offered us the use, as kitchen, of one of the two tiny rooms, not adjoining the church, which he used as vestry. This was shaded by a long veranda, which subsequently served as dining-room. Without further parleying it was arranged that we should start work as soon as we liked; that is, as soon as our doctor and stores should arrive.

The Prefect kindly invited us to "slatko" at his house. We were shown into a drawing-room and were introduced to his wife and daughters, who at once went out to prepare the slatko tray. The rest of us sat round the room talking to our host. Presently Madame and the daughters came back. One of the girls carried a tray upon which was a little silver dish with jam, and another dish with spoons; also tumblers filled with water. The girl came first to me, and I was seized with nervousness; for the life of me I couldn't think what I ought to do. There was water and jam, but no bread. Would bread follow, or must I now take a spoonful of jam? And what about the water? Must I dip my fingers in it or drink it? I slighted the water and concentrated on the jam. I must do something, immediately. All eyes were fixed on me; I made a dash for a spoon, plunged it in the jam, and boldly put a spoonful in my mouth; that seemed right. But the girl didn't go away. Was she waiting for me to take another spoonful of jam? I should have liked to; it was my favourite strawberry, and I was hungry. But I glanced at the girl, and I didn't see consent to that in her face. Ah, yes! The spoon! But what on earth was to be done with the spoon? Ought I to put it into the glass of water? The girl was looking at me critically; it was an awful moment. Dead silence all round the room; the others were all watching me, to get tips for their own conduct when their turns came. I was desperate, and the idea came that perhaps I was expected to put the spoon in my pocket; take it away as a souvenir. Where else could I put it? I asked myself impatiently. I can't put it down, all jammy, on the clean napkin on the tray. And then—huge relief—I suddenly noticed that the little silver basket that held the spoons, had two partitions, and one was empty! I plumped for the empty half, with serene confidence, and—thank goodness!—the girl moved on to the next guest, satisfied.

When we got back to camp, at ten that evening, we found that the doctor designed for Natalintzi, Dr. Iles, had by a curious coincidence arrived from India that evening. Tents and stores did not come till July 13th. But everything was that same day unpacked, stored and repacked, and the next morning at 4.30 tents, stores, drugs and general equipment were stowed in a motor lorry from the town. Our own two cars and another, lent to us by the military authorities, carried the unit, which comprised doctor, two nurses, a cook, and an interpreter, also the sanitary inspectress, Miss B. Kerr, to inaugurate the sanitary arrangements, and Miss Benjamin to put up the tents. With habitual courtesy, Major Protitch came up at 5 a.m. to see us off and to say good-bye, as I was to be away for two days.

SERBIAN WOUNDED ARRIVING AT OUR DRESSING STATION FROM THE BATTLEFIELD NEAR DOBRIDOL

EVACUATING WOUNDED FROM OUR DRESSING STATION

We arrived at Natalintzi at 10.30 a.m. after only one serious breakdown. One of our cars skidded into a ditch, but the motor lorry pulled it out. I always made a rule, on all occasions, that all carts and wagons should keep together when travelling. There were sometimes heartburnings over this, but it was, none the less, a necessary precaution.

The Prefect and the Mayor received us graciously, and lunched with us under our church trees, and by the evening all tents were pitched and stores unpacked. And already next day the success of the dispensary was assured. The good tidings that medical help was at last available had spread, and patients at once arrived. Also, that same evening, the doctor was sent for to attend a woman too ill to be moved; but for the help she then received the woman would have died.

Here, as always in Serbia, we were reminded of the dominance of war as a factor in the lives of the people. I asked one old woman who came to see the doctor, how old she was; she didn't know, but she turned to another old crony who was standing near and said: "Let's see, in which war was I born?" Her friend told her it was the 1848 Austrian war; and thus her age was focussed.

The weather was broiling hot, but many of the peasants wore thick sheepskin waistcoats lined with wool. I asked an old man how he would manage to keep warm in winter, if he were not too hot in such a waistcoat now. He replied, astonished at my question, "In winter I wear two."

I visited this dispensary again in a week's time, and found that more than three hundred people had already been treated. All was working excellently. The peasants had no idea of how to nurse themselves, or how to take sanitary precautions, and their remedies against disease were quaint. To cure a headache, they applied a salad of potatoes and onions, and to heal a wound they rubbed charcoal into it and covered it with leaves.

A woman patient arrived that day at the dispensary in a serious condition; she had been accidently shot in the neck, with bullets from a revolver fired by her neighbour's little boy. It was necessary to take her to our Kragujevatz hospital, and she was placed in the motor ambulance which was taking me back. Her nearest relatives agreed to this; but some of her friends heard that she was being taken to a hospital; that, in their eyes, meant death, so they rushed up to the cart as we were starting, and protested and shouted at us and at the poor woman; a crowd at once collected, and if we had not driven off promptly, the woman would have been snatched from us.

Another day when I went to visit the dispensary and to take stores, I found the little unit struggling gallantly with an epidemic of small-pox, which had broken out in a scattered village three or four miles from Natalintzi. They asked me to go with them to see some of the patients. Major Protitch was with me, and we all drove a little way in the car, and then walked along mud lanes and over fields of kukurus.

One of the nurses (Willis) and the cook (Chesshire) had bravely encamped in a disused school-house, finding that the journey backwards and forwards at all hours of the day and night was impracticable. They met us and took us to a cottage, in which all the members of the family were either ill, or dying, or dead, from small-pox. The walls, both outside and inside, were covered with primitive paintings of figures and of trees. The cottage contained a tiny kitchen-living room and a tinier bedroom. The windows of the bedroom were all closed, the lesson of the necessity of fresh air not yet learnt, for in the nurses' absence the windows were always shut.

In the bedroom were two beds; on one bed a girl of about twenty lay dying, and on the other was a girl of about twenty-two, also in a critical condition. Their faces were smothered in confluent small-pox, their features scarcely recognisable. Another daughter had just died, and still another, younger, was recovering. Willis and Chesshire had been making a brave fight for the life of the dying girl, and had personally fed her day and night, because the relations, in accordance with custom, had for the last few days refused to give her food, thinking that death was near. But they had yesterday, in full view of the girl, who was conscious and had watched the proceedings, prepared the funeral tray, laid with the girl's favourite food and drink.

The people were curiously ignorant about the danger of infection, and friends from their own, and from other villages, would come in and sit on the beds of the small-pox patients, and spend an hour or two, and then go home and rejoin their families. Small wonder that epidemics played havoc in the country.

With Major Protitch, we planned a scheme for disinfection of the village, but without a hospital in which to segregate patients, this was not an easy job.

CHAPTER XIII

The next dispensary to be started was at Lapovo, an important railway junction on the Belgrade-Nish line. On Sunday, July 18th, at 5 a.m., Colonel Guentchitch, the head of the Army Medical Service, accompanied me and one of our doctors to Lapovo to choose the site. The day was, as usual, a feast day, and we stopped on the way, at an artillery encampment, to watch the soldiers dancing the kolo. One soldier stood playing the fiddle, whilst fifty or sixty others were holding hands, and dancing, quite silently, in a circle round him. How could even their enemies have painted these simple-minded, clean-living peasant soldiers, as fierce, fighting-loving savages?

A suitable camping-ground was found adjoining and above the railway, on either side of a long one-storied building which was not yet completed; this could later be used as hospital with eighty beds.

The doctor of the reserve hospital in Lapovo, two miles from the station, invited us to lunch under the trees, in the field of the church compound. A requiem service was being held, and the church was full of peasant women. Upon the floor were many trays of food—the favourite cakes and fruits and flowers of the dead. When the service was over, the women picked up the trays and came outside and handed the food to their friends. They then carried the remainder of the food home; they could not take it to the dead in the cemetery, because the men had been killed in battle.

**THE SERGEANT DISTRIBUTING BREAD WITH THE HELP OF
AN ADMONITORY ROD**
Bread is on the ground in front of him

**SERBIAN ARMY IN RETREAT CROSSING
A BRIDGE NEAR ANDREAVITZA**

These requiem services for the dead, are held first after forty-two days
from death, in accordance with the old belief that the soul takes six weeks to
reach Heaven; then after six months, and again at the anniversary of death.

The women wore tartan skirts, very full; short, loose bodices, of a different colour to the skirt, generally a plain colour, and kerchiefs which completely covered their hair, and were either brilliantly coloured, or else were in black to denote mourning. The men often wore long white tunics, over white trousers, which were tucked into long, knitted, coloured stockings; and opantsi or soft leather sandals.

A funeral peasant party came to the church whilst we were lunching in the field. A man in shirt sleeves walked in front, carrying a tray with the funeral food of the deceased. Next followed a man carrying a cross, and a wreath bearing the name of the dead; then friends with flags; then the coffin, carried by men. On the shoulders of each bearer was pinned a towel, or kerchief, which fluttered in the breeze. Next came the women in gay colours; black as mourning, except in the head kerchief, is thought to be a bad omen.

Owing to delay in the arrival of the unit, the camp at Lapovo was not established till July 28th. Even then the dispensary tents and stores had not come; but some horribly ancient bell-tents turned up from somewhere, and with these and with stores from our Kragujevatz hospital, we began work.

The Doctors Milanovitch and Stoyanovitch met us at the Lapovo Station, and, with the courtesy usual with Serbian officers and officials, offered help, and gave us coffee and cakes under the trees in the garden of the station restaurant. The local Prefect also visited us; he was beautifully dressed in the peasant costume. The day was hot, and he wore no coat, but a soft white shirt, and embroidered waistcoat, brown frieze trousers, tucked into embroidered socks, and leather sandals. He invited us to his Slava feast next day at noon.

The first night was made a little uncomfortable by a violent thunderstorm. The rain treated the tents with the disdain which they deserved, and came straight through, wetting beds and blankets. Next day, therefore, we encamped in the unfinished building, and though there was no floor, and there were no windows, it seemed luxury to have a roof overhead.

Dr. Cockburn, a Canadian doctor, at once won the sympathies of the peasants, who came in hundreds to the dispensary. The first patient, however, gave her much amusement. He was a Serbian officer; he asked to see the doctor, and when she said that she was the doctor, he ran away, and he never came back.

On Sunday evening we were all invited to supper with Dr. Stoyanovitch. He was in charge of a hospital to which were attached field ambulances, for work at the front. We supped out of doors behind the hospital building, in a large yard, and other guests were officers, the apothecary, a medical student, in addition to Dr. Stoyanovitch and Dr. Milanovitch and his wife. At the back of the yard, which was well shaded with trees, were rows of hooded ox-carts; I was surprised to hear that these were for ambulance purposes. I little knew how familiar I should later become with this form of transport for wounded.

The Serbians have a delightful sense of humour, and before we had sat down to the meal, we were all laughing and joking about our places at the table. It is the custom for women to sit at one end and men at the other, but I couldn't allow such a dull arrangement, and I suggested to our host that we had better intermix, and that I intended anyhow to sit next him. He laughed, and said that as we might all be suffragettes he would do as we told him. So we had a "general post" for places, and fine fun. The night was cool, and lovely, and the moon rose dramatically over the trees. During supper, music was provided; a young man, a barber, sat near and played the mandoline beautifully. I asked how he had learnt to play so well, and our host said that all barbers played the mandoline well. It annoyed me not to be able to see the connection between barberism and the mandoline, but I haven't seen it yet.

After supper, soldiers were called to entertain us by singing, and by dancing the kolo, and as usual the kolo infection spread, and soon we were all hand-in-hand, jigging and prancing in the moonlight. Finally, when we said that we must leave, the soldiers all shouted "Shivela Engleska!" (Long live England!); we all sang the Serbian and the English National Anthems; I thanked the soldiers, through the officers, for their entertainment, and expressed our pleasure at the comradeship between the Serbian and English nations, and thus ended an interesting evening. I haven't mixed much in military circles in England, but I wondered whether it would have been possible in our country, for officers and men to consort so freely together. This *camaraderie* was interesting, and if it does not lead to lack of discipline in the field, the relationship is ideal. I came to the conclusion that in the German, the British, and the Serbian Armies respectively, three degrees of discipline are represented, and that of these the German is too severe, and the Serbian perhaps a trifle too lax.

The next day, before returning to camp, I went with our treasurer, John Greenhalgh, and the chauffeur, the Rev. J. Little, to the Slava lunch of the Prefect of Lapovo. The table was laid in the yard, at the back of the one-storied house. Two other houses, belonging respectively to our host's brother and to his mother, were within the same enclosure, in accordance with the old custom of Zadruga, which still prevails to a limited extent. The priest was performing the inauguration ceremony in the two other houses, and we waited, sitting at our table, for our turn. Our host's old aunt, a picturesque old lady, sat with us. On the white-clothed table was the usual big brown candle, and a bread cake ornamented with imitation sheaves and covered with a cloth. The wife and a young son and daughter were preparing the meal. During summer the kitchen was in an outer shed.

The priest was a long time in the other houses, and to keep us quiet, we were given beer and cognac, which we pretended to drink, and bread cake. Our host was dressed in his yesterday's costume and looked beautiful with his clean, white, soft shirt, no horrid stiff collar or artificial cuffs. He could only talk Serbian, and we had no interpreter, but our treasurer, an excellent linguist, and I, had by now learnt a little Serbian, and conversation didn't flag. But we were glad when the priest came. He said prayers at the table, then took a bowl of incense and swung it under our faces; the Prefect next lit the big candle, and the priest said more prayers, and took the loaf and cut it, without severing it, into four parts, and he and the Prefect turned it round and round in their four hands, whilst the priest again said prayers. They then turned the loaf upside down, and each in turn three times kissed the side turned towards him. The priest then broke the loaf in half, put it together again, and replaced it on the table. A portion of the bread was then cut and handed to us all. That was the finish. After that our meal proper was served. On Slava days the host and hostess are not allowed to sit down with their guests; so they waited on us, and ate afterwards. Soup, stewed beef and vegetables, stewed chicken, stewed pork, apple pastry, cakes and wine, were the excellent ménu, and finally coffee and pears, and again coffee.

On Slava days anybody is allowed to claim hospitality, and while we were lunching, we saw women, and children, and gipsies go to the kitchen and sit outside, waiting for the food which could not be refused. Slava feast used to last a week, and was a time of ruination, but now it only lasts for two days in the country districts, and for one day in the towns, and as a rule only invited guests come to be fed.

The dispensary was, as usual, a huge success. Later, when war was renewed, the building—then finished—was made into a hospital, and the wards were filled with wounded. But Lapovo station was singled out for attack by the enemy, and, at the order of the authorities, the unit eventually evacuated the place just before the town was taken.

CHAPTER XIV

The site of the next dispensary was Rudnik: this was chosen on July 23rd, and the work began on August 19th. On the former date, the surveying party included Colonels Guentchitch and Popovitch, Major Protitch and two other officers, our treasurer and Dr. Payne. The prospective Rudnik doctor (Muncaster) had not yet arrived. We breakfasted at 3.30 a.m., and immediately afterwards started on our drive of sixty kilometres to the beautiful mountain village of Rudnik, 2,000 feet above sea level. The day was brilliant, without haze, and the country through which we passed, was a kaleidoscope of colour effects, with purple plums and golden corn, and the rich green, shining kukurus. It is no wonder that Serbians love their country.

We halted at Gorni-Milanovatz, a kilometre off the track, because Colonel Guentchitch wanted to inspect a hospital in the town. So we ate a second breakfast at nine o'clock, outside a small hotel, on the street pavement, under acacia trees. The Prefect of the town sat with us, and rejoiced to know of our intention to help his people. He said the district was destitute of doctors. With the exception of the doctor in the Serbian hospital in the town, who could not leave his work to visit the country people, there was no medical aid available for the thousands of peasants in the scattered villages around. He went with us to Rudnik. The town Commandant also breakfasted with us, and, while Colonel Guentchitch was visiting his hospital, he told us terrible tales of the events which had taken place in Milanovatz during the preceding winter. In December the town was an inferno, filled with wounded, and with victims of typhus. The Austrians came within five kilometres, and the Commandant gained personal experience of their behaviour towards the women and children. His stories as an eye-witness corroborated the worst that has been told of Austrian atrocities in Serbia. One hundred and twenty women and children were tied together and mown down by machine-guns. Again, a crowd of women and children were driven into a building which was then set on fire; our Commandant saw their charred corpses the next morning. His own family was at that time at Kragujevatz, and, thinking that the onrush of the Austrians was inevitable, he was on the point of starting for home, to shoot his wife and children, to save them from a worse fate. But the unexpected happened; ammunition arrived in the nick of time, and

Milanovatz, Kragujevatz and Serbia were saved, alas! only temporarily. Our Commandant was thus spared, by a narrow margin, from killing his family at the moment when it was no longer necessary.

From Milanovatz to Rudnik, the mountain views were gorgeous. This country must not, shall not, fall into the hands of the enemy, was my constant prayer. The village only contained the inn and half a dozen cottages, the latter, as usual, models of picturesqueness. One especially was a great joy: one-storied, with whitewashed walls and red tiles. It contained two rooms, hung with hand-made tapestries, and carpeted with rugs from Pirot, near the Bulgarian frontier. I hoped when I saw the rugs that I might one day go to Pirot and see the rug-making industry. I little thought how soon I should be there; but not to see the rug-making.

We chose for our dispensary site, the school's enclosure, from which there were glorious views towards Valievo, and the south and south-west. There was not enough level ground for the whole encampment, the dispensary and kitchen were therefore housed within the school building, and the staff tents, and mess tents faced a succession of mountains and valleys, which stretched, as it seemed, to the world's end.

We lunched in an open shed attached to the small inn, sat awhile during the heat of the day under the shade of apple trees, and made the return journey *via* Milanovatz and Chachak. At the latter town Colonel Guentchitch inspected another hospital, so we had supper whilst we waited for him, and we fidgeted at not being able to start home before 8.30, knowing the danger of motoring in the dark along those roads.

One of the officers who drove home in the car behind me, had optimistically taken with him from Rudnik, a large jar of honey, which he had, still more optimistically, placed beside him on the seat. Presently he wanted to get up to go out and help to push the car up a steep hill, but he was held in his seat by an invisible power. I heard him say something rather loudly, and I don't think he was praising the scenery; the jolting in the deep ruts had smashed the jar, and the honey had surreptitiously spread itself under the Major's beautiful blue uniform trousers. He stood for the rest of the journey. This car, which was not ours, required help up every hill, and we only reached camp at two next morning.

At last the doctors and nurses, cooks and chauffeurs for dispensaries, arrived from London on Sunday, August 15th, at a moment when the political horizon was again clouded in Serbia. It had always been understood that if active hostilities should be renewed, the dispensary units must be called in. Military considerations were of primary importance, and all available help would be wanted for the wounded. Also it would not be desirable to leave small units isolated in country districts. We had waited three months for the arrival of personnel and stores wherewith to carry out the dispensary scheme. Had these arrived too late?

As a measure of precaution our German-speaking Austrian prisoners—with all the others in the town—were removed on August 17th, much to their and to our regret, to work, it was said, on the tunnel of the railway to Rumania, where doubtless supervision, in case of Austrian success, would be easier. This looked suspicious.

Rudnik was difficult of access, and risk to the little unit must be avoided. We delayed our expedition for a day or two, and on August 17th, I had another talk with Colonel Harrison, and with Colonel Guentchitch, and they considered that next day we might carry out our programme and start work at Rudnik. But torrential rain made the roads impassable. We therefore again postponed, but early on the morning of the 19th, our bales of tents, and stores, and the unit members, were packed in motor lorries and in two cars lent by the military authorities, and we set out to establish the fourth dispensary.

All through the spring and summer the hedges had been gay with flowers in wedding colours, but now they were covered with the black-seeded booryan plant (something like dwarf elder when in flower). Here and there the yellow rag-wort alternated with the booryan, in a passing scheme of black and yellow, or the delicate blue chicory flower made a brave show on the roadside; but the main impression now was blackness: the hedges were already in mourning for the sights they soon would witness.

We lunched under some trees, three-quarters of an hour from Rudnik, and arrived at noon. The long grass in the school enclosure had been cut as promised—Serbian officials never fail to carry out their promises—and by 6 p.m. the camp was established. The Prefect welcomed us on arrival, and placed everything we could want at our disposal.

This unit was especially fortunate in its surroundings, their tent doors opened to a georama of mountains and valleys which seemed to stretch to Infinity and to include all the kingdoms of the world and the glory of them. Mountains did not hide mountains, for we were on the heights, 2,000 feet above sea-level. Ruins of an old fort on the kopje of Ostavitza, a few kilometres distant, a reminiscence of Turkish history, gave the only touch of human reality. The sunset that evening ignored its usual levantine limitations, and ran riot in flaming colours of red, and gold, and nameless greens, all over the heavens: a chord of Nature in the major key; and in antiphon, the mountains gave response, in colours reflected from heaven and earth and all that in them is.

Later, when work for the day was finished, and I lay on my camp bed—the tent doors open—gazing into the black curtain of night, trying to see things that were invisible, the moon came sailing through the sky, tacking in and out of banks of storm clouds. Her wireless was as usual in minor mode. "Joy and colour are ephemeral," was her code message. "Beauty is death, and death is shade and sorrow. The shade of a long night draws near. The dews of death are in the air."

I was going to dispute with her, but she abruptly hid behind a thunder-cloud. An owl in a beech tree hooted; a gust of wind sent a shiver through the plum trees, and I remembered the stirring in the mulberry trees—the warning to David of the coming enemy; a rumbling, like a cannonade, echoed through the mountains; a clap like the bursting of a thousand bombs boomed overhead—Thor's guns, more merciful than man's—then immediately came a fall of rain, fierce, precipitous, as though the dams of heaven had burst; lightning, like a fiery sword, striking an unseen enemy; then a hush, as sudden as the onslaught, and a quiet night.

The successful routine of this dispensary was, under Dr. Muncaster, at once established. From far-off villages and isolated mountain hamlets, the peasants came bringing their sick in ox-wagons, or walking incredible distances. Evidently no simpler or more efficacious system of relief could have been devised.

CHAPTER XV

The site for the fifth dispensary was chosen on August 16th, at Vitanovatz, about six miles from Kralievo. The method of selecting localities was always delightfully simple. I tell Colonel Guentchitch that we are ready to open another dispensary. He at once comes up to the camp, and in my office tent, we spread a map upon the table; the need for help is equally great everywhere, and our aim is to choose a place which shall be easiest of access from as many directions as possible, and within motor reach of our Kragujevatz hospital. "Now, Colonel, where is it to be?" He points to a place where cross roads meet, and we decide to drive there and choose the site next day. Total absence of red tape, and a delightful camaraderie between us.

On August 16th, Major Protitch came with the exploring party. A village along the Kralievo road had been suggested, but it was a one-road place, and uninteresting. "I don't like the look of this, doctor." "All right, let's drive on farther"; and we continued till we came to Vitanovatz—a very different proposition. "Oh, this will do; let's get out here!" We stopped in front of the little inn, asked the landlord to send for the Prefect, and whilst we waited, we drank Turkish coffee at little tables in the stoep. Why should Turkish coffee, the only coffee that is invariably good, be always served in thimble-sized cups?

In a few moments, as though by magic, the Prefect joined us. He was beautifully dressed, in peasant costume: dark-brown frieze coat, trousers tucked into embroidered stockings, a waistcoat braided and hand embroidered, a soft, white shirt, and the leather sandals. Major Protitch explained our intention, and asked if there was much sickness amongst the people? "Yes, indeed." "Was there a large population who would be likely to avail themselves of the dispensary?" "Oh, yes, there were many villages behind the hills, and every person had to pass through Vitanovatz to go to the market town of Kralievo, six miles distant." "And no doctors near?" "None." That settled it. "Now let's go and find a site. Is there any school building handy in case of emergency weather in the coming autumn and winter months?" "No." "Any rooms available later, in case of need, in the inn?" "Yes, three." We saw these, and they were good, and we engaged them for store-rooms for drugs, etc., and then we all walked along the road till we came to a field adjoining the road on our left, a few yards beyond the last house of the village. Near the road, the field was level, an excellent place for the dispensary tent, and above a steep slope, beyond the level stretch, was a fine plateau dotted with apple trees, evidently intended for our staff tents. A footpath behind the plateau would make the dispensary doubly accessible for the people. "Excellent; we'll take this. To whom does it belong?" "To Gospodine —." "Can we see him and make arrangements?" "No, he's away; but that will be all right." "Very good, we shall arrive with doctor, nurses, tents and medicines in a few days." And all was settled.

Later, when we were established, the owner returned, and to his surprise he saw, as he approached, that his field was dotted with white tents, and crowded with sick peasants. It happened that I was visiting the unit. He came up to me, a little perturbed at first, but I pointed out to him what a good work he was doing, and how lucky he was to have been the owner of such a suitable field, and he was soon satisfied.

We drove home, *via* Kralievo, after drinking our tea out of thermos flasks, under the apple trees. As we reached the top of a small rise of road, three minutes from our site, a view of the country in front of us, accustomed as we now were to beautiful scenes, made us hold our breath. Upon our left, close to us, amongst green-grey willows, the broad Morava rushed, silver-grey, through a valley which was green with fields of kukurus; a chain of stately mountains, an untiring guard of honour, lined the river's route; and above the junction of the Morava and the Ibar, came Kralievo, with its white one-storied houses, its round-shaped market-place, its acacia trees, with leaves of delicate green, and with hanging branches of red seed pods, of an exaggerated crimson against the clear blue sky.

We drank coffee with a friend of Major Protitch under walnut trees in the garden of the hospital, and returned to camp by 9.30, p.m., *via* Milochai, Mirchajevli, Bresnitza, and Knish, along the banks of the rivers Ibar, Morava, and Grusha.

On August 31st, the big motor lorries lent by the town authorities, and our own car, and another lent by the military, conveyed dispensary equipment and unit to start the work at Vitanovatz.

We were up at 3.30 a.m., fortunately, as we had many stickfasts on the way, but we were established in our tents by the evening. Dr. MacMillan was in charge, and entered heart and soul into the work, and, as though by wireless, the people soon knew of the help available, and the field was at all hours crowded with patients, mostly from long distances, waiting their turn to be examined.

It was interesting to find that here, as in all other dispensaries, the women expressed satisfaction that the doctor was of their own sex, and the men also found that whilst the skill of the women was equal to that of the men, their gentleness and sympathy were certainly not less. But there was one point on which the sick people were much puzzled. They could not understand why the doctor should want to see their tongues. "But the pain is in my knee, not in my tongue!" said one woman boldly when told to show her tongue. The doctor gave an explanation which must have been extra lucid, for thenceforth it was considered good form to enter the field with the tongue hanging out ready for inspection. How far along the road it was necessary, in the pursuance of good form, to begin hanging out the tongue is not recorded.

On August 27th the site for the sixth dispensary was chosen at Rekovatz. As usual on these occasions we had our first breakfast at four o'clock, and started at 5 a.m. with Drs. Guentchitch, Popovitch, and Protitch. We arrived at nine o'clock, after only one breakdown, and breakfasted at the inn. The Prefect sat with us, and told us that the only doctor in the district had died last winter of typhus, and that medical aid was much needed. We were taken to the late doctor's house, which was well placed in a garden with fine trees and lawns. His widow was still in residence, and warmly seconded the idea that we should establish ourselves in our tents in her garden, and make use of the dispensary rooms at the gate, in the cottage which had served as dispensary for her husband. She offered us in addition the use of her outside kitchen, and later, when the lawn became swamped after much rain, she gave hospitality in her house to the doctor and the nurses. A clever and delightful woman, and she spoke excellent French. She had been left without income, and was now employed at the post office as interpreter at censor work. She was enthusiastically patriotic, but when the Germans came she had no choice but to remain as a prisoner in her own land. I have heard that Rekovatz was treated ruthlessly, and I have often wondered what the fate of Madame has been.

Patients did not wait for us to set up shop, but already that day came clamouring to the inn for treatment.

We were back in camp by 5 p.m. after paying a visit to Lapovo Dispensary on the way home. Here, with Dr. Cockburn, arrangements were discussed with Colonel Guentchitch for building wooden sheds for kitchen and for wash-houses, etc., in readiness for extension of dispensary into hospital should hostilities be renewed.

The dispensary at Rekovatz was started on September 4th. The camp was as usual installed, and in working order, by the evening. The dispensary, in four little rooms in a cottage at the entrance to the garden, and the staff in tents. Dr. Stewart was an ideal woman for the work. In addition to professional skill, she had a keen sense of humour, patience and enthusiasm, and she soon established a success. She was sent for the first evening to see a woman who was too ill to leave her bed. The patient, in a two-roomed cottage, was lying in a tiny room, without any sign of ventilation, past or present. She was closely surrounded by friends; they had already put into her hand the lighted candle—token that she was to die. The doctor opened the window, forced a passage to the bedside through the mourners, gently ousted them, and took stock of the patient. Double pneumonia was the verdict. But there was no reason, except the expressed determination of the relatives, why death should result, if only fresh air, and food, and medicines, at regular intervals, could be assured. It seemed almost a pity to rob the friends of their intended tragedy, but the doctor removed the candle from the victim's hands, and said that there was no reason why the woman should not live; but orders must be obeyed. "Who was in charge?" The mother came forward. "Very well, now you must see (through the interpreter) that your daughter takes the medicine, which I will send, every four hours. Do you understand?"

"Yes, but how are we to know when it is four hours?"

"Have you no clocks or watches?"

"None."

"And none in the village?"

"No!"

"Very well, then you must give the medicine every time you eat your meals."

"We only eat three times a day."

"Then give the medicine three times regularly, and do everything that I tell you, and she'll get better."

The friends in chorus promised that if she got better they would give the doctor a pig—a fat pig. The fat pig was earned, and many other pigs, and fruits, and presents of all kinds were received by the doctor and her staff from grateful patients.

CHAPTER XVI

There was now only one more dispensary to be established, and on September 9th I drove with Colonel Dragomiravitz, who was accompanied by his wife, and little son, to choose the site. We examined the map before we left, and the Colonel suggested Pruyelina. But when we reached this place, I didn't like its appearance. There was only the one road of approach, and Jelendo, a village further along the road, became our objective. But as we drove, the Colonel remembered that at Ovcharska Banja there were 150 Bosnian and Herzegovinian refugees, and that, hidden away amongst the mountains, were many villages, with neglected populations, and he decided that he would like the dispensary to be placed at Ovcharska.

Our road lay through Milanovatz and Chachak. At the latter place we stopped, and Colonel D. and I drank Turkish coffee at the hotel, whilst Madame took her little boy to spend the day with his grandmother. What has now become of them?

Beyond Chachak the country was gorgeously beautiful. The road lay alongside the wide Morava, and we faced, all the time, the forested Ovcharska mountains, 3,000 feet in height, a surprise of beauty even in this beautiful country. But when we turned the last corner, and found ourselves in the Ovcharska valley, I could scarcely contain my joy. A narrow and thickly-wooded valley, between high mountains, also densely forested; on the left of the wood, the adventurous Morava was rushing over boulders, and tumbling down steep rocks, in quest of its long-looked-for Nirvana, in the sea, and on the right of the road, which wound in and out amongst the trees of a thick wood, were again high mountains. Banja is the Serbian for baths, and Ovcharska is a nucleus of hot springs; they are not mineral, but contain, it is said, much radium. These springs bubbled here, there, and everywhere.

A few enclosures with wooden huts served as bathing centres, and peasant women, and men, suffering from rheumatism and other ailments, were bathing, in perfect faith that cures would follow. There was no village, but in a clearing of the forest stood one house, used by the timber contractor. This would, I saw at once, be suitable for emergency winter quarters. The only other buildings were little wooden cabins, which had recently been put up for the poor Bosnian and Herzegovinian refugees. Many of these were, in their picturesque clothes, strolling and sitting in the sunshine outside their huts.

This place was even more beautiful than Rudnik. But to my intense disappointment I saw no possible camping-ground for our dispensary. I told the Colonel; he thought there might be room enough where we stood, but I knew the necessary dimensions, and it was impossible.

"Very well," he said, "then we must go on to Jelendo." But he was evidently disappointed.

"Should we be of more use here or at Jelendo?"

"Oh, here undoubtedly," he answered, "because many paths which you cannot see, and of which you would not dream"—and he looked at the mountains—"all find their way here; whereas at Jelendo——"

I interrupted: "Very well, you stay here and look for a good rock by the river, for our lunching place, and I'll come back presently."

I took with me the head man of the place, the timber contractor, and we followed a little path through the wood for a couple of hundred yards. I saw there was no clear space as far as the eye could reach. But, by the side of us, and adjoining the river, where it was cascading down a precipice, the ground, though covered with trees and scrub, was level. I turned to my companion and pointed in front, and to the right of me. "Look here; you see this tree, and this, and this"—and I made a broad sweep with my hand and pointed to the left. "Please cut down all the intervening trees. Do you understand?"

"Ja, Gospocho" (Yes, madame).

"The trees must be down by to-morrow evening, because to-morrow I am going to place here an ambulance"—as the Serbians called it. "May I rely on this being done?"

"Oh yes, Gospocho, without doubt."

I returned to the Colonel, told him that everything was settled, and showed him the site; we ate our sandwiches by the river-side, accepted an invitation to a second lunch, in the house of the wood contractor, in order not to offend, and started on our homeward drive.

At Chachak we were lucky enough to meet the Prefect of Milanovatz, the district in which Ovcharska was included. The Colonel and I therefore asked him to be kind enough to ensure that arrangements for the clearing of the trees, for our dispensary, should be completed by to-morrow. He began by saying that he would telegraph to me when the work was finished. "Oh,"

I answered laughingly, "I don't want a telegram; I shall assume that the wood will be cleared by to-morrow. But, in any event, we are coming to-morrow evening, and if necessary we will ourselves help to clear the forest." That settled it, and the Prefect promised to do all I wanted.

OUR FIELD HOSPITAL AT DOBRIDOL WITH TENT FOR WOUNDED ON LEFT

ONE OF OUR DOCTORS EXAMINING PATIENTS ARRIVING FROM THE BATTLEFIELD NEAR JAGODINA

But, in case of hitch, I asked the unit to be prepared to help cut down the trees. We accordingly bought and took with us axes and hatchets; but when we, the dispensary party, arrived next day at Ovcharska, lo and behold! the site was clear. The place which yesterday had been forest, was now, though rough, an excellent camp site, and we slept comfortably in tents, on ground which had perhaps never before been directly shined on by the sun. Difficult to imagine a better example of the intelligent response, promptitude, and absence of red tape, characteristic of Serbian officials.

Dr. Hall was to be the doctor in charge, but she was suffering from a touch of fever, and for a few days, until she recovered, Dr. Tate kindly inaugurated the work, with the usual result, crowds of grateful peasants travelled incredible distances for the magic medicine and advice.

Our tents faced, on the south-west, an old church and monastery, picturesquely placed in the trees, about 300 feet up the mountain-side. On Sunday morning some of us, including one of our chauffeurs, the Rev. J. Little (Church of England), went to the service. We were a little early, and as we sat outside the church, on some benches, in a wooden shelter, the monk came and spoke to us. He was middle-aged, with black, thick, crimpy hair and beard. Two priests from neighbouring parishes were with him; one arrived from a long distance, riding a grey pony and holding up an umbrella, as it was raining heavily. The time for the service came, and we were shown into the church, and told to stand near the lectern, on which lay the big prayer book. The elder priest, with long grey beard, went to the lectern to open the book, and tried to find the place, with the evident intention of starting the service. But the sexton by his side, in short sleeves, and peasant dress, had his own ideas as to who was to take the lead, and though the priest remonstrated "Cheka, cheka!" (Stop, stop), the sexton opened his mouth on one side, and emitted a horrible howl, as the first chant. The old priest gave way, and contented himself with chiming in as best he could, with a response now and then. One up to the sexton. But presently the priest seemed to think we'd had enough of the prayers on that page, and he turned to another page. But that didn't please the sexton. He licked his thumb and turned the pages back again, and there was a pretty fluttering of leaves backwards and forwards. "Cheka, cheka!" remonstrated the priest, as he authoritatively turned the pages back again. This time the sexton acquiesced, with grumpy looks. All square. But the sexton ended one up. For, seeing that he was worsted at the lectern, he looked at the priest with a glance which said "All right, you'll see!" and walked smilingly out of the church, and promptly set all the noisy church bells clanging. That was a great success, for inside the church nothing further was audible, except an occasional wail, "Gospodine pomiliu" (Lord, have mercy), from the old priest, whom we had almost forgotten, behind the screen. As a finish to the service, the priest came out from behind the scenes with a saucer in which was bread that had been blessed, for the congregation. He himself gave it to the first three peasants, after they had kissed an ikon on the wall near; then he seemed to get bored, for he gave it up and placed the saucer on a desk, and left the people to take it themselves; and the service was ended. It had been conducted, as usual, in the old Slavonic language, which no one understood. The congregation had stood all the time, and taken no part, except that they occasionally crossed themselves.

Upon the walls of the church were beautiful frescoes of the fifteenth century, and because they were in bad condition, they were about to be whitewashed. Equivalent to saying, if you are ill, don't send for the doctor, murder the patient. The only touch of soulful atmosphere was to be obliterated.

After the service, the monk invited us to his house, adjoining the church, and in the corridor we sat at a table, and talked, whilst cigarettes, rakiya, and coffee were handed round. Mr. Little, our clergyman chauffeur, who generally drove me, was with us. The priests thought it very strange that a clergyman should be a chauffeur; they asked if he was married? He was not. That again was strange to them, because in Serbia a priest must marry whether he wants to do so or not. A monk, on the other hand, must not, even if he wants to. A monk and a priest were both present, so I asked them which of the two had the worse fate—the one who must marry even if he wouldn't, or he who mustn't even if he would. They laughed much, but the question was too difficult; the answer was not contained in their theology.

The priest then wanted to know if English clergymen might marry two wives? No interpreter was present, and our hosts only spoke Serbian, and I thought at first that he meant bigamy, and I held up my hands shocked. But he explained that he meant one wife after the other. He, himself, if his present wife died, would, he explained, never be allowed to marry again. Would our priest-chauffeur, who was sure to marry some day, be allowed to marry again if his first wife died? "Oh, yes!" I answered, "he may drive tandem but not a pair." I added that this chauffeur priest was a very lucky man. He marries a wife; she dies, no matter; he marries a second; she dies, no matter; he marries a third, and so on to infinity. And when I further added that, indeed, the only condition set by law as a premise for a priest's marrying with a dozen successive wives, was the decease of, or divorce from, the previous wife, our priest said he would like to live in England. "And I should like to live in Serbia," I replied. "If I were not already married, I should certainly choose to marry a Serbian priest, for my husband could not fail to put a high value on me; he would know that, though I might not be perfect, he could never get a better wife."

The priests then asked us if we would go with them to meet their Metropolitan (Bishop), who was to pass through Ovcharska. We walked together with all the monks to the tiny station on the railway, which ran from Ushitza to Stalatz, and, when the train stopped, we were introduced to, and talked with, the Bishop; also with two French doctors who were on their way from Ushitza to Nish. I hoped they might have some serum syringes, of which we were in need—much of our dispensary equipment having gone astray at Nish.

As the train was starting, the postman, with letters to be posted in the train, came leisurely along the line; when he saw that the train was moving, he gave a spurt, and dropped half the letters on the ground. He took no notice, but ran on and posted the others. We picked up those he had dropped, and ran after him and gave them to him. He could, with an effort, have put them in the box, but he calmly said, "Sutra" (to-morrow). I wasn't sure whether I envied him his philosophy; I hadn't time to think it out; I wanted to call on the man and woman who had given us lunch on our first visit. They were leaving Ovcharska and going to Chachak, and I wished to make sure of the legacy of their rooms in case of emergency weather in the winter; also I wanted to buy from them a sheep. I accomplished both missions, the latter at the cost of seventeen dinars. A dinar equals about sevenpence. Our sheep, therefore, cost us nine shillings and tenpence. It was destined for supper, and our timber friend said it must be roasted whole, according to custom. He made all the arrangements, and sent us word in the evening that we must come and watch it roasting. A fire had been lighted, in a shed, near our friend's house, as rain was still falling in torrents. The sheep was threaded on a stick, one end of the stick was made stationary, and the other end was held by a man, who turned it round and round, over the red ashes of the fire. It only took two hours to cook. When ready it was carried on the stick by two men, and a third held over it a big umbrella, to keep off the rain. We thus walked in procession to our own tents, where our cook—helped, I expect, by one of our friendly carriers—jointed and carved the poor animal. I can't say I enjoyed the feast: without the usual sceneries to disguise the horrors, it was too realistic.

Everything, however, was interesting and picturesque. It was difficult to imagine where the patients would come from; we seemed to be entirely surrounded by roadless mountains. But through the forests of beech, maple, and Turkey oak, narrow paths wound along, and up and down, the steep mountain sides, and the peasants brought their sick in wheelbarrows, or on stretchers made of branches, or along the main road, in ox-wagons.

The first patient was a boy who was terribly burnt, and already in a serious condition; he would certainly have died but for the help received.

The whole valley and hillsides were the property of the monks, and they asked us if we should like them to bless our dispensary work with an opening ceremony of prayer? We, of course, agreed gratefully.

The monk from our own near monastery, and the monk from the monastery of Sretenya, distant a two hours' climb up the mountains, together with the priest from Chachak, also the Prefect of the district, arrived next day at 2.30 p.m. A heavy shower of rain, as they arrived, made us take shelter in the mess tent. Our monk's pigs ran squawking past the tent doors, having been chased out of the kitchen by the cook. "Ah! my pigs," commented complacently our home monk. "Yes," I replied, also complacently, "and one day Gospodine Svesternik will come and ask, 'where are my pigs?' and," pointing to my central anatomy, "I shall reply, 'Here!'" That started conversation pleasantly, and then came tea. Serbian people like their tea weak, without milk, and with much sugar; and most of us liked it strong, with milk, and without sugar; so that gave us something not too difficult to talk about in the Serbian language. But that tower of Babel business was a confounded nuisance, and I was glad when the rain left off and we went out to the ceremony.

Outside the dispensary tent, a small table had been placed; upon it was a white cloth, and on this stood a silver candlestick holding the familiar long brown candle, with the Serbian arms marked upon it. The sexton now lighted the candle. Upon the table was also an old silver crucifix, with red beads let in (I should have loved to have that crucifix), and a bowl of water containing a sprig of the national plant—boziliac. The monk, on whose land we were stationed, put on a beautiful pale blue silk embroidered robe, and removed his tall black cap. The priest then took an incense vessel, filled with ashes, and swung it in front of us all in turn; prayers were then said by our monk, whilst untuneful responses were chanted by the other two. Then more incense swinging, and prayers, and sprinkling of the holy water from the plant, in all directions. Then our monk, holding the crucifix in one hand and the holy plant in the other, suddenly came and stood close in front of me. Good gracious! Evidently something was expected of me. For a minute I was frightened, but if in doubt in Serbia, kiss. I kissed the crucifix whilst he pressed the wet plant to my forehead. Evidently a good guess, for he passed on, and the act was repeated on the forehead of each one in turn. Finally our monk made a charming little speech about the benefits which the people would derive from the dispensary, and expressed his gratitude and appreciation. The other monk then took my hand and also spoke, with much feeling, of the gladness and gratitude which had filled their hearts at our coming to help their people, and the ceremony was over. They allowed me to take a photograph of them; but unfortunately this photo, with all photos taken during the first six months in Serbia, is now in the hands of the enemy.

The monks gave us pressing invitations to visit them in their mountain monasteries, and I had every intention of accepting their hospitality the next time I came to the dispensary. But I returned to camp on September 16th, the day following the benediction ceremony, and I never, alas! went again to my beloved Ovcharska.

The dispensaries were now all inaugurated, and the scheme, in full working order, was in every way fulfilling our highest hopes. The greatest, in fact the only, difficulty had been the delay in arrival of the dispensary medical equipment; this went wrong at Nish and elsewhere, and we had trouble to secure the necessary scales and serum syringes, etc. But miracles always happened at moments when things looked blackest, and by one means and another obstacles had been overcome.

The six new motor ambulances for the use of the six new dispensaries, only arrived on September 17th. They had arrived at Salonica without a note of authorisation for their delivery, and the port officials had refused to deliver them till weeks had been wasted in communication with London. And even on September 17th, the spare parts had not arrived. We had, therefore, been obliged to work the dispensaries, and to keep up communications, with the one camp ambulance that was left.

CHAPTER XVII

We were now dealing, as seen upon the sketch, with a large area of the Schumadia District, and 20,000 people had already passed through our hands. If the work could only be continued through the winter, substantial results might be expected for the poor suffering peasants. But rumours of a massing of Bulgarian troops on their frontier, and of Germans and Austrians on the Danube front, grew more substantial. If fighting eventuated, all our dispensary work must be stopped, and once more the unfortunate peasants must be left to their fate. But whatever happened, the scheme was an established success, and it was comforting to think that it could be restarted as soon as the war is over.

From talks which I had with various officials, I knew that tragedies were already hovering not far away, and, in order to be ready for eventualities, I visited Rudnik, Vitanovatz, Rekovatz, and Lapovo, respectively, on 19th, 21st, 23rd and 24th September, to arrange, either for winter quarters, if hostilities were not resumed (frosts had already begun), or for plans of evacuation if fighting began. Colonel Guentchitch drove with me to Vitanovatz; he told me that the Austrians, and probably also the Germans, were massing on the Danube, and that fighting was imminent. Our help, he said, would soon be urgently needed. On the 24th, Major Protitch came early to the camp and asked me to go and see the Chief, at the office of the Army Medical Department. On my way, therefore, to Lapovo, I stopped at the office. Colonel Guentchitch was there and he immediately told me that the military situation had become serious, that the Serbian Army was now mobilising, and he asked if I would, with a portion of the unit, accompany the Army as a flying field hospital to the front. It had always been understood, as before mentioned, that our mobile camp was to be utilised in this way, if hostilities should be resumed, and, in fulfilment of the promise which had been made soon after we had arrived at Kragujevatz, I replied that I should be glad to perform service in whichever way was to the Serbian authorities most serviceable.

The Bulgarians had not allowed foreigners to accompany their field hospitals, and I knew that it was unusual to ask foreign units to undertake this work. I, therefore, all the more appreciated the tribute now paid to our unit and to our country.

But a further compliment was yet to come. "We shall be glad," continued the Colonel, "if you will take command of the column. We ask you—without supervision of Serbian officers—to take entire charge of material and equipment, as well as of the staff—British and Serbian. This is, I believe," he continued, "the first time in history that such an appointment has been offered to a woman; but, new times, new customs, and," he added simply, "we know that you can do it." As I listened to these words I wondered if I really was in Serbia, in a country which had for many hundred years been under Turkish rule, and subject to Turkish traditions concerning women. I expressed my appreciation of the confidence shown, my hope that I might prove worthy of it, and my gladness at being able to show, even in a small way, the sympathy which existed between our nation and the Serbian people.

Colonel Guentchitch then arranged how many of the unit from the Stobart Hospital, would be required. Two women doctors, four women nurses, one woman cook, two interpreters, one secretary and two women orderlies; and, in addition, a commissariat under-officer, and a treasurer (nicknamed Sandford and Merton), a Serbian dispenser, a sergeant, and sixty Serbian soldiers were to accompany us. The latter were to serve as ambulance men and as drivers for the thirty oxen and horse wagons which would be used as transport for hospital material, tents and stores.

As the dispensaries must at once be called in, the seven motor ambulances which had just arrived from England for the dispensaries, would now, together with their chauffeurs, be without work. Six of these motors, together with their corresponding chauffeurs, were therefore at once requisitioned for the transport of our future wounded, and for the conveying of our own staff from place to place. This left the Stobart Hospital the richer, with one of the new ambulances in addition to the one which had hitherto sufficed for all the dispensary and camp work. The six motor ambulances were, of course, indispensable for the field hospital work. But the spare parts for these had even now not yet arrived from Salonica, though they were supposed to be on their way, and we must trust to their being forwarded to us. We received them later in Palanka.

I felt considerable reluctance at the thought of leaving the hospital, of which, during six months, I had been in charge, and I expressed my hesitation to Colonel Guentchitch. "But," he replied promptly, "you are needed for the more important work; we will see that no harm comes to the Stobart Hospital." It had been working for six months, and the routine was firmly established; all the doctors and nurses and orderlies and interpreters from the various dispensaries would now be set free, to give additional help, and Dr. King-May, who would be left in charge, was very capable of continuing the work.

There was no time for hesitation, and I accepted the more difficult service, glad of the opportunity of giving practical proof of British sympathy with the brave Serbian Army.

Colonel Guentchitch immediately telephoned to Colonel Pops Dragitch, who at once came to the Army Medical Office and gave the details as to the numbers of oxen and wagons, etc., available. He also arranged for me to meet him next morning at the 6th Reserve Hospital, with our doctors, to see the equipment. I was told to hold myself in readiness to leave in two days' time, if necessary. Thus, within a few minutes, all was settled.

Serbian officers act upon the principle "Trust all in all, or not at all." From that first moment in the Army Medical Office, to the last sad moment of surrendering the command at Scutari, complete confidence was shown, and had I been a male fellow-officer, I could not have been treated with greater trustfulness.

I continued that morning in the car to Lapovo, and with Dr. Cockburn discussed arrangements for the future hospital in the building, which was now ready for beds; returned to camp by 4 p.m.; settled which tents and what stores should be taken; at 5 o'clock discussed further arrangements with Colonels Guentchitch and Pops Dragitch and Major Protitch, who all came up to the camp; and finally tackled the most difficult job of the day, when, after supper, with the doctors, the selection of the staff for the flying field hospital, had to be made. Heart-burnings and disappointments were inevitable, for almost everybody from the camp and from the dispensaries wanted to be chosen, and almost everybody thought that they had special claims. Special physical fitness for the work at the front, as well as the requirements of the hospital left behind, had to be taken into consideration. The doctors selected were Drs. Payne and Coxon; nurses—Cockerill, Collins, Giles, Newhall and Kennedy (six more nurses were on the way from England to replace them); chauffeurs—Little, Marshall, Colson, Holmstrom, Jordan, and Miss Sharman; cook—Mrs. Dawn; orderlies—Miss Benjamin and Miss Chapple; interpreters—Vooitch and George; and the secretary was John Greenhalgh.

At 9 the next morning (Saturday, September 25th) Dr. May and Dr. Payne went with me to meet Colonel Dragitch, to see the equipment at the 6th Reserve Hospital, and they were much pleased with the drugs and surgical instruments. A full inventory was to be given us later.

On September 27th, the flying hospital unit was due at the Reserve Hospital for full-dress inspection by Colonel Pops Dragitch and Colonel Guentchitch. Oxen and horse wagons were packed with tents and stores, and the motor ambulances with personal kit, and by 9 a.m. we were on the parade ground. All the other wagons and oxen and horses were already there. We drew up in line, and the Colonels seemed pleased with the arrangements. Colonel Dragitch then called the sixty soldiers who were to serve with us, and when they were drawn up in line he introduced them to their Commandant, and told them that they must yield obedience and be amenable to discipline. And, through the Colonel, I made a little reply speech to the men, and our unit returned to camp.

At 5 that evening Major Popovitch, Principal Medical Officer of the Schumadia Division, came to see me, and to ask me to go with him next day to see the Colonel who was in command of the division, which was now at Aranjelovatz. Accordingly, next morning early, I called for Major Popovitch in the car, and together we drove to the Colonel's headquarters in the picturesque little town of Aranjelovatz, about sixty kilometres distant. On the way we met large convoys of cavalry, artillery with their fodder, etc., all on their way to the Bulgarian front; this was, I now learnt, to be our destination. Up to that moment, however, it was not known officially whether the Bulgarians were mobilising as a measure of precaution, or which side they might eventually join. If they joined the Serbians, our unit might perhaps go on to Constantinople; if they were neutral, we might be sent through Rumania against Austria. The third possibility, that they might fight Serbia, was unfortunately the most likely, and in that case our destination would be in the direction of Sofia.

Colonel Terzitch had visited the Stobart Hospital; I was therefore not a stranger to him; but though my experience of Serbian officers had invariably been of the happiest, Colonel Terzitch had a great military reputation, and I rather feared that at such a critical moment he might be preoccupied, stern, and unsympathetic towards a woman. But I found him one of the most delightfully human men I have ever met in any country. He received me as an old friend, and at once said how happy he was to know that he was to have our unit with him. There was here no grudging acceptance of service, but genuine appreciation of our desire to show practical sympathy. He at once telephoned to ascertain whether the unit could be conveyed by train to the destination now revealed—Pirot, near the Bulgarian frontier—

or whether we must proceed by road. It was arranged that a train should be put at our disposal, and that we should leave for the front, and be ready at two hours' notice at any moment that we received word from Colonel Guentchitch. The Commandant invited me to lunch with him and with all the other officers of the staff, and he suggested that meanwhile I might like to see the fountain of mineral water known as Kisala, and the Hydropathic Hotel, now a hospital, which were in the town. Major Popovitch came with me, and he also showed me his house, in which he and his family had lived during the summer. He, with his wife and children, had left it three days ago for Kragujevatz. I had seen the children that morning when they came to the gate of his home, to see him start in the car with me. From the moment, a few days later, when he left for Pirot, he has never seen them again, and can obtain no news of them. He only knows that his two houses and all his property have been destroyed, and that his wife and children are in the hands of an unscrupulous enemy. All the married officers who took part in the retreat are suffering similar torture.

The lunch that day was an interesting function, because most of the thirty officers were also going to the front. I noticed that their uniforms varied in colour, and Colonel Terzitch explained that it was not possible to get enough material of any one pattern, so everybody had to get the nearest match available.

The party included the Colonel's mother, a charming old lady, wearing an old-fashioned Turkish head-dress. I wondered if she would be shocked at the idea of my going with the army, but I gathered that, though Serbian women have not yet been launched into the activities of their sisters in the West, they are sympathetic, and I have no doubt that when the war is over, their lives will be fashioned upon Western rather than—as of old—upon Eastern lines.

Everybody, though earnest, was in good spirits, and I parted, after lunch, from Colonel Terzitch and Major Popovitch on the understanding that we should next meet at Pirot. Two officers returned with me in the car to Kragujevatz, one of them commissioned to see that benzine for our motor ambulances was requisitioned, and the other to do business with Colonel Guentchitch.

Next morning, September 29th, Colonels Dragitch, Milanovitch and Pankovitch, and Colonel Guentchitch came to the camp to say that we were to start as soon as a train was available. Colonel Guentchitch brought with him medals for the Stobart Unit, and these he kindly distributed, in appreciation of the services performed by all the various members.

During these days arrangements were in process for evacuating the civilian patients from the hospital in order to make room for wounded, for recalling the dispensary units, for staffing and starting the new hospital at Lapovo; also for establishing the winter quarters for the Stobart Hospital, which was to be transferred to the new barracks, on the other side of the main road which ran along the southern border of our encampment.

On Thursday, September 30th, we knew that we might expect marching orders at any moment. At seven that morning we sighted two German aeroplanes coming towards us. All the patients, as usual, were evacuated within five minutes. Five people were killed and ten were wounded by the bombs, in Kragujevatz.

Some of these bombs had fallen near our camp, and Colonel Guentchitch and other officers came up to be assured that all was well. We had a narrow escape the next day. Again, at 7 a.m., German aeroplanes arrived and began dropping bombs on the town; the intention being, presumably, to destroy the arsenal. But this time they thought our camp worthy of attention. This was tiresome, as we received that morning the order to be at the railway station with the convoy, ready to embark at 3 p.m. The motor ambulances, all in line, would have made an easy target, so we distributed them and hid them as best we could. One bomb fell in the camp, but luckily buried itself in a soft place; another exploded in the middle of our stores, and spare tents, in the new barracks, missing three of the unit, who had just been sorting these stores, by less than a minute. Tents were burnt, and marmalade destroyed, and holes made in the walls, but otherwise no harm was done. I didn't hear how many people were killed in the town, but one man who was brought to us injured, died before he could be moved from the stretcher.

As soon as we were rid of one set of aeroplanes another lot arrived, but they had the decency to clear off in time for us to collect our cortège and be ready at two o'clock to start for the station.

The six Ford motor-ambulances were to carry the staff of twenty-one with their personal baggage; our own ox-wagons and one cart, drawn by two horses, took our personal food, stores, and tents; all the rest of the thirty wagons, including water-cart and oxen and horses, were to meet us at the station. We had been given by the director of the arsenal a field-kitchen on wheels, which had been taken last autumn from the Austrians. This went with us and was a valuable asset.

It was an interesting moment, when, at the sound of the whistle, the little company assembled, said good-bye to the remaining unit and jumped into the ambulances, which were numbered 1, 2, 3, 4, 5, 6, for easy identification by their respective crews, and started for the front (on Friday, October 1st).

Good-bye to our beautiful white camp, in which so many scenes had been enacted—of sorrow, and of work, and some of play; and in which hopes for the Serbian future had fluctuated, now on one side, now on the other, of the balance.

What fate would befall us, and those who were left behind, before we met—if ever—again? But those who were left behind would, at least, I trusted, be protected from harm, for they would be under special supervision, and Kragujevatz was the Military Headquarters. Besides, the enemy would never reach Kragujevatz!

But for one and all there was one word—Good-bye. God be with you; and He was.

PART III

CHAPTER XVIII

The sixty soldiers were already at the station when we arrived, also Colonel Pops Dragitch, and Colonel Guentchitch followed, to watch the embarkation of wagons and motors on the train. We were not to leave till early next morning, so we went in relays to the camp for supper, leaving the others in charge of the goods; and we slept that night in our carriages on the train.

The hospital was to be officially known as "The First Serbian-English Field Hospital (Front)—Commandant Madame Stobart," and we were attached to the Schumadia Division (25,000 men). The oxen and horses were entrained at dawn, but the train did not start till eight o'clock (Saturday, October 2nd). Colonels Guentchitch and Pops Dragitch came to say good-bye. We little guessed that we should next meet at Scutari, near the coast, in Albania, after three months of episodes more tragic than any which even Serbia has ever before endured. I was amused at being told that I was the commander of the train, and that no one would be allowed to board it, or to leave it, without my permission. I don't remember much amusement after that.

We reached Nish at seven that evening, and during the train's halt of an hour and twenty minutes, we dined in the station restaurant. Members of the Second British Farmers' Unit, which had been working at Belgrade, with Mr. Wynch as Administrator, were at the station on their way to England.

After Nish the line was monopolised by military trains, in which were Serbian soldiers, dressed in every variety of old garments, brown or grey—the nearest approach to uniform producible. They reminded me of the saying of Emerson, "No army of freedom or independence is ever well dressed."

We arrived at Pirot at 3 a.m. (Sunday, October 3rd). I was interested and also glad to find that I was not going to be coddled by the military authorities. The assumption was that I knew all about everything, and didn't need to be told; so I assumed it too.

As soon as the train stopped at Pirot, I called the sergeant, and then immediately I realised that I was face to face with a quaint little embarrassment. In the hospital at Kragujevatz, and at all the dispensaries, the soldiers and the people had always called me "Maika." For the position I then held this word was appropriate enough; but now, as Commander of an army column, might not other men hold our men to ridicule if they were under the orders of "Maika"? The sergeant appeared in answer to my summons. He saluted. "Ja, Maika?" he answered. There was no time for hesitation; there never should be; act first and find the reason afterwards is often the best policy, and I quickly determined to remain "Maika." The word "Maika" is already, to Serbian hearts, rich with impressions of the best qualities of the old-fashioned woman; it would do no harm to add to this a few impressions of qualities of authority and power not hitherto associated with women. It was a risk, but I risked it, and I never had cause for regret. I then told the sergeant to disembark the men, oxen, horses, and wagons, while the chauffeurs saw to the handling of the motors. I hoped that meantime a message would arrive giving the order for the next move; but, as nothing happened, I started off at 5 a.m. in one of the cars, with Dr. Coxon and the interpreter, to try and find the Staff Headquarters. Colonel Terzitch having, at Aranjelovatz, said I should find him at Pirot, I went into the town and asked at various public offices where Colonel Terzitch could be found, but no one could, or would, give any information, and we were eventually driving off on a false scent, and in a wrong direction, when I stopped an officer, who was driving towards us in his carriage, and I asked him to direct us. He gave us the information we wanted, and we ultimately tracked the Staff to their Headquarters, in their tents in a field about five kilometres from Pirot, at the moment when Major Popovitch was starting to meet us. Our train had arrived earlier than was expected, and he said he was glad we had pushed on. He took us at once to see the Commandant, who was awaiting us, and he gave us a hearty welcome. He was in the tent which we had given him, but it was wrongly pitched. So we took it down and put it up in the right way, whilst the Colonel told his soldiers to watch and see how it should be done. Then he took us to have slatko (jam) and coffee in the ognishta; a circular fence, made of kukurus, enclosed a wood fire, which was crackling busily in the middle; in a circle round the fire was a trench, about three feet deep and two feet wide, with a bank all round, levelled as a seat. We sat either on dry hay on the bank, or on stools, our feet comfortably touching ground in the trench. The usual slatko and glasses of water, followed by Turkish coffee and cigarettes, were handed round. We were so delighted with the ognishta that the Colonel said he would tell his men to build one for us in our camp, and later in the afternoon this was done.

Meantime we returned to the station, to bring out the convoy. The Colonel and Major Popovitch met us on the road and helped us to choose a site for the camp, about half a mile away from, and on a hill above their Headquarters. It was necessary to protect ourselves from aeroplanes by sheltering as much as possible near trees, and we found, on a reaped wheat-field adjoining a vine-field, a gorgeous site which gave us the protection of a hedge and of some trees, with a view to the east over a valley which divided us from Pirot, and the mountains of Bulgaria beyond.

From over these mountains we might at any moment hear the sound of guns telling of the outbreak of hostilities between Bulgaria and Serbia. The Allies had played into the hands of Bulgaria, and, by refusing to let Serbia strike at her own time, had given Bulgaria the advantage of striking at her time, chosen when support from Germany and Austria on the Danube front, would make the position of Serbia hopeless.

The Colonel had hospitably invited us all to lunch with him, but we couldn't burden him to that extent; and the camp work had to be done. Eight of us, therefore—the doctors, two nurses, two chauffeurs, the secretary, and myself—took advantage of the hospitality, and enjoyed an excellent lunch in a cottage which the officers were using as mess-room.

By the evening our first camp was installed, and next day, Monday, October 4th, Major Popovitch and various officers from Pirot came up, while the nurses were busy preparing dressings and cleaning the surgical instruments in the hospital tent, to see the arrangements. They seemed much pleased. The Pirot officers came up in an English car made in Birmingham.

We only had as patients a few sick soldiers, but there was plenty to do otherwise in arranging the men's routine of work and meals. The soldiers always did what they were told, but they needed constant prodding. In the morning early, for instance, I went to see if the horses and oxen were being properly fed, and I found that the hay and oats sent was insufficient; there was not enough to go round. Though the men knew this, they had said and done nothing, but had tethered the horses on barren ground, and left the oxen foodless in the same empty field. They were surprised when I told them that they must take all the animals to a pasture.

But they were quite as careless with their own food. They had eaten no hot meal since we left Kragujevatz; but, even now, when they had the chance, they were contenting themselves with bread and cheese, because the cook was too lazy to prepare hot food, and I had to insist on a meal being cooked. I made them light a fire, clean a big cauldron, and stew sheep and potatoes, with plenty of paprika or red pepper; then I told them I should come and taste it later. This I did, and the stew was excellent.

We were encircled by mountains, and near us, to the east, the beautiful little village of Suvadol, 1,300 feet above the sea, nestled snugly in its orchards of plums and apples.

The whole valley between us and Pirot was alive with bivouacs of armed men, all ready to march on Bulgaria. At any moment we might hear the rumbling of cannons over the hills, telling us that war had begun. But, as yet, the mountains were silent, their secrets hidden in the blue mist, which, in the evening, under the sunset colours, quickened into rainbows.

On Wednesday, October 6th, we waited all day for news. We noticed that the grey dots in the valley below were fast disappearing; something was evidently happening down there. And that evening our turn came. At seven o'clock twenty-four of us, including the Commissaire and Treasurer (Sandford and Merton, the inseparables), and the Serbian dispenser, were sitting in our picturesque ognishta, round the wood fire, which held a tripod with a cheery kettle for after-supper tea. The opening of our ognishta faced the Bulgarian mountains, but the night was dark, and everything beyond our tiny firelit circle was invisible. We had nearly finished supper, and some of us were lighting cigarettes, when a drab-dressed soldier—an orderly from Staff Headquarters—appeared in the entrance. He handed to me a small, white, square envelope, addressed to the Commander of the Column. I opened it and took out a slip of paper; I put my signature upon the envelope as a token of receipt, and gave it to the messenger, and he disappeared. The interpreter, Vooitch, came and stood behind me, and we read the slip of paper in silence; then he whispered the translation. I shall never forget the looks of eager expectation on the faces which were illumined by the firelight. "What does it say?" "We move from here at five o'clock to-morrow morning," was the answer. The destination, must, of course, not be revealed. Immediately, when the precious tea had been drunk, we all went out and began preparations. As every one was new to the work, it was better to do all we could before going to bed. The men were called, and dispensary and kitchen tents and their contents were packed, and also my tent, to save time in the morning.

From midnight to 3.30 a.m. I rested in the dug-out, round the fire, looking out over the dark valley to the invisible mountains. What a silence! Would it soon be broken by a murderous sound echoing through the valley?

Were those men, those peasant soldiers in the plain below, already rushing to be destroyed, shattered into ugly fragments, by other men—other peasant soldiers—who would also be shattered into ugly fragments soon? Yes, soon, very soon, Hell would be let loose—in the name of Heaven.

I rose at 3.30 to ensure that everyone should be in time at his or her own job, and punctually at five o'clock all was ready for the start. With human beings, as with all animals, habit is second nature; whatsoever thing is done at the beginning, that same thing, rather than some other thing, comes most easily at all times. "As it was in the beginning, is now and ever shall be," is the text for most folks. I took care, therefore, that the start should be methodical. At the sound of the whistle, the convoy drew up in line; first, the ox-wagons, loaded with tents and stores and general equipment, the leading wagon carrying the Red Cross flag; next, the horse-drawn wagons, also with stores and provisions; in these rode the dispenser, Sandford and Merton, and the interpreter; then the motor ambulances, in which travelled the twenty-one members of the British Staff with their personal kit.

Colonel Terzitch had kindly, the night before, sent up four riding horses; no one had said that I was to ride, but it was obvious that I couldn't control the column of men and of slow-moving wagons if I was sitting comfortably inside a swiftly-moving motor-car. I therefore made up my mind to ride at the head of the convoy always, and to take the lead in every deed, for better or for worse, and to share with the men the practical difficulties of the road. So I took one horse, the black one, for myself, and how thankful I was that I was not dependent on a side saddle; gave two to the armed orderlies, who had been told to keep near me always, and one I reserved for Vooitch or for Sandford, whose duty it was to ride in advance and procure food for men and cattle.

Dawn was breaking as the wagons and ambulances came into line in single file; I mounted my horse, shouted "Napred!" (forward), and, followed by the two mounted orderlies, took the lead out of the field and over the ditch, which we had levelled, into a narrow lane which turned abruptly to the right and led down a steep hill into the main road.

Out of the folds of the mountains in the east, white mists were slowly rising, and reflecting colours of purple, and pink, and mauve, from the heralding rays of the rising sun. The valley plains, which had yesterday been alive with bivouacs, were now deserted, the men in thousands were already in procession on the road.

As we reached the bottom of the hill and struck the main road, Colonel Terzitch and our P.M.O. were starting from their encampment, and joining the road, in a carriage drawn by two horses. They waved us a salute, and we took our place in the line already formed behind the ambulance column. In front of this column came the pioneers, engineers, and other auxiliaries, then all the other various columns of our division; behind us were the butchers and the bakers; there were no candlestick-makers.

Our destination was Stananitza, 40 kilometres distant, and the road lay through Pirot. Where was now the carpet-making industry? I had little thought that day at Rudnik, when I so much wished to go to Pirot, that I should visit the place so soon, but that carpet-seeing would not be on the programme.

Congestion of convoys was great, and progress was slow; we were for hours crawling and stopping, and crawling, crawling, crawling through the town. I realised at once that there would be difficulty in keeping the column together owing to the different paces respectively of the cars, the horses, and the oxen. The cars wanted to go fast, the oxen wanted to go slow, and the horses neither fast nor slow; but I determined that first day that, as I myself couldn't go at three different paces, and as I was responsible for the safety of all, we must, by one means or another, keep together. The wagon horses had no objection to going at oxen pace, and the motors compromised by driving on for half an hour and then waiting, or else by starting half an hour after the rest of us. This plan was adopted throughout, with the result that during the whole of the next three months we never lost any of the convoy.

BURYING OUR DEAD BY THE ROADSIDE

THE HISTORIC PLAIN OF KOSSOVO

CHAPTER XIX

After Pirot the country was magnificent: narrow roads wound round and round, ascending the high mountains, and from view-points on the hills, we could see behind us, and before us, only interrupted by the curves of the mountain road, endless columns of the Serbian Army; this was not visible as soldiers, oxen, guns, and transport, but as the sinuous movement of a grey serpent winding itself round and round the mountain passes.

I was surprised at finding that there were to be no outspans. In South Africa it was the invariable rule to rest the oxen for two hours after every three hours of trek. But now we were told that we must only halt when the columns ahead of us halted, and that was very occasionally, for a quarter of an hour at a time. Meals, therefore, were not a prominent feature of the day.

When night fell we were still trekking, and from 5 p.m. the roads were atrocious, and in the pitchy darkness it was impossible to see the holes into which one's horse must stumble. We reached our goal at 9 o'clock: sixteen hours in the saddle without being tired was a good beginning. We were directed to our camping site, which was amongst herds of other convoys; but as the ground was swampy, and there was no room for tents, and we had to move off again at five next morning, we didn't unpack the tents, but slept in the cars. One of the chauffeurs had good luck: he fell into a hole six feet deep, invisible in the darkness, and didn't break his neck; he only cut his head.

There wasn't much time for sleep; there were many things to arrange, and I was up again at 3.30 next morning; it was better to make sure that the men were up, and that fires were lighted, for hot coffee, and eggs, in case there should be no time to eat during the day. And our cook, Mrs. Dawn, from that first day to the last, when we reached Medua, was splendid. She loyally complied with my wish that, as meals during the day were uncertain, we must always, however early the start, have hot coffee and porridge before we left. This meant that she must rise an hour earlier than anybody else—except myself and the soldiers—and she and I were always in rivalry as to who was up first.

The road ran along narrow passes, between precipitous rocky mountains; in these were many large caves. Goats were grazing on the hillsides, and I noticed, away up on the sky-line, on the top of a high mountain, a solitary man, herding his flock of goats, which had found a patch of green grass amongst the barren rocks. He belonged to another world. I don't know why, but I have often thought of that man, and wondered if he is still up there upon his hill-top, happily detached from the sordid, worrying, cruel world below.

We heard that day sounds of distant firing, and we were told that our Army had beaten back 2,000 Austrians in the north-east corner. It rained all day, and as we had again been told that we were to push on without halting, we were glad to reach Knasharevatz at 9 p.m. I had sent the dispenser, who talked German, in advance, to find a camping site, but when we reached the town he had disappeared. The streets were in darkness, the rain was merciless, and things were looking rather gloomy, when an officer in a blue cloak rode up with a message from Colonel Terzitch, saying that the latter would like to see me.

The Colonel was quartered in a house in the middle of the town; so I halted the column, and rode on with the officer. When we reached the house, I was conscious for the first time that the rain was pouring off my hat-brim like a water-spout, that my gloves were so sodden I couldn't take them off, and that my general appearance was a little aqueous. I didn't mind, but I hoped that the Colonel and the P.M.O. wouldn't feel sorry. They, however, were as usual, splendidly tactful; they just said enough to let me know that they knew that I knew that they knew what we were all thinking, and then they told me that they had arranged for us all to dine at a restaurant, and that we had better sleep in our cars in the market square; the men and wagons would take up quarters in a street near by. The P.M.O. came downstairs with me, and I hoped he wouldn't come out and see me mount; my coat was heavy with rain, and I had begun to suspect that I might not find it as easy as usual to spring lightly over the saddle, after a second day of sixteen hours continuously in the wet. He came; but he didn't discover.

I rode back to the doctors and the others with the good news of a real dinner ahead of us, and then we ate the real dinner in the restaurant—the Café de Paris—and went to bed on the stretchers, in the cars, in the square, much to the interest of the native population, who were most of them looking at English women for the first time.

We breakfasted early in the café, and at eight the P.M.O. came and told me confidentially that we should be moving on to-day, and that we had better buy food and stores to take with us. In the meantime, we could, he said, go to a little house, with a field adjoining, for the cars, just outside the town, and have a wash and brush up, and await the order to move. The unit much appreciated the washing interval, and when they were installed, and baths and hair brushing and clothes washing were in full swing, I drove back to the town with cookie, and bought meal, sardines, coffee, bread, etc. We were much helped in our purchasing by a Serbian artist friend, Monsieur Bettich, who was with the Headquarters Staff. We met him in the street, and he told us which were the best shops, and came with us and bargained for us. He was a fine artist; I had seen some of his pictures for sale at the Red Cross depôt at Nish, and I had bought two wonderful scenes of soldier life, little thinking that I should ever meet the artist. These pictures are now, alas! in German hands, with many other prized possessions. We talked to each other in German.

We had now only one interpreter, as the man who had been sent to us at the last moment at Kragujevatz, because I did not want to deprive the Stobart Hospital of its tried men, was suffering from phthisis and tuberculosis, and we had to send him back to Kragujevatz from Pirot.

Before we had quite finished our shopping, our artist friend caught sight of the cavalry moving from the town in the direction of Nish, so he suddenly said "Good-bye! The Staff will be off directly. I must go. You'll be going too. Meet again." I returned at once to the unit, and all day we waited, expecting orders, but none came. At four o'clock, the Major in command of the ambulance column, which always immediately preceded us on the road, came and asked if I had received any orders. He said that the Headquarters Staff had already started for Nish, in their carriages, and he couldn't understand why he had not heard anything. I guessed that we'd been forgotten, so I sent one of the cars and the interpreter, to follow the Staff, and to ask for orders. At 6 p.m. the messenger came back, with the reply that we were to move at once towards Nish. The orderly to whom the original message had been entrusted, had either forgotten it or taken it elsewhere. The P.M.O. was glad that I had asked for information.

I sent word to the ambulance column, and they, in the absence of their Major, who was in the town, started off on trek at once; but when the Major returned, he was annoyed at having been forgotten, and he recalled them and said he was going to wait till the official order came. That was his affair; but his wagons were horse-drawn, so I knew he could catch us up.

I started the column on the road, and went on ahead with the cars to overtake the Staff and get orders. We had a quick supper in the town at our café on the way. While we were mustering and about to start, a man and two women, who said they were members of a Danish hospital unit, came up and asked questions, to which they received no answers. I was suspicious of them, because they told us, as though they were pleased, that Belgrade had been taken by the Germans and Austrians, and that the Armies of the Allied French and English had arrived at Salonica, but that they had been refused permission to pass through Greece, though Nish was beflagged in readiness for their arrival. I didn't at the time believe them, though I had begun to wonder why we were on the road to Nish instead of to Sofia.

The road, in the dark, was a trial for the cars—tremendous hills with hairpin corners—and several times we feared the cars would break down. But the chauffeurs showed great pluck, and as they kept together, they helped each other successively. At 10.30 p.m., when we reached the summit of a place called Vesibaba, we found an encampment all asleep, and we were told by the guards that this was Staff Headquarters; so we ran the cars under a shed and went to bed in them. The rest of the column arrived at two next morning. I rose early to get news of our next move, and had a talk with a friendly major of a telegraph section, who was cleaning his teeth outside his tent. I wouldn't allow him to interrupt such an enjoyment, so he finished the operation, and when his man had taken away the basin, he insisted on giving me a cup of coffee, and then we walked up and down the road—no one else was up—and discussed the political and military situation. Venizelos had just resigned, and it seemed likely that there would be a reaction on the part of the people in his favour. An orderly from Headquarters then came up and presented to me the fateful, white, square envelope—the order to move on, at 6 a.m., to Malça. Breakfast was now ready, and we were on the road by six, forming part of the everlasting grey-brown procession.

The road was downhill, less interesting than hitherto, but better for the cars, and we reached Malça at five o'clock. The only excitement had been the appearance of two Bulgarian aeroplanes, which were receiving attention from the guns at Nish, but they were not hit.

CHAPTER XX

On arrival at Malça we were told to bivouac in a field adjoining the road, just outside the village. It had rained all day, and we ate our supper in the rain, round a wood fire, which had been difficult to light. We sat on the shafts of the wagons, or on anything that presented itself as a seat above the soaking ground, and the night was so dark, that we took the substance of the seat on trust. In the middle of supper there was a sudden earthquake, and two of the nurses were shot from their seat, over the fire, to the other side. We found that they had, unawares, seated themselves on the back of a weary ox, who had apparently found the fire a trifle too hot, and had uprisen. It was not worth while, we were told, to put up tents, so again we slept in the cars, and we revelled in the luxury of seven hours of sleep. I always now, and for the next three months, slept in my day clothes, as the order to move generally came at night, and time spent in dressing could be better spent in hastening the preparations for departure. I learned, during this journey, to economise in dressing and in sleeping, as well as in eating.

Next morning (Monday, October 11th) I was up at four o'clock, and though the men had been told that we were to start at five, I found them all asleep, near the wagons, round their wood fires. No hay had been fetched, and this would mean a serious delay. I saw that the occasion required an exhibition of a little majorly wrath. So I sent for all the men, and, through the interpreter Vooitch, made them understand that a command must be obeyed. When I began speaking, I was not genuinely angry, and I only gave them the external fierce eye and a firm voice; but feelings quickly adapt themselves to contortions of the muscles, and I soon found that I was giving them the real thing, with excellent results. I had not the rifle butt or stick to back me up, but the men understood. But by the time that they had fetched the hay to take with us, for the oxen and horses, and had hauled a stuck wagon out of the mud, we were late. We did not start till 5.30, with the result that the Bakers' Column, which should have been behind us, was ahead of us—a terrible disgrace. But we caught them up, and I made them allow us to pass them, and we were never late again.

We reached Nish at 10 a.m., and found that the town was indeed beflagged in honour of the arrival of the Allies! We guessed that they would not arrive now, and for many weeks to come, those flags of welcome drooped metaphorically in our hearts, reproducing that indescribable feeling of mingled hope, disappointment, and humiliation that we felt as we rode through Nish that day.

We outspanned beside the Red Cross railway station, on a plain which was covered with encamped columns—cavalry, infantry, pioneers, engineers, bakers, etc.—all belonging to the Schumadia Division.

The President of the Red Cross, Doctor Soubotitch, who had visited the Stobart Hospital at Kragujevatz, at once sent a kind message, asking me and our secretary, J. G., to lunch with him and to meet the Commander of our division, Colonel Terzitch, and our P.M.O. The two latter were hurrying to leave by train for the north of Serbia. The secret was now revealed that our division, which was reckoned the best in the Serbian Army, had been ordered to the Danube front to meet the combined German and Austrian attack, which was now inevitable. We went with the President to the station to bid the Colonel and the Major God-speed. Our column was to follow during the day, when its turn for a train should come. Meanwhile, Doctor S. generously, from the Red Cross depôt, filled some blanks in our medical and food stores; he also gave us some extra clothing for the soldiers.

He had suffered much since we had seen him at Kragujevatz. He had lost his only son, the only child, from typhoid; and his wife, distracted with grief, had died soon afterwards. His house was a house of ghosts. He showed us the room in which his wife had died, and the room in which his son had lived. But he could now, he said, face the future fearlessly, for he had nothing left to fear from death. The only living things which were left to him to love were two beautiful and well-bred ponies, which had belonged to his boy. These were capering playfully in the field, and came up to be petted when he called them. Were these also lost to him when Nish was captured by the enemy? In memory of his beloved, he had given all his fortune to a foundation for Serbian doctors, and was then living on his doctor's income. He will now have lost that too.

At the station we saw the first wounded arrive by train from Belgrade. We spoke to them, and they told us that it was true that Belgrade had been taken by the Germans. They also added that the German infantry were of an inferior class, but that the artillery was, as always, terribly strong.

The plain, which had been crowded on our arrival, was gradually discharging its convoys into the trains, which steamed north one after the other in quick succession. But on the Station platform, as the trains departed, there were no demonstrations, no bands, no singing of "Auld Lang Syne." In Serbia there was no need of fictitious aids to sentiment. The work was performed silently, almost automatically; war was no novelty in Serbia.

We might expect our turn to leave at any time after midnight. We placed corporals, in watches, at the station all through the night to warn us, but one, two, three o'clock came and there was no signal. We rested in the cars, and made ourselves hot coffee at 2.30 a.m., found that we should not be called for some hours, and slept till six. Still no call, so later I drove into Nish to pay my respects to the British Minister, Sir Charles Des Graz, whom I had met when he visited us at Kragujevatz, and I told him of my appointment with the Serbian Army. I found that he, too, was very human, with no artificial stiffness or convention. He was not shocked, but much interested on hearing that I was in command, and called his secretary from the next room and told him that I held rank equal to that of major. We discussed the political situation, and asked and answered questions of interest to us both. He asked, as though it were incredible, if it were true that the Bulgars had attacked on the front we had just left. They had not done so as yet. Sir Ralph Paget was still away, or I should have called also on him.

We were to leave in the next train after the Ambulance Column of which Major A. was in command; and at 5 p.m. some of us went to the station to watch their embarkation. This was prolonged, and we talked to two friendly French doctors who were with Major A. Eventually the train steamed out of the station, and I turned to go and see the stationmaster about our train, when, to my surprise, I saw the short, stout, French doctor standing on the platform, still talking animatedly with one of our doctors. "Didn't you mean to go with your column?" I asked surprised. He turned round and saw that the train had gone—without him. It was obviously his own fault, but that was not his opinion, and for a time it looked as though the fury of the coming war, was to be channelled in the rage of one French doctor against the Serbian nation. But I pointed out hurriedly, in passing, what luck it was for him, and for us, that he had been left behind, because now he could travel with us in our third-class carriages, instead of in the cattle truck which would have been his fate.

At that moment the stationmaster rushed up with worried face. "Would I," he asked, "be so very good as to let the Bakers' Column go before us, because the next train contained more trucks than we should need, and they were needed by the bakers?" Our column was already waiting to embark, drawn up in line outside the station, impatient to be off after so much delay; but, of course, I agreed to the stationmaster's request, and we made room for the bakers to pass. We spent the interval eating supper and pacifying the French doctor for the "insult" of having been left behind. By the time supper was finished, he was so far mollified that he was willing to restrict his vengeance to the person of the Major, and to let off the Serbian nation. So I had hopes that after a night's journey under the same pacifying influences, there would be hope even for the Major.

We had great difficulty in getting the cars on to the trucks, which were too small, and the horrible suggestion was made that the cars must be left behind and follow later. I knew what that would mean: we should never see them again, and we could not evacuate the wounded or carry the staff without them. So I insisted firmly that the barriers of the trucks must be removed, and that the trucks must be hacked into the necessary size. And the stationmaster, wearied and overworked, without time for sleep or food, was a marvel of patience and good temper. He let us do what we liked, and our chauffeurs, who were also marvels of resourcefulness, hammered and unscrewed and manipulated, in one way and another, so that before long the task was accomplished, and the cars were all safely on board. Then, as we were at last about to start, we heard shouts of horror, and looking towards the tail end of the long train, which had at the moment no one near it, we saw flames of fire leaping in the air—one of the trucks, containing one of our wagons and, alas! some petrol barrels, was blazing fiercely. At this last moment was our equipment to be destroyed and our work to be stopped? The hood of the wagon was burned and some of the soldiers' clothes, but the petrol was rescued before the fire reached it, the fire was soon extinguished, and no great harm was done.

We left at 7 p.m., and slept as best we could on the narrow wooden seats of the third-class carriages. Our destination had not been officially mentioned, and my instructions were to stay in the train until it stopped. But I knew that we were bound for Belgrade or Semendria. At 8.30 next morning, (Wednesday, October 13th) the train stopped at a station called Velika Plana (Big Hill), and we saw, to our surprise, that the Bakers' Column was outspanned on the platform. Nothing happened, and nobody came with orders, so I asked the engine driver if he had received orders to stop here. He said "Yes"; and he thought we had better disembark, as we were not going any farther. I asked the station commandant, and he said also that we must leave the train; no more trains were to run north; but he had no further orders for us. Something had evidently happened to cause a change in the plans, as Major A.'s column had passed through and gone on safely.

I then disembarked the column, left the interpreter with them, and rode to the town with the German-speaking dispenser, and an orderly, to see the officer in command of the military station. He knew nothing, and we were discussing what could best be done, when the telegraphic machine rapped out a message telling him to tell me to proceed at once, by road, to a place called Palanka. I was to communicate a similar order to the bakers. I returned to the column, who were waiting ready to leave, and while we were making the final arrangements, German Taubes dropped bombs upon the line close to us. But at 10.30 a.m. we left the station. From that moment, and until we reached Brindisi, three months later, on our return to England, we did not board another train.

We gave our French friend a front seat in one of the cars; his wrath against the Major was now modified to sarcasm; the Major's life was saved. And I should not like to swear that at the end of the day, when the doctor rejoined his unit, he did not express even gratitude to the Major for the opportunity that had been given him to "learn English."

CHAPTER XXI

We reached Palanka, a clean, cheery little town, at 1.30 p.m. We drew up in the square, in the middle of the town, and I rode on to see the officer at the military station, to ask for orders. He knew nothing, so I went on to the central telephone station, rang up Headquarters Staff, who were, I discovered, at Michaelovatz, and talked to our P.M.O., who told me to put up our hospital in a field near the railway station, and to arrange to send a motor-ambulance at six to-morrow morning, to Michaelovatz to bring back wounded. That looked like business, and greatly cheered the doctors and nurses, who were getting restless for want of work. We pitched the camp before dusk, and had a peaceful night.

At six the next morning (Thursday, October 14th) I drove with one car, and Dr. Payne with another, to Headquarters—a run of three-quarters of an hour. Colonel Terzitch and our P.M.O. and our artist friend were finishing coffee. They gave us some, and showed us two German prisoners who had just come in. Fighting had begun, and it seemed that though our one division of 25,000 men was confronted with 100,000 Germans and Austrians under von Mackensen, with their biggest artillery, we were holding our own fairly well. Wounded were coming along the road in ox-carts from the battle-field, and along the road were also streams of fugitives flying from the bombarded villages.

The P.M.O. came with me in the car to choose a site for our hospital, nearer to Michaelovatz and the front, than Palanka. We found a camping-place opposite a wood, near Aranya, twenty minutes' run from Palanka. I then went back to the latter town to bring out the column, and we were on the site, the southern side of a sheltering wood, by two o'clock. Tents were pitched before dusk, and immediately streams of wounded began arriving, and continued to come all through the night, and the next day and night. They drove up, in rough, springless ox-wagons, from the battle-field, were removed by the ambulance men, and placed inside our hospital tent. The doctors received them, diagnosed them, and treated them; the nurses dressed their wounds; the cook gave them food and drink (popara and bread, and tea or coffee; and, in the middle of the day, soup or stew); the chauffeurs then drove those who were fit to travel, to the nearest evacuation hospital in Palanka, and the others (fifty) spent the night in our tents, and were transported next day.

Rain fell all day and all night; the mud was horrible, and the wind unpleasantly cold; fugitives, in increasing numbers, streamed along the road; and the thunder of the guns was continuous. But I never heard anyone say anything about the guns; no one gave a thought to anything but work. There were that day one hundred wounded to be tended.

To our relief a courier from Kragujevatz arrived with the spare parts of the motors, and some benzine, and we took the opportunity of sending back by him some tents, which we could spare, to lighten the wagons; also we regretfully parted from one nurse and one orderly. They were both satisfactory in every way, but it was desirable to economise space in the cars, as we were likely to be continuously on the move, and there was likelihood that their services might now be much needed in the hospital at Kragujevatz, or at Lapovo.

On Saturday afternoon, October 16th, a mounted orderly from Headquarters brought, in the usual white, square envelope, the order to move on to Barchinatz. We left at 3.15, and arrived at 7 p.m., pitched our tents, in the dark and the rain, and had supper at nine. We heard, to our intense satisfaction, that the Germans had been beaten back, and that the French and English were fighting the Bulgars. But our joy did not last long. On Sunday, October 17th, the mounted orderly arrived; he brought with him the order to evacuate the camp; I signed the envelope, and he left. Then, as usual on these occasions, I took out the sectional map, provided by Headquarters, to see the direction and the distance of the place to which the column must be moved. Hitherto the direction had been northerly, and that meant, of course, that we were advancing, and approaching the enemy's country. That was good, and the officers and we had sometimes joked about the restaurants we should patronise when we reached Vienna or Buda-Pesth. But now, to my dismay, the map showed that Dobrido, the village to which we were to move, was in a southerly direction. This meant retreat. We hoped, of course, that this was only a temporary check; but from the moment of that first retreat, we never advanced again. But, it must be remembered, to the everlasting credit of the Serbian Army, that though the retreat continued for nearly three months, the Army did not content itself with retreating, but fought rearguard actions all the time. Military experts will appreciate the wear and tear to body and mind entailed in such a performance. We, of course, also, throughout that time, put up our hospital tents, and received and evacuated the wounded. Colonel Terzitch looked in on his way to new Headquarters; he was as cheery as usual. He said that we were making a slight retreat, because one of our regiments, composed of elderly soldiers, with poor guns, had given way. He thought all would soon be well again.

We found this time a delightful camp site in a space enclosed by a fine wood. The routine was always the same on arrival at our destination. Shortly before reaching the village, or place designated, I would ride on, with the interpreter and the sergeant, and choose a site. When the column arrived in front of it, I would beckon to them to follow, and, by hand gestures, indicate the positions respectively for the oxen and horses and the wagons. The position for the motors was decided with the leading chauffeur. The site for hospital tent, kitchen, and staff quarters was then quickly arranged with the doctors, cook, and nurses. Tents were immediately pitched, wood fires were lighted, the surgical boxes were brought to the hospital tent, unpacked, and the contents, arranged by the nurses and the hospital orderlies; kitchen stuff was unpacked in the kitchen by the cook; the doctors put on their white coats, the nurses their aprons; our Red Cross flag, on a pole, was placed in the ground near the hospital tent, and everything was ready for business.

Frequently, and also on this occasion, Major A.'s column was encamped not far from us. He was this time on the other side of the main road. There were no wounded that day, and he and the two French doctors, and the Serbian artist had tea with us round our camp fire. Mons. Bettich stayed the night with us, because we could not drive him back to Headquarters until morning. He was amused at seeing four of the party, after supper, playing bridge, sitting on a ground-sheet by the camp fire, near the shelter of an ox-wagon, as though, he said, they were in their London drawing-rooms. "Ah! you English!" We talked about the arrogance of the Germans, and he told us, as an example, a story of a German officer who had lately been taken prisoner; he was, as usual, well treated and was allowed to write a letter to his friends at home; but in the letter he made reference to the Serbian people as "those Hottentots."

The next day (October 18th) things seemed to be going badly. Piteous processions of refugees, from villages bombarded and threatened by the Germans, were streaming southwards along the roads. In one village only 30 women and children had remained out of a population of 3,000 people. Grenades had fallen in Michaelovatz, which only yesterday had been the headquarters of the Staff; and the thundering of the guns, only five miles away, was continuous. But everybody consoled themselves with the belief that the Allies would soon be here and put things straight. The metaphorical flags of welcome were already fluttering in our minds.

We again received wounded; amongst them was the commander of a division. His foot was badly injured with shrapnel. After the doctors had done what they could for him, he asked to see me, in order to express gratitude for the help of our hospital. Tears were in his eyes, and when he brushed them away, he hastened to explain that his tears had come, not from fear of death, but because he could not go back to his regiment. We drove him and all the other wounded, in the motor ambulances to Palanka station, and they left by train for hospitals farther south. During that evening, and throughout the night, we were kept busy; 102 badly wounded men arrived in batches from the battle-field close at hand. We could see the German captive balloons hovering in the air near us. It was not surprising that some of the soldiers were already dead when they were taken out of the rough, springless wagons. The jolting over bad roads, in the cold and rain, whilst huddled together, half a dozen badly wounded men in one small cart, was bound to be disastrous. Moreover, some of the wagons had high sides, and no opening even at the ends, and the patients, perhaps with broken legs or smashed heads, must be hauled up and over the high sides in the dark, in any fashion that came first.

We buried our dead near the roadside, without coffins, in their torn and bloodstained uniforms. When possible we placed a candle in their hands, and we made plain wooden crosses and wrote upon these the name, the regiment and place of death. The Serbian soldier likes to be buried near the main road, because then he thinks he will not be forgotten by passers by. But surely the Serbian soldier will never be forgotten; the sacrifices he has made in the cause of freedom have made his name immortal.

We continued to evacuate the wounded till 11 p.m. Then the chauffeurs rested till 5 a.m., when they began again. Headquarters lent us a large Diesel French car, which held 10 patients, and this was a great help, as the Fords, on the bad roads, could only safely take four patients at a time.

We were glad to receive that day a second interpreter (George). He knew very little English, but two interpreters were essential. One was always needed in the hospital, and I wanted one for general work, for, though I had learnt some Serbian, I never risked giving important orders, or rebuking the men in a language of which I was not master; ridicule must, at all costs, be kept out of the relationship between us. I was obliged on that day, for instance, to correct, through the interpreter, one of the corporals; I had given him leave to visit his family, who lived near, and he returned 12 hours after his leave had expired, riding one of our horses. The P.M.O., to whom I reported him, said that he was to be punished by being sent at once to the front (he stayed with us, however, to the end).

But my broken Serbian was sometimes effective enough. On one occasion, when the wounded had been arriving continuously all through the night, I noticed, about 3.30 a.m., that the wood fires upon which kettles of water were kept boiling, for tea and coffee for the patients, were all getting low. I called a soldier and told him to make up all the fires. He replied that the fires had eaten all the wood; there was no more wood left. The answer to that was easy in Serbian, for there were plenty of trees of all sizes around us as we stood. I pointed to a good-sized tree close to us. "Isn't that wood?" I asked severely. He shook his head, and that meant "Yes." "Very well, then, cut it down." He shook his head again, and fetched an axe and cut it down, and we had as much wood as we wanted.

George brought us the news that at our Kragujevatz hospital 180 newly wounded soldiers had just arrived, and that at Lapovo already 80 were in the new building. He also told us that the Allies had taken Strumnitza from the Bulgarians and that England had declared war against Bulgaria. Could this be believed?

By noon (Tuesday, the 19th) our wounded were all evacuated. This was fortunate, as at one o'clock came the order to move on at once. News from the front was bad; the Germans were pressing on, and were now close behind us. The guns sounded very near. We had not far to go, only to Uvidno, a two hours' trek. It was difficult to find a camp site; the whole country near the roadside was mud swamp from the continued rain. We pitched the hospital tent between the road and a wood, and three tents, one for the doctors, one for the men, and one for the women, were pitched in the shelter of the wood. The cars stayed on the road. There were not many wounded that afternoon—that was a bad sign. It meant that the enemy were giving no time for collecting them from the field; they were also firing on the ambulance parties, and only the least severely wounded came straggling in, as best they could, by themselves. We evacuated them when their wounds were dressed, from our own and also from Major A.'s hospital, which was on the other side of the road.

CHAPTER XXII

The news grew more and more serious. The Bulgars had taken Vranya, the Germans were at Valievo, and also at Michaelovatz, close behind us. The Serbs had been badly beaten in the morning. An unending stream of refugees passed along the road, and whole families of women and children, babies in arms, infants that could just toddle, boys and young girls, all sheltered at night near us in the wood, constructing as best they could, rough arbours of branches, for protection from rain and wind. We had no time for practical sympathy with these forlorn people, who would, in all probability, never see their homes or their menfolk again. All this was another horrible side-light on the "glories" of war.

The situation was growing hourly worse. Where were the French and English troops? We received marching orders, and were off again by 6 a.m. (October 20th) for Gliebovatz, two miles to the north of Palanka. It was again difficult, owing to mud, and rain, and wind, and no shelter, to find suitable ground for tents, oxen, and the men's bivouacs. Major A., who had, from the first been pessimistic as to the military situation, was now much depressed. He told us that the Bulgars were already near to Nish; that they had cut the line; that the Serbian Government had left Nish; and that the Germans were only three kilometres behind us. The French doctors, however, were always delightfully optimistic, and they and we made a point of trying to laugh the Major out of his forebodings.

On the 20th we received no wounded—again a bad sign, though there was not much firing. We expected marching orders every minute, and we did not put up all the tents. Most of the staff slept in the cars.

On Thursday, October 21st, at 9 a.m., we received the order to go to Palanka, and to establish our dressing-station in the Casino, opposite to the Hotel Serbia, in which Major A.'s column was placed. Rooms for the staff were found in the Hotel Central. I slept in the car, as usual. The cars were drawn up in the yard of a private house. There was a small veranda and a kitchen belonging to the house, and here we cooked and ate our food.

Palanka, when we entered it, was already evacuated in readiness for the Germans. The houses were deserted, the shops shuttered, the mud churned by thousands of oxen, horses, and wagons, into gelatinous paste, was a foot deep. Heavy rain was falling. In the main street a continuous stream of fugitives—old men, women and children—were splashing through the mud, carrying their bundles of household treasures on their backs, and driving hurriedly before them their precious pigs, and goats and little flocks of sheep.

The news from the front, which was, alas! behind us, continued to be bad. Work, therefore, for doctors and nurses was slack; there is never time, in a retreat, to collect all the wounded. At this point we were troubled to know how to carry the benzine for the cars. It was too heavy for the wagons, and we optimistically decided to send some of it by train to Lapovo, to await us there. I stopped a refugee woman with her cart and commandeered her, against payment, to take some barrels to the station. The barrels left for Lapovo, but we never saw them again, because Lapovo was in the enemy's hands before we reached it.

BROKEN BRIDGE AT FRONTIER BETWEEN MONTENEGRO AND ALBANIA
Our route lay across the basaltic rocks

SERBIAN SOLDIER (2nd RESERVE) DURING THE RETREAT

Our P.M.O. seemed this day more than usually sad, chiefly on account of the people. He calculated that at least half a million unoffending peasants must die of starvation. This has proved to be an underestimate. But as we should probably, he said, be remaining that day in Palanka, he asked if I would like to go and exchange greetings with our commander. The latter was as delightful, and cheery as usual, and it was easy to understand one, at least, of the reasons why he made a good commander. I was much interested in all he told me about the general position; some day, when the situation was more favourable, I was, he said, to go with him and watch a battle at close quarters.

Shortly after I had left Headquarters the mounted orderly came up with the white envelope: marching orders, and we moved on immediately. This was inopportune, as Dr. Coxon was in need of boots, and, at the moment, she and I were on the point of breaking into a locked and shuttered boot shop. We were obliged to go without the boots; the doctor's crimeless record was left unsullied, but her feet were left unshod, and this at the time seemed more important.

We arrived at dusk, after much trouble with the cars owing to the mud, and took up quarters near some old stone quarries. The guns were growing noisy again, and it was curiously interesting to watch the fire from shell and shrapnel on the hills close behind Palanka. Wounded came again during the night, and we evacuated fifty in our cars and in wagons supplied by the ambulance column, to Ratcha. The wounds were terrible, and some men were already dead when they arrived. The transport of the wounded was always an anxiety, lest the job should not be completed, and the motors should not have returned, before the next order to move should come, as that would complicate the question of staff transport.

I went to bed at one a.m. and was up again at four. I saw that Major A. was on the move, and I knew that our order must come soon. Just then a captain of infantry arrived, and said that we ought to go at once; he had been given orders to dig trenches on the place of our encampment. I told him that he could dig his trenches, but we could not go until the order came. We made ready for departure, and packed everything except the surgical dressings, and then more wounded came, so they were tended. One man died at dawn, and we buried him. At 6 o'clock the order came to go towards Ratcha, to a place only distant 1½ hours. We encamped in a field by the roadside, and immediately wounded arrived.

The outstanding feature of this camp was the behaviour of the dispenser. I noticed during the morning that he was haranguing in a loud voice, and that all the men were gathered in a circle listening to him and laughing. I went to see what was happening, and I found that he was drunk. When he saw me, he stopped talking and ran away and jumped on an unsaddled horse, saying that he was going to ride to Headquarters. The soldiers and I followed him, and the former held the horse, and I told him to dismount immediately. He refused, and promptly pulled a loaded revolver from his pocket. At that moment a friend, with whom he had been drinking, an under-officer from another column encamped close to us, came up and persuaded him to dismount. He took him off to his camp, and said that he would keep him until he had recovered. I took the revolver, and found that it was loaded with five cartridges, and I sent it with a messenger to the P.M.O. In the evening, when I was in the car preparing for a few hours' sleep, the dispenser suddenly arrived and demanded his revolver, and when I told him that it was in the possession of the P.M.O., he was furious and vowed vengeance. He would smash the cars and destroy everything we had, etc., but I got rid of him. The sergeant and the soldiers were very angry, and volunteered to put extra guards round my car, and no more was heard of him. When a fitting opportunity came he was removed. That was the only case of drunkenness I saw from start to finish of that three months' retreat, and he, the dispenser, was not a Serbian proper: he was an Austrian Serb, and, like most of these semi-Austrians, he was hyper-nervous of falling into Austrian hands.

The next morning (October 24th) at 5.45, we again retreated, this time to a field beyond Ratcha. The roaring of the guns was now terrific, and the scenes along the roads, which were crowded with refugees, who were all mixed up with the retreating convoys of the army, were heartrending. But this day, for the first time since we left Pirot, the sun shone, and we were at least physically warm for a few hours.

In the afternoon we witnessed a strange sight. A German aeroplane was flying over our heads, when suddenly from behind some clouds, a French biplane appeared, and the two flew towards each other. And then, as though to hide from us on earth the prostitution of science to murderous ends, both birds of prey dived into a huge white cumulus cloud and disappeared; and immediately, though both biplanes remained invisible, the sound reached us of pit-pit-pit-pit from their spiteful quick-firing guns, as the aviators played hide and seek amongst the clouds. Strange to think that even the heavens are now invaded by the murderous machines of man. We watched for a long time, but we never saw anything emerge from the thick cloud.

That day we heard a rumour that the Germans had been driven out of Ratcha by two regiments who had rushed on them with bayonets, in disregard of the general order to retreat. I tried to believe it was true. On the evening of that day, when again marching orders arrived, I wondered, as I opened the white envelope, whether, on the strength of the last rumour of a German repulse, we might not at last be going to have the joy of an advance. No one who has not experienced the depressing effect of retreating, day after day, in the home country of the retreating army, can picture the eagerness with which the slightest hope of a change of fortune will be hailed. But, alas! a glance at the order soon dissipated hope.

The direction of the place detailed for the next halt was still southerly. It was nine p.m. when the order came. Immediately everything, tents, surgical boxes, kitchen materials, etc., were packed in readiness for departure, when suddenly, as we were about to start, a batch of fifty badly wounded soldiers arrived in ox-wagons, from the battle-field, to be dressed. We could hear that the Germans were now close behind us; their big guns were banging ominously, as the wagons discharged their burdens on the ground, and disappeared. At once I gave the order for the necessary surgical boxes to be unpacked. The night was cold, and dark, and by the light of hurricane lamps, the doctors and the nurses set to work and cut away the torn and bloodstained garments and dressed the wounds of the gory, groaning, battered objects, who were placed upon the ground, round impromptu bonfires, which we made of hay, and straw, and wood, to give warmth. One man was already dead; I ordered a grave to be dug, saw that it was the regulation depth—three feet—and then sent to another column for a priest.

For the Serbian soldier is like many another of us, he is not particular about saying his prayers during his lifetime, but he is very particular that prayers should be said over his dead body. Then I stood beside the priest, a few yards behind the scrimmage round the bonfires, whilst he, in his gay embroidered robe, chanted, all out of tune, in the old Slavonic language, which no one now understands, the words of the Greek Church burial service. He held the prayer book in one hand, and read by the light of a small piece of tallow candle held in the other. The groans of the wounded, and the thunder of the guns, coming ever nearer and nearer, made an effective accompaniment. The only incongruity was the frequent repetition in the priest's prayers, of the word "Allelujah!" Why "Allelujah!"? I asked myself in the intervals of my "Amen" responses, as the scene round those bonfires burnt itself upon my mind.

The Germans were coming on fast behind us. They had taken Palanka in the afternoon, and there was no doubt that as we had received the order to move, a couple of hours ago, we ought not now to be here; but we still had our fifty wounded to evacuate. We had been told in the morning that we were to send all the wounded to a hospital along the road leading to Kragujevatz, in a south-westerly direction. It was evidently, then, intended that the retreat should follow that route. But now the orders were to move the column to a place which was, as the map disclosed, along the road leading to Krushievatz, in a southerly direction. I knew that the Germans had, since the morning's order, taken Palanka, close behind us, and that if I now obeyed the morning's order, and sent the wounded and the chauffeurs along the Kragujevatz road, they would almost certainly be cut off by the enemy. I also knew that to disobey a military command is to incur grave responsibility; but I incurred it, in obedience to common sense; and as there was no time for hesitation, I decided at once that the wounded must come along the Krushievatz road with us. I was sure that there would be a hospital, sooner or later, along that road.

But how were we to move the patients? Three of our motors had gone with wounded, earlier in the afternoon, along the Kragujevatz road, and had not yet returned. That left us with only three motors for the staff and for the wounded. The ox-wagons which had brought the patients from the field had disappeared, and, owing to the nearness of the enemy, no other wagons would be available unless Major A. could spare some. He was stationed a quarter of a mile away, across some marshy fields. I must ask him; a messenger would be useless; I must go myself. I tumbled into half a dozen ditches and a bog or two, in the dark, and found him. But he was in the same straits as we were, with many wounded and no transport; he could give no help. I ran back to our column. There was only one thing to be done, if the whole hospital was not to be taken by the enemy. The staff, who usually travelled in the motor ambulances, must walk, until the three motors from the Kragujevatz road caught us up, the worst wounded must go in the motors, those who could crawl, must crawl, and as for the others— well! the usual miracle made everything quite simple, for at that moment empty artillery wagons were passing, and they gladly took the residue of the wounded; and two soldiers were left to tell the three cars to follow on.

The road was abominable, with mud and holes, and narrow and broken bridges, and in the dark, dangerous. We were continually, all through the night, obliged to lift the wounded out of the ambulances, and carry them over the dangers, and hold our breath whilst the motors—those wonderful Ford cars, wonderfully handled—performed acrobatic feats inconceivable to orthodox chauffeurs at home. The three other motors caught us up after we had been trekking for two or three hours, and the staff were again able to ride. This was, fortunately, just before we came to a bridge which was the scene of six motor miracles. I was riding, as always, in front of the column, and when I was half-way across the bridge, I discovered, just in time, that the planks on either side, a few yards in front of me, had been broken off, presumably by the wheels of the heavy gun-wagons which had preceded us. There was no parapet, and the bridge was so narrow, that it seemed doubtful whether there was room for a car, even if it could steer straight enough, to avoid the precipice on either side. If the wheels skidded in the mud, the car must overturn; and just beyond the bridge there was a mud-hole three or four feet deep; and there was no other road. The wagons, being warned, passed safely, though some stuck in the mud-hole and had to be dug out. But the men then cut branches of trees and found some kukurus stalks. We stopped the mud-holes with the trees, and laid the kukurus on the skiddy mud on the bridge, and the road was now mended for the motors. The wounded were lifted out and carried on stretchers over the bridge; the first chauffeur had a final good look at the place, then mounted the car and made a dash. Well done indeed! We breathed again—he was safely past the precipice, and only stuck in the hole beyond. That was nothing, for the advantage of a Ford is that you can lift it out of mud-holes. It seemed impossible, however, that the other five chauffeurs should all be equally skilful and equally lucky. And what about the nerve of the woman chauffeur? It was as good as the men's, and that is saying much. And we left that danger safely behind.

There were plenty of others ahead of us, and continually, all through the night, the cars had to be pushed and lifted out of mud-holes. Sometimes, as a variety, a wagon would overturn and block the road; but everything developed the wholesome habit of righting itself, and we reached Gradatz at 9.15 next morning. I was growing accustomed to small allowances of sleep, and I never felt physical fatigue; but on this occasion, although I was not tired, I grew sleepy about four in the morning, when the road became less dramatic, and I was surprised to find how uncomfortable it was trying to keep awake on horseback. I fell asleep for a second or two, then felt myself swaying in the saddle, pulled myself together and gave my mind some active thoughts, only to fall asleep again and go through the same performance. But by the time we arrived I was thoroughly awake.

CHAPTER XXIII

Our encampment was in a field, near a small stream, with high hills on the other side of the road. The sun was shining inspiringly when we arrived, and after the wounded, who had come with us, had been attended, we had some coffee, and a couple of hours' rest was the next order. We were only about six miles from Lapovo, and I sent George with a note to Doctor Cockburn, asking for news, and telling her that we were near. I was on my way to take a rest, when an officer, who was riding past, stopped when he saw our camp. He dismounted and came up to me, so I stayed to give him some breakfast and to talk with him. He was very depressed; he did not see how his country could be saved; and he horrified me by bringing out of his pocket a loaded revolver—he said he should end his life if the Germans took possession of the land. I tried to comfort him, both with food and cheery thoughts, placing most reliance on the former. He had eaten nothing since mid-day of yesterday, and at first he refused food, but I compelled him to eat a good breakfast, and I hope that happier thoughts were the result. Serbian officers, though particular about their food in peace time, seem to ignore the importance of food when their swords are girt. My friend rode away, and I was just going to rest for an hour, when at noon the Staff mounted orderly rode up; I knew what that meant—instant departure.

I was not surprised, for the guns were making a deafening noise close at hand. We had already despatched our last wounded, so we packed and were away within half an hour. There was no time for lunch. Berzan, the other side of Batuchini, was our goal. Rain was again falling, but we found it a good plan to take the Serbian view that rain was a blessing (because it checked the progress of the big German guns), and we accepted it cheerfully. We had travelled a few kilometres along the road, when we met a convoy coming towards us in obvious haste. It was curious that they should be coming towards us, as the retreat was general. The under officers who were in charge shouted to me as they passed, that we had better turn back at once. It was not possible, they said, to go through Batuchini, the next village, as this was now under bombardment, and the shells were dropping in the street through which we must pass. Our sergeant, and dispenser, and Sandford and Merton, all came up and urged that we should go back, according to the advice of the returning column; but I had been told to go to Berzan, and no other road led there. I did not know enough of the language to argue in it—it is a mistake to know enough of any language to argue in it—but I listened to what the men had to say, and then I replied firmly, "Napred!" (Forward!), and led on. When we reached the village, shells were, it is true, whizzing over our heads and falling clumsily rather close to us; a brisk cannonade was going on round the corner, and cannon fire was spitfiring busily on the near hill. But this was a good thing, as it had the effect of hurrying the drivers, who were a bit scared, and we reached our destination rather quicker than we should otherwise have done, at 4 p.m., hungry for the delayed lunch.

We pitched camp in a field at the back of a disused café, specially designated in the orders as our site. The approach was down a narrow by-lane, which was a bog of mud. Wounded arrived at once and kept us busy with the hospital, and evacuation work, but when the cars finally came back, about 11 p.m., we sat round the wood fire and enjoyed a supper of turkeys, which had been spitted over the wood fire by our cheery cook.

I had a few days previously sent a messenger with a note to Doctor May, at Kragujevatz, asking for news. He now returned with a letter, saying that our hospital there was then being evacuated, and that the military authorities were sending the unit to Novi Bazaar. They were sent ultimately under the charge of Doctor Curcin to Petch, and thence over the mountains to Scutari, Medua, and Brindisi. The unit say that no words can praise too highly the kindness and devotion of Doctor Curcin, and he says that he cannot cease to marvel at the courage and resourcefulness of the women who, under his care, faced indescribable difficulties with invariable cheerfulness and good temper.

The messenger from Lapovo had also now returned with the bad news that our hospital there had been evacuated, by order of the military authorities, two days before he arrived, whilst Lapovo was being heavily bombarded. Doctor Cockburn and her little unit ultimately joined the Kragujevatz party, and escaped to England under Doctor Curcin's care. We, ourselves, now at Berzan, expected marching orders every minute; the firing line was close upon us, and the guns made such a noise it was difficult to sleep. The quartette (dispenser, sergeant, Sandford and Merton) all came up and suggested that we should move on without waiting for orders. But the shells were not dropping in our camp, and I saw no reason for interfering with the arrangements for evacuation made at headquarters. It would never do to allow a panic or "skedaddle" principle to invade our camp. That would be a worse enemy than the Germans. And—in House of Commons language—my answer was in the negative.

The order to move came at nine next morning, Wednesday, October 29th, and the speed with which the column put itself this day in marching order was exemplary. Rain was falling in torrents as we trekked along the muddy road to Bagrdan. Would this place also be evacuated, or should we be able to buy some much-needed articles of clothing here? But from the first moment of retreat, during the next three months, we never entered a town or village that had not either just been evacuated or that was not about to be evacuated for the enemy. Houses deserted, shops shuttered, all eyes, as it were, closed, that they should not see the scenes of sorrow as the fugitives fled in silence through their streets; that they should not witness the galling spectacle of the triumphant entry of the enemy. Evacuation meant, of course, cessation of all means of communication with the outer world. During three months we were without letters, or news of any sort from home. Powers of mind, soul, body, were all concentrated, driven inwards, on the tragedy in which we had literally a walking part.

It was terrible enough to see town after town abandoned to the enemy; I pictured what we should feel if our English towns from Newcastle to Falmouth, were all to fall, in regular routine, as prizes to the triumphant Germans. But the abandonment of stations on the railway line, the main artery of national life, that seemed an even sadder sight.

When we arrived at Bagrdan the station was already dismantling. We encamped, according to instructions, in a field near the station, but when heavy rain made the ground a swamp, I asked permission to shelter in the station rooms. In the morning these were not available, and we were obliged to do the best we could with sodden tents, but in the afternoon we were allowed to take possession, because by then the station was dismantled in readiness for evacuation.

The line behind the station, to the north, had already been cut; bridges, as we could hear from the noise of explosions, were then being blown up; the telegraphic and telephonic apparatus was destroyed, and the station entrance hall, and waiting rooms were littered with the débris of torn official documents, and old telegraphic paper strips.

The last train, filled with wounded whom we had tended during the day, left in the evening, as usual, in silence—no scene. The stationmaster was leaving in the guard's van. He knew that the next train to leave the station would be working under German rule; he knew that for himself exile and ruin stared him in the face; but, as the engine puffed and snorted, and the train began slowly to move, he called to me and to a few remaining officials on the platform, "Sbogom!" (Good-bye!) and nothing else. But could other words have added to the pathos? Was not the history of a gigantic crime against his nation revealed in that one word?

Next day was full of interest. For, though our division was holding its own fairly well, another division, the Drinske, was having a bad time, and all the morning, streams of cavalry from our division passed along the road. They were to cross the Morava river, three-quarters of a mile down the line from Bagrdan, by pontoons, and go to the rescue. Then a rumour reached us that 25,000 Bulgars had been taken prisoners, and that there were now no more Bulgars on the Serbian front, and that the French and English were on their way to help us! Much too good to be true, and I began to suspect that these rumours were floated to keep up the spirits of the soldiers from time to time.

At seven the next morning, came the order to move the column to the other side of Bagrdan. Rain continued all that day, and I was thankful to be able to commandeer three small houses for shelter for hospital and staff in the village. The wagons and oxen outspanned in a field behind the hospital houses. There were many wounded and some dead, and these we buried in graves half filled with water, in the rain.

Major A. and his column appeared again, and told us that they had journeyed by another route, and had been obliged to wade through a river, neck deep, to get here.

As usual, I slept in the car. This was stationed in the one and only street, outside the house belonging to a teacher. He had already sent away his children, and his wife was to leave next day. He said that he should wait till the last moment in case of a miracle. He showed us his honey hives, of which he was very proud. Several had been stolen in the night, and if he left the town he would lose everything.

The firing on the near hill was now terrific, and there seemed very little chance of the miracle, though another rumour, that English guns were on their way, gave us hope.

The teacher's wife left at seven next morning, October 30th. We moved at 8.15. We were told to encamp on the other side of a bridge, near Kriva Alpregan. The bridge was difficult to find, and the whole country was a swamp, but we found the bridge, and as there was no village, we took shelter in a wood. Between the field and the wood, was a deep and broad ditch of mud, which we had to cross continually, but we were glad of the shelter of the trees. We put up a hospital tent between the road and the wood, and a mess tent amongst the trees, and we lit our kitchen and dining-room fires inside the tent, and enjoyed a supper of little chickens spitted on a stick, the only way of roasting which was available. We generally arranged that the field-kitchen should cook for the soldiers once a day, when possible, their much-loved stew, when outside fires were difficult, and we then managed for ourselves.

That field was a sea of liquid mud whilst rain was falling, and it became a gelatinous pulp when it began to dry. I slept in the car on the road, and all night long, in a continuous stream, wagons rumbled past me with guns, with fodder, with all the material for the existence of an army of 200,000 men, and intermixed with these were wagons filled with fugitives.

In the morning I had seen the P.M.O. His news was extremely gloomy. The rumour of Bulgarian defeat was quite untrue, and my friend, though outwardly calm, was suffering anxiety not only about the life of his nation, his heart was also filled with fears as to the safety of his wife and children, who were in Kragujevatz when the town was taken by the Germans. Communication with them was, of course, impossible. Thousands of other officers and men were suffering a similar anxiety. How could I help sharing some of this grievous load of sorrow? I think my ears will never lose the sound of creaking carts, and rumbling wagon wheels, for in the sound, as I lay awake that night, and many other nights, there was mingled with every revolution of the wheels, the anxiety and the misery which were gnawing at the heart of this exiled nation.

CHAPTER XXIV

On Sunday, October 31st, the order to leave for Voliovtza came at 10.30 a.m. On the road, Major A. and one of the French doctors, who were both riding, joined us, and we pitched our respective camps on either side of the road, just outside Jagodina. While we were pitching our tents, a German aeroplane dropped bombs within a few yards of Major A.'s camp. No harm was done, though in Jagodina many were injured, and six people were killed, including the brother of one of our men, by bombs dropped a few minutes later by this same aeroplane.

Major A.'s mother and sister were living at Jagodina, having fled there from Belgrade, from the Austrians, some months earlier. The Major was now much troubled, because it seemed that they must remain in the town. Where, he asked, could they go? If they went south, they ran grave risk of being captured by the Bulgars. If they stayed in Jagodina, they would, it is true, be taken by the Germans, but they preferred the Germans, as the lesser, they said, of two evils.

This time we were able to pitch our bivouac on dry ground, on short, sheep-eaten grass by the roadside; and we received at once some wounded. But it was discomforting to find that the number of our patients was in inverse ratio to our losses in the field. This evening we only had a dozen, and they walked in. They told us that the severely wounded were being left upon the field; the enemy would give no time for collecting them, and they were, as usual, firing on the ambulance parties. Only those men, therefore, came for treatment who could move themselves. Also wagons for transport, usually commandeered from the local peasants, had now all been taken away by the refugees for their own uses. Fighting was continuous, and the thought of the wounded lying untended on the field, was nearly unbearable. I knew that fierce battles had been raging near us, and yet there were only a few wounded in our dispensary tent. I spoke next morning about this condition of affairs to Major A., but he said, and I knew that it was true, that the P.M.O. was doing all that was possible. I was for the moment, however, sorely tempted to go with our own ambulance cars to the battle-field and pick up as many wounded as we could, but I remembered in time, that I had been entrusted with the command of a column which had its own deputed work, and that such command had, for the first time, been entrusted to a woman; it would be a dereliction of my responsibilities if, for any purpose, I neglected these to take upon myself somebody else's responsibilities. I resisted the temptation, but with a sore heart.

The French doctors and Major A. spent the morning with us, the former and we trying to assure the Major that the situation must change for the better before long. He, however, was convinced, and rightly so, that his country was doomed. In the afternoon J. G. and I went over to his (the Major's) camp and had coffee in an arbour, placed in a vineyard of American vines; these were of a light green colour, and looked beautiful against the purple mists upon the mountains. They had been imported as a check to the vine pest, the phylloxera.

On Tuesday, November 2nd, the situation looked desperate. It had never looked so black. Even rumours as to the arrival of the Allies, were now less frequent, though poor old King Peter, remembering, no doubt, how a year ago he had, by his presence at the front, inspired his troops to further effort, drove that afternoon past our camp to the trenches, saluting us as he drove past, and told the men that if they would only stick to it bravely for a few more days, help would be forthcoming. But it was obvious to us all that the Serbian Army, with its inferiority of artillery, might check, but it could not stem the tide of the enemy's advance. The big guns now roared and thundered mercilessly, louder and nearer, almost continuously day and night. I could never understand why, being so near, the enemy did not make a dash and cut off our retreat. It might be expected any minute, and the tenacious defence that was made by this Serbian Army, in the face of terrific odds, was indeed worthy of admiration.

The Germans had taken Kragujevatz; this town had, whilst we were there, seemed to us like a second home, and now it was, together with its inhabitants, who had been so friendly to us, in the enemy's hands; all our wealth of hospital material and equipment was being fingered by Germans, and German soldiers were bivouacked within our much-loved tents upon the racecourse; and—and this was the saddest thought of all—the fine arsenal was now being used to fashion German munitions to be used against our Serbian friends. The Germans were also at Milanovatz, and our dispensary headquarters at Rudnik would be in their possession.

From our present position we could watch the battles raging on the near hills; these were ablaze with fire from shell and shrapnel. We were already, as Major A. pointed out, surrounded on three sides. Could we—that is, could the Army—possibly escape?

The Major thought it was impossible, but the French doctors were as usual delightfully optimistic. They had, with me, confidence in the Serbian *état-major*, which had formerly done excellently against the Turks, the Bulgars, and the Austrians; and they were not likely to fail us now. They must have some way of escape up their sleeve; the retreat was being conducted in such a dignified fashion, it was clear that the control was in capable hands. But faith was a useful companion.

Then came a sudden influx of severely wounded—96 that day up to 10.30 p.m., and with a bound, up went the spirits of the doctors and the nurses. But it was piteous to see these wounded. We knew that most of them must die, for there was no time for them to rest anywhere; they were evacuated from station to station. After we had treated them they must, according to our instructions, continue, in the ox-wagons which had brought them, to Treshnitza—14 kilometres distant. Two officers were in a pitiful condition—their brains were bulging through their skulls, and they had also been shot in the stomach. They must die in the carts.

At sunset I climbed a small hill with Major A., and on three sides we saw the battle—many battles—raging. White smoke, and black smoke, and flashes of fire, were belching forth, with thunders, and roaring, and occasional silences, which were worse than the noises, for in the silence you could feel the agony of the wounded—the passing of the dead. On the fourth side, and just below us, was a sight which would, a few years ago, have been no less remarkable. By the side of the road, along which were passing at that moment, guns damaged in the action which we had just been watching, the various columns of an army in retreat, and refugees in flight, we saw a small white camp. Moving in and out, quietly, and leisurely, amongst the tents, were some women, who seemed to have no concern with the tumult that was raging all around them. One of them was cooking supper over an open wood fire. She was apparently joking with the Serbian cook-orderly and threatening to hit him on the head with the frying-pan. An ox-wagon stopped in front of—ah! yes!—that was a Red Cross flag. Immediately, a woman in a long white coat, and two women in white aprons, stepped out from the tent nearest the road. The white-coated woman climbed up on the wheel of the wagon, and stooped down to examine a mangled form, which was immediately taken out, placed upon a stretcher, and carried into the tent. And we realised that the picture formed a tiny fragment of the European mosaic of war; it was a scene in the routine of the First Serbian-English Field Hospital.

That evening we ate supper in the open, round the fire, but it was difficult to take our eyes off the absorbing scenes that were being enacted all around us. Occasionally an extra loud and startling outburst of cannon-roar, quite close to us, made us jump; but no one took any further notice, and we went on with our supper. After supper we received a message that we were to hold ourselves in readiness to depart at any moment, and we accordingly packed our hospital tent. But the wounded continued to arrive. For this we were always thankful, and the doctors and nurses now attended them in the open, by the light of hurricane lanterns; our acetylene gas lamp was packed. But then came a further order that we were not to move until the morning, so we put up the hospital tent again, for it was raining, and shelter for the wounded must be provided.

CHAPTER XXV

Between Bagrdan and Jagodina, rain had fallen almost incessantly, and though rain was, the Serbian soldiers always said, the best friend they had, because it checked the progress of the big German guns, it had a depressing influence on the men, and made the roads almost impassable, with deep, gelatinous, marvellous, mud. We had, on this night, put up the tent, and I had just gone to my car for an hour or two of rest, when the dreaded orderly rode up to the car and presented the order to leave at once. It was 1.30 a.m. I sent for Vooitch, who always aroused the soldiers; camp was immediately struck, and I rode round as usual, to see—a little difficult in the darkness—that nothing was left behind, then I sounded the whistle to collect the unit, and as the oxen and horse-wagons and motor-ambulances came into line in single file, I shouted "Napred!" (Forward!) and, followed by the two mounted orderlies, took the lead. Within twenty minutes of receiving the order to move, we were on the march. Rain was, as usual, falling, and the night was so dark, I could scarcely see my horse's head, as our column jolted over ditches, and struck into the road. One of the orderlies, riding a little behind me, held the lantern to throw light upon the road immediately in front, to give us warning of danger from mud-holes, and broken bridges, and we entered Jagodina.

The usual story: abandoned by its inhabitants; houses shuttered and deserted; the whole town in darkness, except that along the walls of the houses, wherever space permitted, camp fires had been lighted, and refugees, women, children and old men, were crouched in groups, sleeping, or sitting in silence, waiting for the dawn. The fires illumined the faces of the fugitives and showed suffering not easy to forget. When the camp fires were left behind, the darkness was complete, and even objects immediately in front were only visible because they showed black against the shining mud. It was a world of shadows, and of dreariness, of wet and cold. And never for a moment had the sounds ceased, of the creaking of wagons, and the squish, squish of oxen-hoofs pressing glutinous mud. Sometimes my horse would stumble, in the dark, over a little flock of sheep that was being driven with a convoy for the purposes of food; or a scared and tiny shrew mouse, absorbed in its own affairs, would dart across the road and escape death by a miracle.

I looked behind me, and saw, only darkness and sorrow, columns, and confusion. Thousands of unoffending people were suffering heartache, separation, desolation; and, as the guns reminded me, thousands of brave men were, a couple of miles away from us, facing at this moment, a murderous death. How could I help asking myself where, in all this hell, is God?

And immediately the answer came. As if in purposeful response, the mountains in the east threw off the blackness of the night, and showed rich purple against the lightening sky. Over the mountains rose clouds of gold, and pink, and aerial blue, and as the rays of sunlight shot triumphantly into the sky, white mists, thick and soft, that had lain hidden, became, for a moment of pure joy, bathed in all the rainbow colours; and one daring cloud of brilliant gold spread itself in the shape of a great dragon across the dark sky. Glories and beauties everywhere, if we could only catch the meaning.

But while I was wondering at it all, the glories vanished; the time for understanding had not yet come; the hills became commonplace, the prosaic light of day was with us, and I saw once more the nightmare picture of drab-dressed, mud-stained soldiers, splashing with their sandalled feet, in the sloppy mud; sometimes stumbling, then rising, smothered with mud, without a word; weren't there worse troubles than that? "Hleba!" (Bread!) "None for three days," were the first words I heard.

I don't know whether I liked least trekking by day, or by night. By day nothing of the horrors by which one was surrounded, was left to the imagination, but by night there were added difficulties. For, apart from danger from the enemy, the roads, or tracks, were full of risks and hazards, even when by daylight these were visible in advance; but they were dangerous when one was dependent on the light of a small lantern, to reveal mud-holes, boulders, fallen trees, precipices, or broken bridges.

Also, there was at night the added danger that in the darkness, the column might be intercepted by other greedy columns butting their way through. But the officers of other convoys were always extremely courteous: they frequently helped us to recover a place in the line, and we were fortunate in never losing, even temporarily, any of the column.

Commanders of other columns often urged me to sleep during night treks in the wagons, or, like the staff, in the motor ambulances, but I preferred to be at the head of the column by night as well as by day; partly because it was obviously the only way in which one could be always on the alert, and partly, also, in order that the men should feel that I was not asking them to endure what I would not endure myself, and that I was sharing with them the practical difficulties of the road.

We reached Treshnitza at 9 a.m. Wednesday, November 3rd, after the night's trek. The cars had a troublous time with mud and holes and were, on several occasions, hauled out by the oxen.

The P.M.O. came to see us as soon as we arrived, and he asked us to take some wounded officers next day in the cars to Krushievatz. It was dreadful to look at the map, and see how far south we had now been driven.

We had commandeered the empty village school-house for dispensary and kitchen, and the column was camped in the orchard behind. The P.M.O. laughingly said we had found a better site than they had, though they— Headquarters Staff—were only a couple of hundred yards away.

Next morning early, we sent off the two wounded majors in motors to Krushievatz; we ourselves received the order to leave at 11.30 a.m. for Shanatz, and we met the returning motors on the road.

In the afternoon, as we were trekking steadily, having been told not to halt till we reached Shanatz, I saw by the side of the road, on a grass common, a hay-cart, a woman, and half a dozen soldiers. The woman was evidently in trouble: she was weeping, gesticulating, and shouting through her tears at the soldiers, who were in possession of the hay-cart. I guessed what had happened, so I halted the column and asked the woman to tell me what was the matter. I found, as I had suspected, that the soldiers had bought hay from her—for the sum of three dinars—and when it came to payment, they had discovered that they had no change, only a ten dinar-note, called in Serbian "banka." I told the soldiers if they didn't pay the woman what they owed her, they must leave to her the hay, or I should report them to the commander, and I took their names and regiments. But they swore that they had no change. I didn't believe them, and there was not time to investigate, but I couldn't let the woman be robbed, so I said I would buy the hay and pay for it, and I gave her three dinars. "Now then," I said, "the hay is mine," and I shouted to our men to come and take it off the cart. Our men were delighted; they leaped to the road and ran quickly to the cart. This worked magic, for hay was difficult to procure, and in an instant, the leader of the dinarless soldiers, produced three dinars; they had, he said, got hidden in his pocket; I handed them to the woman, telling her that she could also keep the other three, and I graciously allowed the soldiers to take away the hay.

HEADQUARTERS OF THE MONTENEGRIN POLICE (AT PETCH) ON RIGHT, GAOLBIRD'S HOUSE ON LEFT

CONVERTING FOUR-WHEELED WAGONS INTO TWO-WHEELED CARTS, IN CEMETERY AT PETCH

The evening colours were a recompense for a wet and dreary day; this side of the broad Morava, yellow beech leaves, caught by the red rays of the setting sun; beyond the river, green-grey mountains, and over these a rainbow, which seemed unwilling to touch the bloodstained earth, and dispersed amongst the clouds. Along the road everything was drab and dead, or dying; the ghost-like procession of convoys and of fugitives was not dead, for it was moving; but it was movement without life, for the soul was stunned.

The town of Varvarin, which we reached at 6 p.m., was in darkness; shuttered and deserted; mud and rain, as usual, in possession. We halted in the broad, main street, ambulance wagons all in line, in a foot and a half of mud, for the column to eat some food, for which there had been no time all day. Immediately on arriving, I received a message that a certain artillery major had been waiting for some hours to shake hands with me. He had once visited our camp at Kragujevatz. I remembered him as a vivacious and intelligent officer, and I was proud that, in the midst of his strenuous work of placing batteries in defence of the retreating Army, he had time to think of his English comrade. It seemed that Serbian officers, indeed, in whatever circumstances they found themselves, always did the right thing at the right moment. They were truly chivalrous, not with the chivalry which rushes to open the door to let you out, but with the chivalry which leaves the door open for you to come in.

The congestion of convoys on the other side of the pontoon bridge, leading to Krushievatz, was terrific. A narrow mud lane led to the bridge, and when we arrived at the entrance to the lane, at about 8 p.m., we found that the column ahead of us, were taking things philosophically and had lighted fires in the road, and were cooking food, and warming themselves; the oxen were lying across the road. There was no possibility of getting past them, though Shanatz, as I then discovered, was on the left bank of the (Western) Morava, and we should therefore not cross by the pontoon. But we eventually moved, and we reached Shanatz, a tiny scattered village, at 3 in the morning, to my great relief, for no other convoys had followed us, and, as the night passed, I had begun to be afraid that we had taken a wrong road. On arrival, we roused the Prefect, and he gave us the keys of the school-house, for our hospital, and we requisitioned a couple of rooms for the staff. Wounded were waiting for us. We cleaned the schoolroom; the doctor and the nurses who were on night duty attended to the patients, who were also given hot coffee and food; and the oxen, wagons, and men, settled in the school enclosure. I went to rest in the car at 5 a.m. and was up again at 6.

The Morava, broad and magnificent, flowed by the side of the village, and in the evening, after dark, some of us seized the rare opportunity of a bathe and a wash.

CHAPTER XXVI

The situation was growing more and more serious. We had retreated forty miles in the last two days, evidently not without reason, as the Germans had entered Jagodina, at noon, on the day we had passed through at 2.30 a.m. and, as there were other columns behind us, that did not leave a large margin of safety. I was always aware that delay caused by mistake in taking the wrong road, or by dalliance with accidents, would be fatal; but neither in our column, nor in any column that I saw during three months of retreat, was there ever anything but calmness and apparent unconcern. Had there at any time been panic, the narrow defiles would have been catacombed with dead, in addition to the thousands who perished from other causes.

But remarkable indeed was the dignity and orderliness with which, from start to finish, the retreat of the Serbian Army was conducted. And the silence! Hour after hour, day and night after day and night, week after week, thousands upon thousands of soldiers, trudging wearily beside their slow-paced oxen, or with their regiments of infantry, or driving their gun-carriages, or, as cavalry, riding their horses—in silence. No laughter, no singing, no talking; the silence of a funeral procession, which indeed it was; a silence only broken by the cries of the drivers to their oxen: "Svetko! Belia! Napred! Desno! Levo!" ("Svetko! Belia! Forward! To the right! To the left!") and the ceaseless rumbling of wagon wheels, which sounded like the breaking of an angry sea on a distant pebble beach. I have, since my return, re-read accounts of the retreat of Napoleon's army from Moscow, and though we were spared some of the horrors they endured, there were two features in our Serbian retreat, which were happily absent in the other. For the retreat in which we took part was the retreat, not only of the Serbian Army, but of the Serbian nation. This meant that thousands of women, children, and old men, driven from their homes by the advancing enemy, were, in ever-increasing numbers, as we progressed southwards, adding to the difficulties of the safe retreat of the Army, by mixing with the columns of artillery, cavalry, infantry, engineers, field hospitals, and swelling the procession.

Wagons filled with household treasures, beds, blankets, chairs, frying-pans, even geese, slung head downwards at the back of the cart, or balancing themselves with curious dignity, upon the uneven surfaces of indiscriminate luggage; a look of pained astonishment on their faces, at their rude removal from their own comfortable pastures.

Or, more frequent and more painful still, wagons filled with little children; the oxen, weary and hungry, led by women, also weary, hungry, and foot-sore. I saw one woman, dragging by the rope, two tired oxen drawing a wagon, in which were eight small children. I saw a tiny boy leading two tiny calves, which were drawing a tiny cart containing a tiny baby, who was strapped to the cart. I saw a woman, evidently not wealthy enough to possess a cart and oxen of her own, carrying her two babies, one on her back, and one in front; and, in one of the crushes which frequently occurred, the baby on her back, was knocked off by the horns of a passing ox.

We wondered, at Shanatz, why we were on that side of the river, with no bridge near us, when all the other columns were travelling towards Krushievatz on the other side. We received no orders all that day, and I wondered more and more, for there was always the possibility that the order might have gone astray. But at 3 a.m. on Saturday, November 6th, the order came to start at once for Kupçi, beyond Krushievatz, via the pontoon bridge, which we had left on our way here.

It was still dark when we reached the bridge. A lengthy convoy of artillery was crossing, and behind them again were endless other convoys. We halted, and it seemed likely that hours would pass before we should get a chance of butting in. But, to my joy, I found that the artillery column was under the command of my Varvarin Major. He saw us, and at once came up and said that he would arrange for us to cross the bridge immediately after his guns. We had not more than an hour to wait. A short, steep bank of mud, and we were up on the approach road to the bridge. I was told to dismount, and, following close upon the guns, and followed by our own Red Cross wagons, I led my horse across the pontoon. Dawn was breaking, and I was glad, for my eyes would surely never again see such a sight. Purple mountains, wrapped in white mists, and crowned with soft pink clouds; the broad grey river, rushing wildly to its fate; and a bridge of boats. Upon the bridge, dimly visible in the growing light, soldiers, leading wagons which were carrying cannons and heavy guns—motives of murder and destruction dominant—closely followed by women leading Red Cross wagons—the cross of Christianity waving in the breeze.

On the other side of the bridge, refugees, streaming along the road from Stalatz to Krushievatz, converged with the stream of columns and refugees who crossed the bridge, and made confusion even more confounded than before. But I found my friend, the Major, waiting for me on the other side. He had seen his column safely across, and now he would, he said, ride with us to Krushievatz, to show us the road out of the town. He did this, and then rode off to place his battery for a rearguard action.

The town was a solid mass of convoys and fugitives, and it was anxious work steering the column safely through, intact. The road leading through the town was broader than usual, and the wagons of refugees and of columns were jammed together three abreast in hopeless tangle. "Many oxen were come about us; lean bulls of Basan closed us in on every side."

Later, the Headquarters Staff overtook us, and I rode for a while beside our Divisional Commander. He told me quietly, as though he were talking of the death of a distant relative, that Nish had been taken by the Bulgars; those flags of welcome which we had seen, were now welcoming our enemies. Where, we asked each other, were the French and the English? But not a word of bitterness passed his lips; "there was doubtless some good reason," was his only comment. And I could only say what I always said, "Never mind, we shall get it all back one day," but I sometimes almost wished, for the first time in my life, that I was not English.

We arrived at Kupçi at 3 p.m. The noise of the guns was continuous, and in the afternoon we also heard violent explosions—the destruction of the powder factory, before the entrance of the Germans, who took possession in the evening.

The river Raçina ran close beside our bivouac, and after dark we had time for another bathe. The artillery major had tea with us; he was a cheery philosopher, and no one could have guessed the feelings that were gnawing at his heart, whilst we exchanged experiences and joked about minor incidents of the trek. One of the cars had broken down during the day (the raybestos band had given way), as we came through Krushievatz, and we had had difficulty in commandeering animals to drag it. Eventually we secured four cows; but after a few miles, the owner came and took them away, and we had been obliged to readjust our oxen transport arrangements on the road, not an easy matter, in the crush of convoys, all clamouring to push on. But the sick car was safely steered into camp, and the chauffeurs, by working at it till 10 p.m., put things straight again.

Amongst the refugees who swarmed along the road, were thousands of Austrian prisoners. They were under orders to evacuate themselves from place to place, according to instructions from the various military stations, to which they must report every evening; but they were without guards. They were mostly Serbian-Austrian soldiers, and their one dread was that they might fall into the hands of their former rulers. But their plight was now pitiable. Food for everyone was getting more and more difficult to procure, even for money; for prisoners without means, it was almost unprocurable. They had to rely on scanty bread rations. Half a dozen of these prisoners straggled into our camp at Kupçi, and their eager gratitude when we gave them some food—which we could ill spare—was horrible to witness.

CHAPTER XXVII

That evening I had a talk with the Commander and the P.M.O. They told me confidentially that the situation for the Army was, at this point, critical. The road from Kupçi to Blatzi led through a narrow defile, and there was grave fear that the Germans, who were already at Krushievatz, might overtake us in the rear, and enclose us on the northern entrance, and that the Bulgars might dash across from Nish, which was now in their hands, and cut us off on the southern exit. The Austrians also were on their way to Mitrovitza, and might wish to have a hand in drawing the net around us, and in annihilating or, at least, capturing the Serbian Army. Hope of help from the Allies was now extremely faint, and all efforts must be concentrated in the endeavour to save the army, intact, if possible. I must, therefore, I was told, push the column through the defile as speedily as possible—as speedily, that is, as the oxen and the congestion of convoys would permit.

But the order to move did not come till next evening at 4.30. We were bivouacked near a narrow bridge on the main road, over which convoys of artillery, cavalry, infantry, pioneers, bakers, butchers, field hospitals, etc., with their innumerable oxen, and horse wagons streamed ceaselessly day and night. Whilst I was waiting for our column to collect, I saw two men busy under the bridge. I was not sure if they ought to be there, and I jumped down into the ditch to see what they were doing. One of them had now climbed a ladder and was placing something in the rafters overhead; the other man was standing with something mysterious in his hands. It was melinite explosive, and the men told me that they were going to blow up the bridge as soon as our column and a few others had passed; the Germans were close behind us.

By this time our convoy was ready to start, but it was one thing to be ready, and quite another thing to have the chance of starting. It was not an easy matter to force, with the column intact, an entrance into the line, and to prevent other and more influential columns from shunting us aside. The sergeant, who should have done the shouting and protesting, was slack and afflicted with amiability, and amiability, though it may be useful at garden-parties, is not an effective weapon with a retreating army. But we eventually forced an entrance, and left Kupçi at 5 p.m. on November 7th.

During night treks the staff slept in the motor ambulances; the sergeant slept in one of the wagons, and I did not miss him. The mounted orderlies took it in turns, respectively, to sleep in a wagon, or to ride behind me and carry the lantern, which showed the only light available upon the road in front of us. The second interpreter was useless. I liked him best when he was asleep. But Vooitch was always at hand. He, too, was slightly tainted with amiability, but it was not of the paralytic kind, and he was excellently helpful. I could always rely upon his help by day or by night.

The cars had that night a difficult time, as the road was for the greater part of the way too narrow for them to pass other columns and go ahead, and in places where it was broader, a solid phalanx of wagons blocked the way.

When we entered the gorge (Maidevo end) it was pitchy dark, and the murky mountains, almost meeting overhead, shook their sides, echoing and re-echoing the thunder of the guns. The Psalmist's words flashed through my mind, "Yea, though I walk through the valley of the shadow of death, I will fear no evil, for Thou art with me" — and He always was.

On our right, the narrow road adjoined precipitously the river (Raçina) which, below us, surged, white-lipped, frightened, impatient to reach the freedom of the sea. The mountains descended vertically, from hidden heights, to the river's farther bank, and on our left, they towered perpendicularly by the roadside.

It seemed laughable to try to lighten such darkness with one small, flickering lantern, but nothing is less perfect for being small, and the orderly, Millyvoy, rode as usual behind me, throwing the best light available on the pitfalls immediately in front, and the rest of the column followed close behind.

It was raining, but there were other things to think of. Progress was at snail's pace; there was no one in control of the way, and wagons belonging to Army columns, or to refugees, all intermingled, blocked every inch of the road, either in single file or two deep, according as the breadth of road allowed.

A stoppage in front, caused increased congestion and confusion behind, as everybody then tried to pass everybody else, and the result was an entanglement of wagon-wheels and a general jumble, which was as big a nightmare as human brain could picture—with the cannons bellowing on every side.

If a wagon stuck in the mud, which was sometimes two feet deep, it held up the whole procession for miles. Then the drivers, urged by the impatience of those behind, lightened the load by pitching the contents of the wagon into the river. The example was contagious, and soon barrels of benzine, packing cases—some, alas! containing food—tents, chairs, beds, were hurled indiscriminately over the precipice, and bobbed, or floated, or sank, in the narrow swift-flowing waters. If a wheel came off, the wagon, with its contents, was hurled over the precipice. It was necessary to watch carefully, lest our own drivers should adopt this simple method of easing the burden of their oxen, and use their discretion as to what should be discarded.

Undercurrents of anxieties were always struggling to gain possession of my mind; the anxiety to procure bread, meat, hay, wood, shelter, for my weary, hungry column; anxiety for the health of the staff; anxiety lest the cars should break down, or benzine fail; anxiety lest any of the convoy should be left behind; anxiety to secure position in the line, the narrow line of flight; and above all, anxiety lest the column should, owing to error on my part, be captured by the enemies. But, as it's impossible to have more than one real anxiety at a time, I reduced all these to one—the anxiety to save that tiny portion of the brave army which had been entrusted to my care. For what were our troubles compared to the sufferings of this driven nation? For them the future held no break in the darkness and chaos which were only transient for us.

And this night I understood, as I had never understood before, the meaning of the words, "brought to silence by their enemies." For the multitude in front, and the multitude behind uttered, as they fled, no sound, except cries of encouragement to their oxen. "Ide! Terrai! Stoi! Chovai!" ("Go on! Hurry up! Stop! Get out of the way!") Grief, when it wails, is pitiful enough, but grief borne in silence, betrays a tenser tragedy. Had the misery in those breaking hearts, been uttered in a single cry, that cry caught and re-echoed through the mountains, must have broken the drum of the ear of God.

And, as I rode through the black night, amongst this suffering host, in rain, in wind, in cold, in storm, deafened by the roaring of the guns, which reverberated from rock to rock, all through the defile, thoughts, though not consecutive, had a fierce intensity. The thought dominant in my mind was the irreligion of the world. Crimes—the most gigantic crimes were triumphant everywhere in Europe, and the exponents of religion were silent. For prayer is smoke unless it is determination, and religion is only sentiment if it is divorced from action. "Thy will be *done*," is the ideal prayer.

During the first part of the night, I was joined by our friend, the artillery major. He had placed his guns, and as we passed his camp, he had been about to sit down to supper, but he saw us passing, and he joined me, and rode with me for an hour, for a talk—a talk which I shall never forget. For this Serbian officer was a philosopher, well-read, and with an intellectual breadth of vision, and depth of thought, which would certainly have been unusual in an army major of Western Europe.

There was, that night, neither moon nor stars. Black clouds hung over the mountains, which were dimly discernible, precipitous, close upon either side of us. The darkness was complete, and all night long the guns thundered ceaselessly against the mountain sides. (At home, canaries were singing in their cages.) Death was near for many; it might also be near for us. At any moment annihilation of our columns was possible; the scene of what might happen, in this narrow gorge, if the enemies overtook us—from both ends—was easily imagined. We both knew the peril of the situation, but we did not talk about that. And perhaps it was because, in the physical world, there was no light visible, that we sought light in the realm of thought, and discussed the problems of death, and of life beyond. He was one of those few who can discuss without argument; we both knew that we knew nothing; but we listened with eager interest to each other's guesses concerning the great truths which are still so dramatically withheld from our conscious intelligence. Why are they withheld? Is the God who withholds them—is the God who is now permitting our European holocaust—is He, in fact, all-powerful? Can anyone be all-powerful unless he exists without conditions? But why crave an all-powerful God? May not all-powerfulness have to go the way of jealousy, anger, and all the other human attributes with which primitive man endowed his deity? May not the germs of human evolution be within the human soul, for us to develop or to neglect at will? Eve was free to take, or to reject, the fruit of the Tree of Knowledge—material knowledge; are not we, perhaps, also free to take, or to reject, the fruit of the Tree of Life—spiritual life? It is largely because we are taught that we have no power of ourselves to help ourselves, that we tumble into crimes of militarism. To leave ourselves in God's hands, is often an excuse for idleness, and the result is that we find ourselves in the hands of a war-lord. Autocratic government is giving place to democratic government, on earth; may not our view of an autocratic God also be doomed to disappear? If the Kingdom of Heaven is within us, the King of Heaven must be there too, reigning not in solitary glory, in empty space, but within each one of us. The souls of men are the prism which should refract the radiant Spirit of God, and we must not be disappointed when, in times of trouble, the human spectrum shows the dark lines only. If we knew more about the laws of Nature, we should know that the dark lines are due to local conditions, which give invaluable proof of the Universal Law of Light.

My constant ejaculations—"Chovai! Stoi! Terrai! Napred!" ("Get out of the way! Stop! Go on! Forward!") were like tugs at the tether, which tied us to the material world, reminding us that we still had small material parts to play.

I was specially interested during our talk to find that it was not only in the older, and, as it might be thought, more effete civilisations of Western Europe, that a consciousness of the incongruity of war with twentieth century ideas, is becoming current. This officer, representative of the best traditions of Eastern European soldierhood, described how he had formerly been an enthusiastic lover of war, a believer in its glories, and had once even sacrificed a good position on the Staff, in order to be in the thick of the fighting line. And now, though he suffered, as his personal record testified, from no lack of courage or virility, war, in his eyes, was murder, and its glories tinsel. I compared this Serbian major with our German devil-major at Tongres. Which of the two was the more truly civilised? I realised that Kipling's "East is East, and West is West, and never the twain shall meet" does not apply to the east and west of Europe. The west of Europe must, and will, unite with the Slav portion of the east, as a safeguard against the Central Powers of darkness. This war is bringing clearly before human consciousness in the east, as well as in the west of Europe, the fact that it is logically impossible for civilised mankind to preserve simultaneously two opposed standards of conduct: for individuals, a high form of morality, in which life, honour, and justice are revered; and for nations, a cynical non-morality, in which murder, dishonour, and injustice are inculcated as the highest virtues. We must raise the international standard or we shall inevitably debase the individual standard of human right and wrong.

The fate of humankind, whilst this war lasts, is in the balance. The fight between the Allies and the Central Powers is not merely a struggle between one form of civilisation and another; between a society which believes in full-blown militarism, and a society which believes in a milder form of militarism. There is more than that at stake. The struggle is between militarism and human evolution. Europe is in travail—the travail preceding the birth of a new race. We prayed God that the birth might not be still-born. For fear of this, and for this reason alone, deliverance must not be prematurely forced. The Central Powers, the arch exponents of militarism, must be vanquished.

My friend and I were agreed, that in the future, militarism must be exterminated, root and branch, if mankind is not to regress towards a monstrous sub-humanity. There was no one and nothing to contradict us, and we felt that if we lived a thousand years, our thoughts would never be more appropriately leaded to plumb the depths of the sea of Truth.

After an hour, the Major left me, and went back to his murderous guns, and as I rode on alone, I welcomed the ideas which we had exchanged, to a place in my memory, but I warned them that they were not there for ornament; ideas are lumber until they are expressed in action. The thinker should also be the doer; the world's trouble is that too often thinkers only think and doers only do. Society understands how to translate into action its hatreds—the hatreds of a minority; it has not yet learned to translate into action the love and sympathy of the majority of mankind. Hatred is expressed easily enough in war; love has no such dramatic mouthpiece. Hatred is positive; love still only negative in expression. Love is still blind, and the poets shouldn't joke about it. Love has not yet seen that there is a greater love than for a man to lay down his life for his friend; to take up your life for someone who is not your friend, requires a more difficult sacrifice.

The warmongers have an advantage over the peacemongers; they don't talk, they act; the peacemongers don't act, they talk; and until their talk is translated into action, they will be ineffective in conquering war. It's no use sweeping, unless you get rid of the dust.

CHAPTER XXVIII

The crush of wagons in the gorge grew worse and worse, as the night went on, till at 1 a.m. all movement stopped, and the block seemed permanent. Were the Bulgars closing in upon us in front? Or were the Albanians taking this easy opportunity of attacking convoys? There were no officers about, and the soldiers of our column and of neighbouring columns, who were unaware of the full danger of the situation, all assumed that there was a bad hole or a broken bridge ahead of us, and that the stoppage was irremediable. But nothing is irremediable till all remedies have been tried, and then others can probably be invented.

There was barely room to pass, but I rode forward with Vooitch, scraping and bruising my legs against the wagon wheels and hard wooden pack-saddles, to try and discover the reason for the long halt. If there was a serious reason, it was as well to be prepared. But we found, as we had suspected, that a little way up the line, some of the oxen had decided that, enemies or no enemies, it was now bedtime, and they were calmly lying across the road, and the complacent drivers, in the absence of officers, had acquiesced, as there was no space by the side of the road, on which the animals could rest. The soldiers were seated around the promptly lighted fires; they were not sleeping, they never seemed to sleep; or eating, one seldom saw them eat; they were gazing into the red ashes, in apparent ignorance, or indifference to their pending fate. There was only one remedy. Vooitch and I were both wearing thick boots. We dismounted, and with the optimism of Mark Twain when he tried to push the glacier forward with his stick, we walked along the line of the columns ahead of us, kicked the oxen out of their slumbers, called the men from their dreams, and provoked a move; we may thus possibly have prevented the capture of some of the rearguard columns.

We then journeyed continuously, except for short compulsory halts, due to congestion of convoys, all through that night, and the next day, till 6 o'clock in the evening—a 25 hours' ride—till we reached Ravni, in an opening which ended the first, or Maidevo, half of the gorge. This opening was also the entrance to the second, or Yankova, portion of the defile.

We bivouacked by the side of a small river. We economised time in those days, and pitched as few tents as possible—one for hospital, one for doctors, one for men, and one for women. This evening we made our kitchen in the open, under a large walnut tree, by the side of the stream. Four or five officers, including the Colonel who had been the head of the powder factory at Krushievatz, joined us for supper, and we gave them blankets, and straw, and the shelter of the hospital tent, for the night. The Colonel, like most officers, had been obliged to leave his wife and children in Krushievatz. How could he have transported them, and where could he have taken them? He hated the Germans, although, or was it because, he had a German wife, but he trusted, he said, that they would be cavaliers. But he was nervous and excited. Is it a wonder? He asked the question which I always dreaded, "Where are the English?" And I could only reply, as always, "Oh! they'll turn up some day." But I never, during our three months' retreat, heard either officer, or soldier, utter a word of bitterness, or reproach, about the non-arrival of the Allies. They always said, with quiet dignity, that there was some good reason why they had not yet been able to send help.

We were, of course, happy to offer these officers hospitality, and we were glad to be able to show, even in a tiny way, British sympathy with the Serbian nation. But now our little stock of stores was coming to an end, and there was no prospect of renewal, and on this evening we shared our last pot of jam with these Serbian friends. Could they, we asked, have a more practical proof of sympathy than that?

Some of the oxen were lame, and I found that it was because the men had carelessly omitted to reshoe them. Next morning, therefore, early, I summoned all the drivers, and told each man to bring his oxen before me, that I might examine their feet. Oxen parade. I then reminded them that the time might come, any day, when we in our turn should be in pursuit of the enemy, and how would they feel if they had to stay behind because their oxen were lame? I was told it was not possible to shoe them now, and this, that, and the other plausible excuse was offered. But this was no time for excuses; fierce eye and deep voice were summoned, and then at once the sergeant acquiesced. "Ja! Ja! Dobro! Dobro!" ("Yes! Yes! All right! All right!") Then I heard him murmur to Vooitch, as he shrugged his shoulders, "It's no use. If she says it's got to be done, we've got to do it." And it was done. (I knew there were shoes and a smith in another column near us.) That little affair was scarcely finished, when I heard that one of the kitchen boys was playing cards, when he had been told by the cooks to fill the lamps. Fierce-eye business again. I don't believe in corporal punishment, but I couldn't begin teaching the Serbian soldiers abstract reasons for the necessity of obedience, and obedience was essential. So, hoping to teach the sergeant a little elementary discipline, I called him, put my whip in his hand, and took him with me to the bivouac tent in which the delinquent was playing truant, and told him he was to use the whip if I gave the word. We arrived in front of the kitchen sleeping tent, and there, sure enough, was the naughty Nicola, playing cards with three other soldiers. Very fierce eye, and very fierce voice this time. They could play cards, I told them, in leisure hours, not in work time; I took away the cards, tore them in pieces, and told the sergeant to use the whip. He thought it would be a pity to discriminate between Nicola and the others, and he belaboured all four, and we had no illegitimate card-playing after that.

My next job that same morning concerned Sandford and Merton. We had, two days ago on the trek, failing to find oxen, commandeered some cows to help draw the wagons, as our oxen were exhausted. They had with them two calves, and last night, on arrival, Sandford and Merton had killed the calves, and, with their own little group of friends, they had eaten them, without asking permission and—here was the rub—without offering us any veal. Sandford was stout and lazy, and was catering very badly for us, and if we had relied on his services, we and the cattle should have fared badly, and now food was getting scarcer, and he gave himself less, instead of more, trouble. So I took the opportunity of a fierce-eye talk. I used to disbelieve in the necessity for anger, but, with the soldiers, I found that an ounce of anger was worth a ton of argument. But, for the sake of the interpreter, the wrath had to be broken up into sections, else Vooitch forgot what I had said and, then he invented, and his inventions were not the same as mine. But to bring the wrath duly to the boil, then let it wait, simmering, whilst the interpreter translated, then again boil and simmer, boil and simmer, in quick alternation, as often as required, needed, in order to be effective, a little stage management. So far, I had got on without "damn," for which I didn't know the Serbian.

Our Artillery Major looked in for coffee and a talk after mid-day dinner. News was as bad as ever, but he was as cheery as usual. There were only a few wounded, and that was the worst sign of all.

At 4 p.m. came the order to move on. Night treks seemed now to be the rule, and this night we must tackle the second half (Yankova portion) of the defile.

The first stretch of road was terrible for the cars, very soft, and deep in mud and holes, but the soldiers all helped to push and carry, and the chauffeurs, as usual, mastered all difficulties. Before we entered the gorge, we passed our divisional commander, who was watching some of the artillery wagons enter the main road, from a by-track to the hills, where the guns had been in position, and as we were held up, we had a short talk. He was, as always, delightfully genial, friendly and cheerful. If we passed safely through the gorge to-night, the Army would, he said, probably be saved. There was renewed hope that the French and English—and even the Russians were mentioned—were on their way from Salonika. Possibly we might join them at Velles. He also gave me the good news that our dispenser was to be removed next day.

The congestion last night had been so great, and had caused such dangerous delay, that to-night steps were taken by officers to control the way, and to get the columns in a single line, to allow of passing up and down. Officers were also stationed at intervals to prevent wagons and refugees from butting in from side-roads and causing confusion, which it would take a Dante to describe.

The cars were allowed to go short distances ahead and await us at intervals, but in view of the possibility of capture by enemies, at either end of the gorge, it was not desirable that they should be beyond easy reach of the rest of the column. The guns were making their usual din, resounding noisily against the mountain sides, as we entered the gorge, but the valley seemed less full of forebodings than yesterday, and we reached Blatzi at the astonishingly early hour of eleven p.m.

I left the column outside the town, and went on with Vooitch to find shelter. But the town was choked with troops, and every house, though deserted by its own inhabitants, was full of soldiers. Eventually we found a side lane for the encampment, and by one o'clock we were all asleep. At six the next morning, some officers vacated two rooms in a house near, and we took possession, for kitchen and hospital. Wounded arrived, and we had to evacuate them to Kurshumlya, about twenty kilometres distant.

Major A. and the French doctors were bivouacked at the other end of the town, and came to see us at tea-time—the former much depressed, the latter still full of optimism. A cousin of our Artillery Major, so like him that he might have been a twin brother, presented himself, and from talks with him and with other officers, I gathered that the situation was extremely black. The numbers of the infantry were rapidly diminishing; 1,000 had been left, dead and wounded, on the field near Bagrdan. It had been impossible to move the wounded; the Germans had fired on the ambulance parties. Officers were now reduced in numbers by one third. The absorbing consideration still was, "should we meet the French and English before the Bulgars caught us up?" Skoplye was already in Bulgarian hands, and now I heard for the first time that, if there was no hope of being joined by the Allies, the Army must retreat across the Montenegrin mountains, to the coast of Albania. But conversation still ended always with the hope that the Allies would come.

CHAPTER XXIX

We left Blatzi at 10.30 a.m. on Thursday, November 11th, for Tulari, half-way to Kurshumlya. The road was less bad, and shortly after passing the Nish turning, we were temporarily cheered by an officer who, as he rode past, told us that he had heard that the Allies had taken Nish; but, of course, it was not true. We arrived at Tulari, at 1.30, in pelting rain and sleet. The fields were all under water, and we were lucky to secure rooms in two of the few small houses of which the village was composed. We were kept busy with wounded and evacuations and burials. Major A.'s column arrived a little later, and one of the French doctors had supper with us. He told us that the other doctor was mislaid: he had ridden in advance, and had evidently lost the convoy. He turned up, in a starved condition, two days later.

We left Tulari at 2 p.m. on November 12th for Barbatovatza, and the order said that we were to go via Choongula. But the first 200 yards of road were, fortunately, so bad with mud and holes that, though the cars tried, as in duty bound, they could not get through it, and I was obliged to let them separate from the rest of the column, and go *via* Kurshumlya along the main road. And the road followed by the column was throughout so bad that it would have been impossible, even for our wonderful cars and chauffeurs; the authorities, when they ordered us to take this track, must have forgotten that we had cars with us, for there was no attempt at road, and the way lay over ploughed fields, and the mud was often up to the axles of the wagon wheels. The oxen had heavy labour all the time, and in many places we had to outspan oxen and, with their help, drag the wagons one after the other out of deep bogs.

There were so few other columns going our way, and the firing line was so near to us, that I wondered if I had, after all, made a mistake in taking this route. But I had acted according to instructions. The way for some distance ran along a high plateau, parallel with the road on which we had travelled from Blatzi. On our left was another plateau, and all around, and in the distance, were mountains which were now snow-capped. Blatzi village seemed to be ablaze, and the hills between us and it were red with the fire of cannons, and reeking with shrapnel smoke. But the view was magnificent:

dead, yellow leaves of the scrub of Turkey oak—not the common oak, nothing was ever common—made a gorgeous show of colour against the dark blue mountains.

At 4.30 p.m. the daylight vanished. There were no roads, but tracks led in all directions, over ploughed fields, and through woods, and it was difficult in the darkness to know which to take. But, by good luck, we steered straight, and at 10 p.m. I saw with joy the fires of bivouacked columns, and knew that we were near our goal; and, to my intense relief, the cars containing the British Staff arrived an hour later.

We encamped under trees by the roadside. At one o'clock, when I was about to go to bed in the car, an officer came up. He was very excited, and asked why in the name of—I think he said Heaven—we had encamped in this place? He had been told, he said, to put his guns here, in position for a big battle that was to be fought early in the morning against the Germans. I told him that we, too, were here by order. That must, he said, be a mistake. So I showed him my order paper, and he shrugged his shoulders and went away. Major A. was encamped on the other side of the road, and I went across. I heard sounds like small guns being fired in quick succession. I tracked them to their source, inside a tent, and found the Major, the two French doctors, and one or two other officers, all asleep. I woke the Major, told him what the Captain had said, and asked him if he thought that the Captain had known what he was talking about. The unshaved Major sat up in bed, much interested, and suggested that I should send a line of enquiry to Headquarters Staff, who were lodged in the school-house near; and he asked me to let him know the result. I went, with Vooitch, to the buildings in which the P.M.O. was supposed to be, and I asked the guard, who was walking up and down outside, if the Staff were there. He said, "Yes." "Were they asleep?" "Yes." So I said "Thank you," and came away, and went to bed. If they were sleeping there couldn't be any hurry for us; all must be well, and I took a four hours' rest. But it was sometimes a little difficult on such occasions. For I was, above all things, anxious to avoid giving the impression that we were nervous. We were not; but, at the same time, I must not, for the sake of my own pride, expose the column to unnecessary risk.

In the morning I had a talk with our P.M.O. He had now, he said, lost everything. His house and possessions in Arangelovatz had been taken by the Germans, and, worse still, in Kragujevatz, not only his house and property, but his wife and five children were in the Germans' hands. I knew that the pessimism of both the P.M.O. and of Major A., with whom I also talked that morning, was only too well grounded, and I felt half ashamed to be able to talk cheerfully, whilst I was only suffering vicariously; but I always argued with them, that France and England were big nations, and that they would not have intervened, and have sent troops to Salonika to help Serbia, if they had not meant to aid effectually; their prestige was at stake, and they would never allow Serbia to be expunged.

On the other hand, all Serbians realised that England had not yet begun to understand the groundwork of Serbian politics. Even admitting that England felt now goodwill towards Serbia, it was a goodwill which was accidental, and due to extraneous circumstances, rather than to appreciation of the motives which had actuated Serbia in taking the field against superior enemies. And nothing in all history is more wonderful than the way in which the Serbian people have, during centuries, struggled, then suffered passively when struggle was useless, then struggled again for their ideal; for an ideal which must have been sub-conscious in the minds of a people who had lived for centuries scattered amongst their tyrannical conquerors—the ideal of race freedom.

The Serbian people could, at a price, have bought exemption from this present annihilation, but at a price which would have killed for ever, hope of the eventual freedom, not only of the four million Serbian and Montenegrin Slavs, but of the seven million Slavs, now living in a neighbouring and hostile State.

All Serbians also realised that England still had only a superficial acquaintance with the Serbian character, and was still in the habit of judging them by the unfortunate act which had first brought their nation to the knowledge of the British public. Of that act they had heard only through newspaper comments circulated by their enemies: the extenuating circumstances had never been learned.

But England had not only exaggerated the shortcomings of the Serbians, she had also exaggerated the virtues of the Bulgarians, and probably never believed till the latter crossed the Serbian frontier, that which every Serbian peasant had known from the beginning of the war—namely, that the ambitions of the German Ferdinand were not based upon the ideals of a democratic people, but upon the designs of a Prince who was in sympathy with the military autocracy of the Central Empires. Every Serbian knew that between Bulgo-German autocracy, and Serbian democracy, there could be no affinity. England would, they knew, discover this in time, but meanwhile Serbia was being sacrificed.

The confidence with which Serbians believed that when England understood the ideal for which Serbia was struggling, she would extend, not only the little finger, but the whole hand, of fellowship, moved me almost more than their sufferings. And if, as a nation, we do not fulfil the expectation that we, who have won our own freedom, shall help the Serbians to win theirs, we can never look a democratic country in the face again.

But the continuous retreating could not fail to have a depressing influence on everybody, except those who were commanders, and this morning at Barbovatz we had an illustration of the different spirit which actuates respectively a defeated or a victorious soldier. One of the ambulance men came up and suggested that the big brown tent which had been brought for hospital purposes, should now be abandoned. It filled two wagons on the treks; the oxen were growing weak with the continuous journeying; corn was never now obtainable, and hay only in insufficient quantities, with the result that the roads were already strewn with the dead bodies of oxen and of horses. The man said, and truly, that we did not use this tent now—there was never time to put it up—and the other tents were large enough. But it belonged to the Serbian hospital equipment, and I would not abandon it till we were compelled. "What you say is all very well," I said, "while we are retreating, but when we, in our turn, pursue——" "Ah!" interrupted the man eagerly, "I will carry it on my own back then."

We had a momentary gleam of hope that afternoon, from a rumour that the German troops had withdrawn from our front, and had gone, it was thought, to meet the Russians, who were believed to be advancing from Negotina, through Rumania. The Austrians, without the Germans, would be manageable. But this, like all other rumours of good news, was false. It served, however, as a temporary tonic to the spirits. It is always easier to bear disaster than the fear of disaster. Disaster has a bracing influence, but fear paralyses action, and I came to the conclusion that these rumours served a useful purpose.

We left next morning, November 14th, at five o'clock, for Spantzi, only a two hours' trek. We found a dry field for the camp, and a farmhouse for kitchen. The guns were very near and noisy that day.

CHAPTER XXX

Next morning, November 15th, we moved, at five o'clock, for Marzovatz, where we arrived at 8 a.m. We were lucky in finding a delightful camping-place, in an orchard, surrounded by fine mountains. Our oxen were getting exhausted, so I sent the corporal to try and find others, also additional wagons, as the animals could no longer pull their full loads.

We now heard, to our regret, that our division, which had all this time borne the brunt of the fighting, was to have a rest, and the Drinske division was to take the first line. This would probably mean fewer wounded for us, and our doctors and nurses would grow restive.

At 9.30 that evening, Monday, November 15th, the order came to go on to Podyevo, some distance beyond Kurshumlya. We were away by 10 p.m. The night was fine, but very cold. Kurshumlya, as we passed through, was in darkness, and deserted except for the usual groups of refugees, huddled round camp fires, in the streets. One of the cars broke down in the town, and we had to leave the car with a Serbian soldier-chauffeur who had turned up and had offered his services. He was to repair it, or find oxen, and bring it on as soon as possible. If the Germans overtook him before he had done his work, he must destroy the car and follow us. But we never saw the car again. The man mended it, and was on his way to join us, when, on a steep and narrow road, it stuck, and some officers, who were following, blew it up with gunpowder and set fire to it, to prevent it from falling into the enemy's hands.

Our way lay through a narrow gorge, and the road was atrocious, and, in the dark, dangerous; and as the chauffeurs were exhausted, with the constant strain, and lack of sleep, we decided at 3 a.m. to call a halt till dawn at 5.30. After that came a steep hill up to Prepolatz, the old Turkish frontier.

At the base of this hill lay Banya, and a long stretch of flat muddy road, which was blocked, from end to end, with a solid phalanx of wagons, all motionless, as if they were carved in stone. Round the far corner the hill began, and what was happening there, no one could see. I was waiting on my weary horse for our turn to move, when a young captain of a commissariat column came up, and in excellent English, invited me to come and drink a glass of tea with him in his camp by the side of the road. He recognised me because he had visited our Kragujevatz hospital in the old days. He was encamped with his large column in a sea of mud, and we sat round his fire on little stools which sank deep into the slush; but I enjoyed the tea, which helped to keep me awake during a weary halt.

It was sometimes a little difficult to discriminate between times when it was right that we should be shunted out of the line by a more important column, and times when we must hold our own. For artillery columns, of course, we always gave way, but sometimes extra officious under-officers, in control of columns, would try and bounce us out of the line illegitimately, and that required the fierce-eye business. Serbian officers were invariably courteous, and though I refused to take undue advantage of sex, they often smuggled us into the line when we might otherwise have had long to wait.

At Banya, our Artillery Major's double, who was also an artillery officer, appeared, and he immediately arranged that our column should follow his convoy, and others had to stand aside. Soon after that, the Major arrived, and rode with me for a little while on his way again to place his guns. He introduced me to another officer who had lately been embarrassed by the arrival from Berlin of his German wife and seven children, who were all now travelling with the convoy.

The cars, as usual, took the hill wonderfully, and went on and waited for the column at Prepolatz, near the old Turkish fort. This was the boundary of Old Serbia, the entrance to the newer Serbia of recent conquests, and my heart ached for our Serbian comrades, who must now say good-bye to the best-loved and most-prized portion of their country, and leave it, with all that was most precious to them, in the enemy's hands; knowing that the enemy would now eat bread from corn which they had not sown, and drink wine from vineyards which they had not planted; whilst the sowers and the planters, the owners of this fertile soil, were fleeing, a spectral nation to a spectral land, without clothes, without money, without food; but, all honour to them, never without hope, because they were never without an ideal. Will the day ever come, I wondered, when "the arrogance of the proud shall cease and the haughtiness of the terrible be laid low?"

The Major and I were glad to rejoin the cars which carried the food, and to eat a hurried sandwich. I had had nothing since the captain's glass of tea in the early morning; the Major never seemed to eat. We reached Dubnitz at 9.30 p.m.—a twenty-four hours' trek. Our field-kitchen oxen had broken down, and we had to send others to help bring the field kitchen in. It arrived next morning after we had left for Dole Luzhan, and it followed us.

We left at 8 o'clock, on a twelve hours' trek. A snow blizzard, with intense cold, made the conditions unpleasant for us, and deadly for the beasts. Continued cold, exhaustion from forced marches, and increasing lack of food, made the track a shambles. The well-aimed ball of death was knocking down oxen and horses, like ninepins, all along the road. One of our riding horses died also to-day from cold and exhaustion. It was bad enough to see these poor beasts dead along the road, but it was still worse to see them dying, and to know that all they needed for restoration to life, was warmth and rest and food. I thought of the Blue Cross Society, but even they could have done nothing, as there was no time; enemies on three sides were always close behind us.

When we arrived at the village we found that the cars, which had gone on in advance, were standing in two feet of water. The chauffeurs and the staff had gone into a cottage to dry their clothes, and in the meantime, a stream which ran across the road had expanded into a lake. The cottage was also surrounded by the flood, and the doctors and nurses were carried out by the gallant chauffeurs, who then waded up to their knees and rescued the cars.

We found camping-ground for the column in an Arnaut (Albanian) village, and we ourselves slept in the cars upon the road; the snow was too deep for tent pitching.

CHAPTER XXXI

We left next morning, at nine, for Prishtina. Progress was very slow, the road being more than ever blocked with columns and refugees. The cold all day was bad enough, and but for straw-covered stirrups and my wonderful rubber canvas boots, worn over three pairs of stockings, I must have had frozen feet, but between 4 and 10 p.m. the cold was intense.

Amongst many memorable days, that day stands conspicuous, for at dusk we began to cross the historic battlefield of Kossovo. Upon this desolate plain, which extends southwards to Skoplye, was fought, in 1389, the Waterloo of Serbia, the battle of Kossovo Polye (the field of blackbirds). Upon this plain, the Serbs had suffered, at the hands of the Turks, a defeat which robbed them of nationhood during nearly 500 years; a defeat which must have been the harder to bear because it came after 200 years of flourishing empire; this empire had begun with the Nemanya dynasty, under Stephen, in 1196, and had reached its zenith under another famous Stephen—Stephen Dushan—who died mysteriously in 1355.

It was only in 1878, and, strangely enough, through the Treaty of Berlin, that the Serbs regained their independence.

This Kossovo battle, more than any other in Balkan history, seems to have gripped the imagination of both Turks and Serbians, conquerors and defeated. Poets relate that the Turkish Amurath the First, though a Sultan, and presumably accustomed to such pastimes, was enjoying a honeymoon when he received news that the Serbs and Albanians had routed his legions, in the fastnesses of the Black Mountain; he, therefore, bade a hurried farewell to his bride, and, as there were no cars or aeroplanes in those days, he galloped to Kossovo, accompanied, it is said, by so many men "that a horseman could not ride from one wing of his army to the other in a fortnight. The plain of Kossovo was one mass of steel; horse stood against horse, man against man; the spears formed a thick forest; the banners obscured the sun; there was no space for a drop of water to fall between them."

But also on King Lazar's side, many Serbs, Bosnians, and Albanians were banded together. They must have made a formidable array, for legends record that at the last moment, Amurath hesitated to attack the allied hosts, and that his doubts were only allayed by a dream which came to one of his counsellors, bidding him to "conquer the infidels." Lazar, also, seems to have been in touch with the heavenly powers. They, metaphorically, rang him up just before the battle should have begun, and asked him if he would rather have a heavenly, or an earthly kingdom. If he chose the latter, he would be victorious over the Sultan, but he could not have both, and if he wanted a heavenly kingdom, he must submit to being defeated by the Sultan. Lazar appears to have asked the exchange to hold the line whilst he made up his mind; he finally decided upon the Kingdom of Heaven. The poets seem universally to have approved his choice, but though it may have been wisdom for himself, it was bad luck for his army, his dukes, and his nine brothers-in-law, who perished with him. He should either not have fought, or he should have fought meaning to win.

And now, when we set foot upon that steppe, it seemed that those 500 years that had passed since the first Kossovo day, had been expunged. For the Serbian Army, now defeated by the allies of those same Turks, was still, like a ghost from the past, fleeing across the silent plain. The panoplies had fallen from their horses, the armour from their men: it was now a skeleton army, in skeleton clothes, but it was carrying the same soul, of the same nation, to guard as a holy treasure, till the day of the Lord shall come. In the darkness, the physical wonders of the place would have been hidden, but for the white snow which outlined the low hills, and transformed their rolling ridges into the foamy waves of a tempestuous sea, which seemed, on both sides of the narrow road, to be advancing in tidal waves to engulf us, as we moved slowly onwards, co-partners in that spectral flight.

At every few yards, corpses of oxen and of horses, and bodies of oxen and of horses not yet dead, but unable to rise, kept the image of Death foremost in the mind; and then, as though to give her cold, green-blooded sanction to the scene, the moon rose over the hillocks, sailed defiantly across the sky, revealed dead horrors of the present, and recalled to the eye of the imagination, horrors which had lain hidden during 500 years.

The moon revealed, also, one picture of dumb and hopeless misery never to be forgotten. Apart from our funeral procession, nothing living, not even the famous blackbirds, had been visible during mile after mile, mile after mile, in all the wide expanse till, at a turn in the road, I saw, a hundred yards to our left, standing up to his fetlocks in the snow, abandoned, because it could no longer pull, a lean bay horse. It was too weak to move, and it knew that if it lay down it would never rise, but must succumb to a lingering death from cold and hunger; so it stood, staring into nothingness, knowing that no help would come. It was the dumbness of the misery that appealed, and I realised that the misery of many of us who are suffering in this war, is almost as dumb as the misery of that poor beast. And we shall remain dumb until we have the courage to wrest the flaming sword from the hands of the cherubim who guard the Tree of Life. The dictionaries tell us that cherubim are second-class angels, so there ought to be no difficulty, if the attack were only determined enough.

It was 9 p.m. when, cold and hungry, we sighted the picturesque town of Prishtina, with its square-roofed houses and narrow streets. At the entrance there was bad congestion—a phalanx of wagons were all struggling to pass through a narrow alley, and whilst waiting our turn, one of our men, who had gone on with the cars in advance, gave me a shock. He told me that our two women doctors, and the nurses, were all in a Turkish harem. It was true, and they much enjoyed the hospitality of a kindly old Turkish gentleman.

The only possible site for the wagons for the night was in a muddy square. I slept, as always, in the car, in one of the side streets, but not till our faithful cook had given me some much-needed supper, as we sat on little stools in the mud, round a fire which the soldier-cook, Demetrius, had lighted for us in the street.

Next morning, early, a camping-site must be found, and I rode with Vooitch along the Prizrend road. Very soon we saw, on our left, a large hospital building, with an open grass space between it and the road. This was the military hospital; we went in and asked the commandant to allow us to encamp in the garden. He agreed, and he also kindly gave us a room in the hospital for sleeping quarters for the doctors and nurses, and in the garden a round summer house, which could be used as kitchen, dining-room and sleeping-room for some of the men.

At Prishtina we were now, as I understood, at the parting of the ways. If there was still hope of our joining the Allies, the Army would continue on its southward journey, *via* Prizrend, and we noticed, on our arrival at the hospital site, that all the convoys were passing along this road, in front of our camp, and that was a good sign. But if this hope must be abandoned, then all hope of victory and all hope of saving Serbia was at an end, and the only aspiration would be to save the Army; for this there was only one road of salvation open—over the mountains of Montenegro and Albania to the coast. This road, which branched off from the Prizrend road, nearly opposite our camp, was at present lifeless, and that was good.

In the town we met, to our astonishment, our Doctor MacMillan and Mr. Rodgers. They gave us the news that Nurse Clifton had been accidentally shot (as before mentioned). She was now lying ill at Mitrovitza, and they had been to Prishtina for stores, and were now on their way gallantly to rejoin her and Doctor Iles, and Nurse Bainbridge, with the certainty of being taken prisoners by the Austrians, as "Ginger," though better, was too ill to be moved. (They returned safely to London in February, 1916.)

Next day a young German officer strolled into our mess hut. He was a prisoner, but the only restraint upon him was that he must report himself at the military station every night. During the day he was as free as we were, and he came and took meals with us several times. His views upon the military position were interesting: the war had been brought on by England; France had been the first to violate Belgian territory; and the war would be finished in a month; there was no chance at all for the Allies; we could not win; the Germans had practically won already. Our hospital party would certainly be taken prisoners in a few days. We told him that some of us had enjoyed one experience of being prisoners in German hands, and that, though we had no intention of being taken prisoners by anybody, we would rather fall into the hands of the Bulgarians, the Turks, or the Austrians, than of the Germans. We told him of our devil-major at Tongres, and he replied, "Ah! you'll find you will be much better treated this time; you mark my words." We have marked them ever since.

Other visitors were two blue-jackets from Admiral Trowbridge's unit, which had done such fine work on the Danube. They were now, with their guns, also in the general retreat, and were encamped near Prishtina.

But all day long, columns were still passing along the road in front of us, towards Prizrend. "Terrai! Ide! Desno! Levo!" ("Get on! Make a move! To the right! To the left!") was in our ears all day and all night.

The difficulty of getting hay for the animals became greater every day. I found this evening, when I went my round, that nothing had been provided for the oxen, or the horses, for the night, or for the next morning. So I routed Sandford out of his slumbers, and sent him to neighbouring villages to search for fodder. He must have hated me. But I have never wished to be popular; popularity is a drag on the wheel of effort.

Prishtina was, of course, in process of being evacuated, and though we were too late for food stores, we secured for the soldiers, from the Red Cross depôt, a number of under-garments which were much needed. There were, unfortunately, no boots, and the men's footgear was deplorable.

November 20th arrived, and still I received no order to move. I was a little uneasy lest the message should have miscarried, as the P.M.O. had told me, when we first arrived, that we should be moving on at once, and I noticed that the convoys which had, a day or two ago, passed along the southern road to Prizrend, were now returning, and taking the western road towards Montenegro. That was disquieting, for I guessed that it might mean that the dice were loaded against us, that the Allies had failed us, and that the intention of the Serbian Army to continue southwards, through Prizrend to Monastir, there to join with the Allies, must be abandoned. The

Bulgarians were already at Skoplye, and it was obvious that, if the Serbian Army risked encountering the victorious Bulgars, and was not successful, the fate of the Army would be sealed, for the road of retreat to Montenegro and Albania would then be blocked by the Germans and the Austrians.

The moment of decision for the Headquarters Staff, between going south, and risking the annihilation of the Army, upon which the existence of a future Serbia depended, or going west, and abandoning their beloved country to the enemy, must have been as bitter as any moment even in Serbia's tragic history. We should learn the decision when our order came to move.

But still no order came, though the columns all around us, artillery, cavalry, and the pontoons on the other side of the hospital building, had all gone. All the staff of the military hospital had gone. The Secretary was a Russian. He was very bitter, and consequently unjust, to the French and English. He said that the former were drinking absinthe, and the latter whisky, at home, whilst Serbia perished. He was busy evacuating his hospital, and he kept urging me to go, and not to wait for the order. He said we should certainly be cut off by the Bulgars, if we did not get away at once. Convoys which had gone towards Prizrend, had been recalled, and all were now hurrying to the Montenegrin frontier. Could I not hear that the Bulgarian guns sounded louder and louder as they drew nearer every hour? But I wouldn't go till the order came.

All that day I tried in vain to procure more oxen and wagons, as the men said our oxen could not possibly carry all the material, but without success, and I was obliged at last, reluctantly, to abandon the large brown tent. The Russian Secretary allowed me to put it in his hospital, which was then empty.

And still no order came. On the evening of Sunday the 21st, I sent an orderly to try and find the Headquarters Staff, and to enquire if there were any instructions for us. The man came back saying that our order had been sent yesterday. "Has the P.M.O. sent the order by you now, or given you a message?" "No, he said it would come." I could not, therefore, leave, as I had not instructions as to where to go, and didn't even know whether our road would be towards Prizrend, or Montenegro. I couldn't send the orderly again that night, as the Headquarters were a long distance away. We only had three riding horses now, and they were exhausted, and must be spared for the next trek. And every hour the Bulgarian guns thundered louder and nearer on one side of us, and the German guns on the other.

Early next morning (Monday, November 22nd) I sent the orderly to Headquarters, and told him that he must this time bring back a written order, and at 7 a.m. he returned with the small white envelope. He had seen the Divisional Commander, who was very angry when he heard that we had received no order. We ought, he said, to have left two days ago, and I must now make up for lost time.

Then came an exciting moment; were we to go towards Prizrend or Montenegro? I have never opened an envelope with more acute anxiety, for the fate of the Serbian Army, and of the Serbian people, would be disclosed. And if the fate of my own army and my own people had been contained in that small envelope, I could not have felt more deeply concerned.

The order said: "Take your column at once to Petch (near the Montenegrin frontier) *via* Valorno Han, Kievo, Lapushnik, and Dresnik, and *don't halt till you get to Dresnik.*" That was, I knew, the temporary death sentence of the Serbian nation. It meant that our backs, the backs of the Serbian Army, would now be turned to hope, Allies, and victory, and we must face—better not think of what we might have to face. Thoughts and energies must be concentrated in saving all we could of the Serbian Army, for future effort. This thought must be our beacon to lead us on with firm step and determined heart.

We were ready to start when the messenger returned at 7 a.m. (Monday, November 22nd), but the difficulty of getting into the line was great, because convoys and fugitives were now converging from all directions, on this one road of escape.

The cars went on first; they were to wait for us after half an hour's run; but when we came to the first cross road, we discovered that they had taken the wrong turn, so I had to send messengers flying after them, and we waited for them, with the column, by the side of the road, on an open plain. The cars returned, but we could not get back on to the road or regain our position in the line. We were by then surrounded by a solid block of convoys, on the plain beside the road. A glove could not have been dropped clear, amongst that chaos of wagons, horses, oxen, soldiers and refugees.

When the cars arrived I sent for the sergeant; he couldn't be found, so I searched, and found him playing cards with the sergeants of other columns. He said it was hopeless to expect to move to-day; some of the columns had been already waiting here for two days; we had better make up our minds to spend the night here. It was true that the columns around us had outspanned their oxen, and the men were sitting complacently round their ubiquitous fires, though the Bulgarian guns were dinning louder and louder every minute in their ears. It certainly looked hopeless to expect that jumble of wagons, animals and men, ever to disentangle themselves and break away into the serried line of convoys, artillery, transport, and refugees, which were all streaming without a break, along the road beside them. A more complete nightmare it would be difficult to picture. But I told the sergeant that we must get on at once; our oxen must not be outspanned; I didn't care what other columns did; if they chose to be taken by the Bulgars, that was their affair. He said it was impossible to get on to the road; we couldn't move either forward or backward, and between us and the road, and parallel with the road, was a broad deep ditch. There was, he said, nothing to be done but to wait patiently—the fatal doctrine of Kismet, by which he had been all his life impregnated. He was never resourceful, and now despair had paralysed him. But I had no intention of calmly letting the column be captured by the Bulgars, so I examined the ditch near to us, sent for some of the soldiers, told them to bring spades, and then ordered them to level the ditch. This was soon done. I then warned the column to be ready to move at a moment's notice, and, with Vooitch, I stood on the road watching an opportunity to break in. We stopped an officer who was commanding a passing column and asked him to insist on our having a place after his column; as we were a hospital we had, by right, precedence over many others. He responded by immediately stopping the columns behind him, and he gave us a place just behind the carriage in which was riding the General of the Kossovo Division. I heard afterwards that some thousands of the people whom we left behind on the plain, when we crossed that ditch, were captured by the Bulgars.

CHAPTER XXXII

But the congestion occasioned by the retreating of all the various convoys of an army 200,000 strong, with their innumerable oxen and horse wagons, plus the fugitives, with or without wagons, along bad and narrow roads, was now the more dangerous, because four enemies—the Germans, the Austrians, the Bulgars and, henceforth, the Arnauts or Albanians, who made sporadic and murderous raids upon the convoys for the sake of loot—were all close upon our heels. From Barchinatz, in the north of Serbia, to Scutari, near the coast of Albania, the sad cortège was winding its way, like a writhing snake, without beginning and without end, slowly, at oxen's pace, along roads, which sometimes looked impassable, with mud, and holes, and broken bridges.

The poor old Kossovo General had a narrow escape from drowning, or from a bad ducking, soon after we began to follow him. We came to a swollen river, over which there was no bridge; the water came over the steps of the four-seated pony carriage in which he drove, and, as the bottom of the stream was mud and boulders alternately, the carriage nearly overturned many times. I was ready to rescue him, but I expected every minute to be submerged myself. When I had forded safely through, leading a way for the others, I found that the fool of a sergeant had let another column break in, and intercept our rear wagons, which ran the risk of being left behind; so once more I was obliged to plunge into the water and splash up and down, and risk being overturned by angry, desperate drivers, and riders, whilst I insisted on our wagons getting a passage, and showed the drivers the treacherous places to avoid. The General soon got ahead of us, and we never saw him again.

We travelled all through the day and all through the night, with the exception of an outspan during two hours from 11 to 1 p.m., when we had supper by the roadside.

At 5 a.m. (Tuesday, November 23rd) we waited for the cars, which had stayed behind to rest awhile, but they got blocked, and did not reach us till 10 o'clock a.m. The cold during the night had been intense, and I was often obliged to dismount and to walk, in the thick mud, to keep my feet from freezing. Soon after starting again on Tuesday, November 23rd, we came to a wooden bridge, from which some planks had been removed by the column ahead of us, for firewood. An army on the march will commit any crime for firewood, and to a Serbian soldier, firewood seems of more importance than even bread. Before the cars could pass, we had to cut down some trees, which were, fortunately, available, and mend the bridge. It seemed certain that the time would come when the cars must be abandoned. How would the staff and their baggage then be carried? The wagons could carry no more; but I always remembered the old woman, who complained that "she 'ad indeed 'ad many troubles in 'er life, though"—she added, as an afterthought—"most of 'em 'ad never com'd off." We, too, had a few troubles that day which didn't come off. At one deep and bridgeless stream across the road, steep mud banks led to it and from it; the cars made dashes and scrambled through marvellously, but some of the wagons overturned in mid-stream. The drivers then waded into the water, above their knees, to drag up the fallen oxen, shouting "Ide! Ide! Terrai! Terrai!" and beating the poor, panting beasts till they struggled to their feet and scrambled out somehow. When they were out, they couldn't be given time to recover breath, because of the multitudes following behind.

Evening came and no outspan could yet be made, and it was now obvious that a second night must be spent without sleep. Sometimes our column, with others, would be shunted to the side of the road, to make way for artillery transport, which must, of course, have precedence. At twilight, on this evening, at the top of a steep descent, we had been thus halted, but finally, an officer in command at this point of the road, ordered way to be made for us, and we started, in the dark, on a narrow road, which was worse than anything we had yet met, with deep holes and mud up to the axles. I could not believe that the cars could possibly get through, but Mr. Little walked ahead with me, and said it might possibly be done. The cars made the descent safely and, finding that a road which was being reserved for artillery was better than the road which we and all the other columns must follow, we obtained leave for the cars to take that road and to meet us at Dreznik. And thankful I was that this was done, for the road on which we travelled would have been impossible, even for our wonderful cars and chauffeurs.

There were now only five motors, and they were overweighted. So J. G. and Mr. Little came with the column and drove in one of the horse wagons. At the bottom of the descent, the road ceased and became a track across a narrow, swampy, grass plain. Here there was a congestion of convoys which blocked us from 2 to 5 a.m. This was a blessing, as the animals were exhausted. Rugs and coats were in the cars, but we sat round the fire on some straw, made coffee, and pretended that there was no frost and that we were quite warm.

Before dawn (on Wednesday the 24th) came the moment when we had to take advantage of other columns who might be dozing, and get into the line before them. There was no road, only a track through beech scrub and up a steep ascent. I was accompanied, for a portion of the way, by the Artillery Major, whose wife and family had lately joined him; two of his sons, well-grown and well-mannered boys of about 15 and 16, were with him, in Serbian uniform.

On the top of the hill, when we reached an opening in the forest, we were told that we must halt while the road ahead of us was being mended. That sounded hopeful, and we always cheered the men with every scrap of hope that came our way. Meantime I was invited by some officers to have breakfast with them—coffee, and little chunks of fat bacon and bread—a huge treat. Soon afterwards we continued our journey—the mended road was, alas! like all other good news, only a rumour—over ploughed fields, feet deep in mud.

In the middle of the day, after a time of terrible straining for the oxen and horses, we were about to outspan for an hour's rest, but I was told we mustn't stop, even for a quarter of an hour. The animals, however, were exhausted, and we gave them a ten minutes' breathing interval, and the men time to swallow some food, and we went on. Would Kievo ever come in sight?

We continued all through that day (Wednesday, November 24th) in one ceaseless struggle with mud and ploughed fields, and through scrub of Turkish oak and beech woods—no road anywhere. Towards evening we climbed a steep hill through scrub, and reached a plateau which would, under normal circumstances, have given great joy, for a more gorgeous view it would be impossible to find. At first I thought that the snow-white peaks in the high heaven, to the west, and south, were fleecy clouds, but I soon saw that they were snow-capped mountains, away up in the sky at an incredible height, as far away from this troubled earth as they could get. I envied them. But there was no time to look at scenery. Before us was a steep descent, and thousands of wagons, converging from tracks running east and west, were streaming down the steep hill and blocking us. I rode down, and then up and down again, for some time, vainly trying to find an officer who could break the line for us; when I saw an officer in the distance, he had always ridden away by the time I reached the place. But eventually we got into line and descended, and found ourselves once more upon a road.

At 9 p.m. (Wednesday the 24th) the oxen could go no farther, and we outspanned for two hours in a wood by the side of the road, and we slept in the wagons for those two hours till 11 p.m. Then into the line again. But soon we were shunted to make room for artillery, and the difficulty of getting a place again was greater than ever. Some of the columns comprised two to three hundred wagons each. The sergeant, as usual, suggested that we should wait till to-morrow, but at 2. a.m. (Thursday the 25th) I found an officer of a munition column sitting by his fire by the roadside; I sat and talked with him for a while (J. G. and Mr. Little were asleep in the wagon), and then, when the chance came, he helped us into the line again. I am afraid that this officer will have a poor opinion of the intelligence of Englishwomen if he judged by my conversation that night; for I had been without sleep for seventy hours, and sometimes I couldn't prevent myself from dozing in the middle of a sentence, and then I had to try and tack the interrupted words correctly on to the next sentence, and I don't feel sure that they always fitted.

At 6 a.m. (on Thursday the 25th) we halted, again blocked. Some officers on the other side of the road were drinking coffee. I could manage to keep awake whilst moving, but during a halt it was too difficult; the officers saw me trying to keep awake, and dozing every few minutes on my horse, and one of them, who was Commander of the Staff of the Schumadia Division, second reserve (our division was first line), came across and made friends. He asked how we managed always to get a place in the line; he had noticed, he said, that we were generally to the front, and he then asked if I would allow him to join our column; he only now had eight horse wagons and carriages left, and he would not, he said, incommode us. I was, of course, glad, and he rode with us to Dreznik, which we reached at 4 p.m. on Thursday, November 25th. We had left Prishtina at seven on the morning of Monday, the 22nd, and had thus travelled continuously, with only occasional short halts, during three days and nights, but though I had been 81 hours without sleep or rest, I was quite fresh and untired, and the only inconvenience I had felt was from occasional fits of sleepiness when nothing important had to be done.

CHAPTER XXXIII

We were disappointed to find that the cars had not arrived, but we discovered that the road which they had been told to take did not come to Dreznik; we should, however, we were assured, find them at Petch (Ypek). The continued lack of rugs and baggage seemed of little consequence, for there never was time or opportunity for playing with such relics of past civilisation.

But at Dreznik we had a lovely dry camping ground, near a farmhouse, and we slept in a tent, on beds, for the first time and the last for many weeks. The night was cold but dry, and we had a real supper round the camp fire. Our kindly Captain (a barrister in the reserve) bivouacked in the field next to us, and joined us for supper, and we arranged to start together at daybreak the next morning. We knew that there would be difficulty in getting into the line, as myriads of wagons were already blocking our road of entrance. I hoped that Captain W. would do the fierce-eye business, and secure a place in the line, but he thought melting-eye business would be more effective, and he asked me to make the arrangements. So I rode on to see the lie of the land, as we were encamped away from the main road (I had sent Vooitch with the motors and the staff, and I was, meantime, without interpreter, as G. was useless). It was sometimes a little difficult to carry on in a language which one only understood imperfectly, but everything in Nature and this world is in a language which one doesn't understand, and we have to carry on. A big munition column of 200 wagons was the next in order of progression; I found the officer in charge, who, as usual, could talk German and French, and I asked him to let us follow immediately after him, and he cheerfully agreed. This was great luck, as oxen and horse wagons—all struggling and fighting for places—were clustered like bees before swarming-time, at every angle of the entrance to the narrow road of flight, and Captain W. was mightily pleased at the quick success. A snow blizzard began whilst we were waiting, and continued all through the day.

OUR CARTLESS COLUMN OF PACK PONIES AND OXEN HALTING
Discarded Shells in foreground

"I DIDN'T MISS MY SUNRISE, AFTER ALL"

The word "road" is a euphemism for the river of mud into which we immediately plunged; indeed, all day long we met no road, but journeyed over ploughed fields, bogs, now covered with snow, rivers, mud banks, and stick-hills. My horse was continually over its knees in mud, and was growing weaker every hour; but it was necessary to ride up and down the column, through the slough of mud, whenever this was possible without getting legs broken against the wagons and hard wooden packs, to watch that when a wagon stuck or broke, and had to be left, that the load was not thrown away, but was distributed amongst other wagons, whose drivers strongly resented extra burdens.

Horses fell, and their riders were thrown into the slush; wagons overturned, and were then, with their contents, destroyed as the quickest remedy; the road was one long pandemonium. At one bridge, over the River Drin, the scrimmage was even worse than usual. The bridge was so narrow that passage could only be effected in single file, and an officer near me estimated that 5,000 wagons were, at one moment, struggling at the entrance for places in the line. The loud voices of officers on horseback, shouting, and sometimes quarrelling, and of drivers urging their weary oxen, was like the noise of a thousand furious football crowds. Then suddenly above the din I heard my name, and an officer, wishing to expedite our column, shouted a dramatically worded biography, as an appeal to the soldiers to let us pass. But while we were still waiting to cross, I saw one desperate soldier, who was angry because an officer would not let him pass, seize the officer by the arm, with the intent to strike him. Promptly the officer took out his revolver and aimed it at the man. Fortunately the weapon was not loaded, so the officer, thwarted, turned round and seized a rifle from a soldier standing near. The culprit fled. The officer dismounted and pursued, caught up the man, whanged him on the head with the butt end, and was evidently intending to shoot. It was a horrible moment, but the man pleaded, others intervened, and the man was led away. Everyone's nerves were overwrought, and suffering and discomfort were so universal, that I don't believe that one death, more or less, would have seemed a great thing to those who were watching.

But once across the bridge, and on the tramp, all was again silent, except for the monotonous and automatic cries of the drivers to their oxen: "Terrai! Chovai! Ide! Napred!" The route all day was roadless, through sloughs of mud, and unbroken scrub, and over boulders, and everywhere it was strewn with the dead bodies of oxen and of horses.

At dusk we outspanned for the night, in the snow, at the top of a hill, near an Arnaut village. We had now, presumably, made up for the time lost at Prishtina, and rest for the animals was imperative. Captain W. supped with us.

We were away again by 6 o'clock next morning (Saturday, November 27th). We ate mealie porridge at 5.30, as it was impossible to stop for food during the day, and it was good to have some physical basis of energy. This meant an hour's less rest for me and for the cook (now, in the temporary absence of Mrs. Dawn, Demetrius, the soldier man). But it was worth the effort. We trekked, this day, first through an Arnaut village; the houses were one-storied, mostly of stone, as protection from enemies and from Serbian vendettas, and, indeed, they were so substantially built that only cannons could have dislodged the inhabitants; and then we came into a vortex of columns converging on all sides from their various encampments.

One officer (a doctor) told me that he had been blocked with his column at that spot during two days, and it was now seven days since he had left Prishtina. We got into line behind the guns, which soon, however, got ahead of us, as they were horse-drawn, and at a narrow bridge we were again blocked for hours. Thenceforward there were no roads, only tracks over fields and through scrub of Turkey oak, and mud incredible; and another of our riding horses collapsed.

The view, as we neared the snow-covered mountains, of which Petch was at the base, was magnificent. We encamped at dusk, on the slope of a hill, in the valley. Captain W. had supper with us. During the day, to my relief, Vooitch reappeared; he had left the motor party safely ensconced at Petch, and I was thankful to have his help again and to know that the others had arrived.

At 6 a.m. Sunday, November 28th (Advent Sunday), we were on the march. As usual now, there were no roads; we scrambled and stumbled over ploughed fields and every variety of rough country, but there was less block, because, as there was no road, we could choose our track. Hard frost, too, helped to make swamps more manageable. We had to abandon another wagon, because the oxen were growing weaker, and the kitchen wagon needed extra help.

The worst block of that day, after the start, occurred at the end of the day. I had scrambled through a hedge, in advance of the blocked column, and, with Vooitch, had chosen as camping site a grass space, partially sheltered from the icy wind by the wall of an Arnaut village. When we returned to the hedge we found that the Bakers' Column had intercepted ours, and refused to let our wagons pass. They said this was in revenge for their having been forced, by another officer, to let us pass them earlier in the day. When our men eventually got through, they were so angry at having been kept for an additional hour from fire and supper, that when they got through the hedge, they placed their wagons close under the hedge, instead of coming across to the other side of the enclosure, where I was awaiting them and keeping the ground from other columns. So, with fierce eye flaming, I stalked across to them, through intervening convoys, and told them to come at once. They said that they had already outspanned their oxen and lighted their fires. Full of wrath, I kicked their fires out, with my impellent boots, and gave the order to inspan and to follow me at once. They came meekly, and were soon glad of the shelter of the wall. How could I help loving these men? For they never sulked or bore malice when they had to do things they didn't like; perhaps they remembered that we, also, were doing things which we didn't like, for their sakes.

That evening I had the good fortune to be able to buy, for 90 dinars, a pony to replace my horse, which was exhausted. We took the latter with us to Scutari, but it was never again ridden on trek.

In the evening a rumour came that the town crier at Petch, was crying that the Russians had been victorious in Galicia, and that the Germans were leaving Serbia. It was also rumoured that we might be ordered back to Mitrovitza. And much as the men wanted to return to Serbia, they all shouted in chorus, "Never again along that Prishtina road."

J. G. and Mr. Little and I slept in the wagons that night. We were up at five next morning (Monday, November 29th), and when we were starting, the local Prefect came up and said he had only just heard that we were here, or he would have invited us to his house for the night. He made a charming speech of appreciation of our work, and asked me to come and drink a glass of new milk at his house. I had not time to dismount, but I shall never forget that drink of milk. It was half cream, and the daughter of the house warmed it. I had not realised, till I found myself gulping like a greedy puppy, that we had lately not been overfed. I called the other two, and they also had a gulp.

The cold was horrible all day, and the route was worse than ever: over hedges, ditches, rivers, bogs, ploughed fields and slippery ice, all the way to Petch, which we reached at 4 p.m. Major A. and his column, with hundreds of others, were encamped on the bare, frozen marshes outside the town, and he suggested that we, too, had better stop on this side of the town. But it was a bad place for a camp, no wood for fires, or shelter from the icy wind, and the ground was a swamp. Our cars were on the other side of the town, near a monastery, and that sounded very hopeful and peaceful. I was told that we should not be allowed to go through the town, but we risked it and got through. I found that the doctors and nurses and their cars were inside the monastery walls; the other cars, with the remainder of the staff, were outside, beside a stream. On the other side of the stream we placed the column. There was no wood available, in or around Petch. A Serbian soldier would sell his soul for firewood, as our Tommies would for a long drink, and I had to consent that one of our wagons, the most dilapidated, should be cut up, in order that the men might make their magic fire circles, and, whilst sitting round them, dream of past and future, and forget the present. The continuous strain and lack of food were exhausting the oxen. Every day now loads had to be readjusted, and if there was one wagon less, the men would be helped.

It was pleasant to be welcomed "home" again by the staff after a separation of six days. We took up quarters near the wagons outside the monastery. Doctor May and the unit from Kragujevatz, who had all been obliged to evacuate the Stobart Hospital, by order of the military authorities, were now, I heard, in the town on their way to England, so I went to see them, and I found that Doctor Curcin, who had at Kragujevatz been officially responsible for the welfare of foreign units, was in charge of the party, and that all arrangements had been made for their journey with ponies to the coast. They were returning to England as quickly as possible, and it was now decided that the two doctors of our Serbian-English Field Hospital, two nurses and three chauffeurs should go home with the Curcin party. I could not guarantee that I should return to London immediately. I was pledged to the Army and to the column as long as my services were needed, and I could not yet foresee what might be required of me, and it seemed wise that those who wished to make sure of being in London before Christmas, should take the opportunity of Doctor Curcin's escort. We helped them to buy ponies, and they left Petch on December 1st, for Andreavitza and Podgoritza.

CHAPTER XXXIV

The cold that first night at Petch was intense, and in the morning we couldn't put on our boots till we had unfrozen them at the fires. In the morning (Tuesday, November 30th) I went into the old Turkish town, picturesque with mosques and narrow streets, to get orders, on the telephone, from the P.M.O. I was told to do whatever was done by the Fourth Field Hospital. They were out on the frozen swamp, so I sent an orderly and told him to report their movements. In the meantime, as my hands when I was riding were generally frozen, I tried to buy some warm gloves, for though shops were all shuttered, and their owners had for the most part gone, it was possible here and there still to buy a few odds and ends, if you knew where to go. But there were no gloves to be had, so I bought a pair of short white woollen socks to wear as gloves. A clumsy, but on the whole a useful contrivance.

On Wednesday, December 1st, we had received no order to move. I went into the town to see the Kragujevatz party start on their long mountain walk, and I took possession of a couple of rooms vacated by them, for kitchen and for dining and sleeping-room. The only available site for the column was in an old Turkish graveyard, close to the house. This house, which was near the headquarters of the Montenegrin police, belonged to a Montenegrin man, who was not at home when we arrived. I wanted to take down his fence at the back of the house, as it enclosed a grass space convenient for the cars, and I asked the police if I might do this. They said perhaps I had better wait till the owner returned in the afternoon. About three o'clock, a tall, dark, heavily-built man, looking like the villain in penny novelettes, appeared; he had been in America, and spoke a very little and very bad English. Serbians in America pick up marvellously little English. We met many who, though they had been years in the United States, could not make themselves intelligible in our tongue. Our friend said he was sorry to be late, but that he had only this minute come out of gaol. "Ah, yes," I said, as though that was the place from which one naturally expected one's friends to be arriving, "and what business took you there?" "Oh!" carelessly, "I just killed a nozzer fellow here," and he pointed to his own doorstep. It seemed that his wife and the "nozzer" fellow had been on too familiar terms, and our Montenegrin giant had taken the law into his own hands, and had promptly rid himself of the enemy. He had not yet been tried, though he had been in prison for ten months and three days. But now, as Petch was being evacuated, all prisoners were set free, to escape as best they could. He gave us permission to destroy his fence. As the moral fence around his home had already been destroyed, the wooden fence must have seemed of small importance; besides, his house would soon be in the hands of the Germans, and nothing could have seemed of much consequence now except his freedom. He was lame, he had no money, and his horse was too small to carry him, so he asked if we would let him go with us over the mountains to the coast, and if we would let him ride our biggest horse in exchange for his pony. He must, otherwise, he said, be captured by the enemy. We couldn't let him be taken prisoner again, and as he said he knew all the Montenegrin roads and might be useful, we let him come with us. He came, but he didn't know the tracks, and if ever I asked his judgment as to direction, he was invariably wrong. But he was kindly and harmless, and we took him as far as Podgoritza.

In the street at Petch, I met our P.M.O., who was on his way to see me. He gave me the cheerful information that henceforth the roads would not be good. With remembrance of the road between Prishtina and Petch, still in my mind, I laughed. The P.M.O. smiled grimly, and said, yes, the roads would be even worse now, and I must at once cut our four-wheeled wagons in half, and make of them two-wheeled carts; I had better see how the Fourth Field Hospital were doing this, and do the same. Then he told me that he and Headquarters were very pleased with us, that we had done well in difficult circumstances, and he referred, with congratulations, to the fact that we had had no deserters, a trouble which had befallen other columns. He was glad, he said, that having come through so much, we were still sticking to the work. His kind words cheered me very much, for having had no previous experience of this kind of work, I didn't know if I had been doing all that was expected of me.

We were now, he said, to start to-night, or at daybreak to-morrow, with our two-wheeled carts, for Scutari, near the coast of Albania. The route was to be *via* Roshai, Berani, Andreavitza, and Podgoritza.

Thursday, December 2nd, was a busy day; the first job was to cut the wagons in half; the back portion would be left behind, and we should carry on with the front portion. It was difficult to procure saws, especially as some of the wagons belonged to the drivers, and they were not anxious to cut them up. "Nema" and "ne moshe" ("There is none" and "not possible") lurked ominously amongst the tomb-stones, but fierce-eye prevailed. Then came the sad business of sorting hospital material, for, as half a wagon is only half as large as a whole wagon, half the hospital material must be left behind, (we gave it to a hospital in Petch), also most of the equipment, and the tents, except one bell tent, to which we clung in case of desperate weather at night.

We guessed that it might be possible that even the two-wheeled carts would not be able to continue to Scutari, so we set to work to buy ponies, upon which to pack food and kit, in case the carts must be abandoned. Jordan, Colson, and Vooitch cleverly managed to find a dozen ponies, in various stages of decay; these were subsequently our salvation. But they must be rough-shod, or they would be useless in the ice and snow, and there were no blacksmiths left in Petch. Nearly everyone had now gone, and the town was deserted except by the passing soldiers and fugitives. But this difficulty, too, was overcome by the triumvirate. It was also important to procure a store of food. We tried in vain to find tinned foods, and we only had a few Serbian meats left; but we luckily found some of our precious mealie meal, also a little rice and a few beans, and we carried these in sacks, and these three things ultimately saved us from starvation.

At dusk, when I went again to the cemetery to superintend the packing of the two-wheeled carts, I found a murky atmosphere. A Turkish graveyard is, under any circumstances, a melancholy place. The ground is uncultivated, and rough, cuneiform stones, a couple of feet in height, are strewn pell-mell to mark the graves. In this cemetery every yard of ground was covered with disembowelled animals, dung, broken carts, and refuse from past encampments. The night was, as usual, pitchy dark, and it was raining heavily as I stumbled over graves, and carcases, and horrors of all kinds, to find the men, guided only by their camp fires.

I arrived at a moment of excitement. One of our drivers had just let off his rifle, whether accidentally or not, I never discovered, and he had nearly killed an officer who was passing. The officer was a little upset, and was now in a loud voice threatening to punish our man. But I invented an explanation for the incident, and expressed regret, and the officer, who was luckily otherwise preoccupied, agreed to forgive the driver.

But our men were in sulky mood. Was it a wonder? For they were now face to face with the mountains of Montenegro, which would henceforth lie between them and all they loved on earth. And now this man said he couldn't take more than one package in his cart, and another couldn't take anything: "Nema, ne moshe; nema, ne moshe" met me at every turn. The situation must be tackled; so I called the men together, round one of the camp fires, that I might see their faces. I told them how much I sympathised with them in having now to leave their country behind, and to make this journey over the mountains, into a strange land; the situation was bad, but they wouldn't make it better by bad behaviour; two "bads" did not make a "good." Prudence, as well as patriotism, required that they should go forward. If they attempted now to return to their homes, they would be imprisoned, or starved, or shot. It was only the spirit of Serbia which could some day reconquer Serbia, and they, the Serbian Army, were the guardians of that spirit. Up to now they had a splendid record of behaviour; would they not keep it unsullied to the end? Then the personal touch. Was my task an easy one? Did they wish to make it more difficult? Had I not come from afar to help their country, and would they be less patriotic than the stranger from another land? Had I not shared with them—Before I could say more, my voice was drowned in a chorus of "Ja! Ja! Maika! Ja! Ja! And don't you know that ours is the only column that has lost no men from desertion? Ja! Ja! Maika! It is hard, but we won't grumble."

And content was restored. I told them all to bring tins, or paper, for some extra rations of tea and coffee, for the trek, and the naughty mood of these impressionable, child-like, affectionate peasant soldiers was put away.

CHAPTER XXXV

We were up at 3.30 the next morning, Friday, December 3rd, to pack the ponies and get ready to start at daybreak. We must now leave our much-loved and faithful cars behind; we gave them to the Prefect, with instructions that he must burn them if the enemy arrived. We should badly miss their sleeping accommodation, but for me personally it was one anxiety the less. Possessions are at the root of all anxiety.

At 6.30 a.m. our reduced column, with its deformed carts, set out through the narrow streets of Petch, to be swallowed up in the great mountains; these already seemed ashamed of what they had in store for us, and were hiding behind thick mists of cloud and rain. Nothing was visible except the endless stream of two-wheeled carts, oxen, horses and soldiers, behind us and ahead of us. The road that day was not worse than usual, and we encamped at dark in a tiny but dry field, behind a farmhouse in which Headquarters Staff were spending the night. The P.M.O. came and had a talk with us, and said we were to move on at one next morning. That was the last time we saw or heard of Headquarters Staff till we reached Scutari.

We departed soon after 1 a.m., December 4th, and in a quarter of an hour, we arrived at a block, which, in the darkness, seemed to be composed of all the carts and oxen and soldiers of the universe—apparently on an open plain. It was too dark to see what lay ahead, blocking progress, and no one knew anything, except that movement was impossible. So we lit fires and sat around them till daylight at 6.30, when we had coffee, and moved with the multitude, a few hundred yards. But we were at once again hopelessly blocked. Then suddenly appeared, for a few minutes, our old friend, the cheery Artillery Major, who had just performed the heartrending task of destroying his three batteries. What were our little discomforts, in comparison with the grief which this keen officer and patriot must have suffered, in the destruction of his beloved guns—the last defences of his country?

We took advantage of the halt to send the drivers for hay for the oxen and horses, and we outspanned for two hours. The snow was now melting under a hot sun, and making a miry slush, which was not warming for the feet; but by the time we had procured hay, it was daylight, and as we could then see that there was no road, there seemed to be no object in waiting, so we wriggled out of the chaos of other columns, and took a track of our own—an awful track over rocks, and scrub, and amazing mud, but in the right direction; and at night we bivouacked on the slopes of a wood, overlooking plains and mountains which lay in the direction of Macedonia.

We could see the shrapnel fire, and hear the mountain guns close to us all the evening. In deep ravines in the track in front of us, lay dead horses and oxen and broken carts. At daybreak I took an excursion, on foot, with Vooitch, to inspect the route ahead of us, and it seemed impossible that carts could travel on it; the spaces between the maze of ravines, twelve feet deep, were, in places, only two or three feet broad. And, indeed, no carts were now visible, only pack ponies, and oxen with blankets strapped upon them. I was wondering what was to happen; but I had determined to make the start with carts, as I had received no order to leave them behind, when a message came from an officer in charge of the way, to say that we were to abandon wheels, and continue as best we could, with any ponies we might have had the prevision to buy at Petch. How thankful we were that we had bought some; we could otherwise have carried no food or blankets. Our oxen were now reduced to thirty-two. They could carry nothing, but they must, of course, go with us, and be saved if possible.

There was no time for sentiment; we were obliged to harden our hearts, and burn or otherwise destroy the carts.

The abandonment of carts, meant the abandonment of our beautiful hospital material and camp equipment; all our treasures must be left upon the ground. But I determined to save the instruments, and to carry them with us at whatever trouble they might cost us; they were valuable and belonged to the Serbian equipment. But, to my horror, the man in charge of them, had taken upon himself to loot the box, and had already begun distributing the knives, and other useful implements, amongst his friends. I was just in time to save them. I wrathfully made the man return the instruments. I then took them out of their box, which was heavy, and placed them in my own brown canvas rug bag, to be carried with my personal goods, instead of something else, which I left behind. But, notwithstanding this precaution, they were, to my great disappointment, stolen on the way.

We were now about to start upon a more difficult and uncomfortable phase of the journey, and the men would need heartening. At daybreak I called them together, and as I stood on a tree stump, at the edge of the wood, facing the plain and the mountains of Macedonia, the men came up and grouped themselves, in the grey light, in a half circle. "Dobrdan!" ("Good morning!") "Maika, dobrdan, dobrdan!" The sun rose blood-red over the mountains as I spoke. We must now, I said, be prepared to meet discomforts and difficulties; but though we were abandoning much, we could, and we must, take with us, goodwill and a courageous spirit; these would be of more use to Serbia, than the ointments and bandages which we were leaving behind. And now, if any man wanted to turn homewards, and risk being shot by the Germans, the Austrians, the Bulgars, or the Arnauts, he had better go now, at once, and save us from the trouble of feeding him over the mountains. Those who wanted to stay, and be loyal to their column, their Army, and their nation, could put up their hands. And every hand went up, with a shout of loyalty, and determination to keep together to the end.

Our British chauffeurs, William and Jordan, also the Serbian Ilia, and Vooitch, now adapted themselves finely to the new task of packing loads for the ponies' packs. We had only been able to procure one pack saddle, and all the other loads, containing food and blankets, we tied to the horses' backs, with string and cord, which we had brought with us. At 11.30 a.m. we turned our backs on the ruins of our column—burnt and broken carts, beds, tents, personal clothes, and, worst of all, surgical boxes and hospital equipment. Our bivouac looked as though burglars had been interrupted in looting operations, and in their flight, had left the ground strewn with the spoils. Good-bye to our hospitable field-kitchen and all its useful appurtenances; good-bye to tents and beds and the last relics of comfort; good-bye to all hope of hospital work; and, worst of all, good-bye to all hope of rescue for Serbia.

For now, all hope of help from the Allies had vanished, and the intensity of the tragedy to the Serbian nation was revealed. The journey which we were then about to take—on foot—over the mountains of Montenegro, and Albania, to the coast, is now, for thousands of human beings, a memory of mental and physical suffering, which will cause life henceforth to be seen through darkened spectacles.

CHAPTER XXXVI

Into the land of Montenegro, the land of the Black Mountains, which already threatened precipitously to bar our way, we must now force an entrance. Our first path, about two feet wide, ran through a thick wood; I went first, and led my horse, for, though there were plenty of men to lead it, I guessed that I should better be able to sympathise with the difficulties of the road, if I had to overcome them first myself; and I wished to choose the route. Colson, Jordan, Vooitch, George, and Ilia also each led a pony, and the Serbian men led the others, and the oxen. Our skeleton column was followed by other skeleton columns, and during all that day we tramped and splashed, and slipped, and scrambled, over rocks, and through scrub, in mud, and over slopes of ice and snow—a route impossible for carts.

Roads had now ceased, and even the tracks were only those which had been trampled by the multitudes in front of us; over passes 5,000 feet high; between mountains 8,000 feet high; through snow, ice, boulders, unbroken forest, mud-holes, bridgeless rivers. And always those pitiless mountains glaring at the tragedy; mountains with steep, snow-covered slopes, or mountains of grey, bare rock, precipitous, shutting out, for thousands, all hope of return to home and nationhood.

It would be impossible now to trek at night, and at dusk, I noticed ahead of us, a mountain slope covered with trees, which would give us partial shelter from the cold wind. Only another half hour's scramble, down a steep incline, in a thick wood, and rest, and fire, and supper would reward us. The last 100 yards of descent were precipitous, and at the top, my horse and I slipped on the ice, and we rolled together to the bottom. We picked ourselves up, shook ourselves, looked at each other—I was still holding the reins—and walked on. There was no one to say "Poor dear, are you hurt?" so it wasn't worth while to be hurt. Men who were passing, passed; they took no notice. Why should they? A broken leg, even a broken neck, more or less, of what consequence would such trifles be in the general havoc? During war, new values—are they better values?—are found for many things.

We were now in a narrow valley, with steep mountains close upon either side of us. We scrambled a little way up the slope on our left, and found that the whole mountain side was becamped, and we secured a small level space for our fires, with difficulty. We scraped away the snow and made a fire, with wood, of which there was, fortunately, plenty, collected some clean snow for tea water, warmed some tinned food, and had supper. Except from snow, there was no water available during the next three days. No hay was procurable for the animals, and all we could give them to eat was dead beech leaves, which we unburied from the snow. We slept round the fire, and prevented ourselves from slipping down the mountain side, by logs of wood placed at our feet. The men, with their fires, and the horses and the oxen, were close to us. And then I noticed that not only was our own hillside ablaze with camp fires, but that the lights amongst the trees upon the mountain opposite, from which we were only divided by two hundred yards of valley, were also camp fires, and not, as I had fancied, stars. Where did camp fires end and stars begin? Were there still such things as stars? Or was heaven quite shut out by earth? There was only a small piece of sky visible between the towering and overhanging mountains, and, in the darkness, heaven and earth seemed merged in a huge amphitheatre which was outlined by myriads of flickering lights. During the precious moments just before sleep—the only moments, in these times, available for thought—stars and camp fires, earth and heaven, became hopelessly mixed. I couldn't sort them, and I went to sleep, convinced that stars were the camp fires of the heavenly host, which is now out in mortal combat against the hosts of evil on our earth.

It took us, at first, a long time to pack the ponies, but we were away by dawn (Monday, December 6th), climbing up the mountain, through the fir trees, over slippery ice, and rocks which were half hidden in snow. There was no longer a defined way; the whole earth was now an untrodden track, from or to perdition. Whichever way you looked, oxen, horses, and human beings were struggling, and rolling, and stumbling, all day long, in ice and snow. Soon after we started, I saw a long column ascending a steep hillside; near the top, a horse slipped, and knocked down the man who was leading it; they both fell, and as they rolled down the slope, they knocked down all the other men and horses in the line, and these all fell like ninepins, one after the other, all the way down the mountain side.

As the physical difficulties of the route increased, the difficulty, for all the columns, of securing bread for men, and hay for oxen, and for horses, increased also, with the result that the track became more and more thickly lined, with the dead bodies of oxen, and of horses, and worse still—of men. Men by the hundred lay dead: dead from cold and hunger by the roadside, their eyes staring at the irresponsive sky; and no one could stop to bury them. But, worse still, men lay dying by the roadside, dying from cold and hunger, and no one could stay to tend them. The whole scene was a combination of mental and physical misery, difficult to describe in words. No one knows, or will ever know accurately, how many people perished, but it is believed that not less than 10,000 human beings lie sepulchred in those mountains. The route of escape, which led through Monastir to Durazzo, was even more disastrous. From amongst the army reserve of 30,000, composed of boys below, and of men above military age, 10,000 only reached Durazzo.

Many of the fugitive women, when they saw the mountains, and were faced with death from cold, fatigue, and starvation for themselves and children, went back to their Germanised villages in Serbia. Poor souls! They were between the devil and the deep sea, and they chose—the devil! The wife and two children—two boys—of one of our drivers, who had trekked with us, in one of our wagons, since Palanka, also turned back when we came to the mountains, and for their sakes I was thankful.

Except from time to time, the congestion this day was not so great, because the mass of columns was now outspread over the mountains, and the commanders chose their own tracks; but this was in some ways worse, for it meant that the responsibility for route lay now with me. Gaolbird had no sense of topography, and it was all he could do to drag his poor lame leg along; he was too heavy, in every sense, to be of use. A false track might lead to disaster, and we only vaguely knew the direction of our goal. But why should anyone fear responsibilities that come in the course of work? We can only act according to our lights. Life is a sequence of choices during every moment of existence. Even if we choose not to choose, that is equally a choice; and I risked prompt decisions to scale or descend this, that, or the other height, with audacious confidence. Progress was slow, the ponies often fell, and their loads had to be readjusted. My horse and I had many a stumble, but that served as useful warning to the others behind. I shall never cease to wonder at the pluck and endurance of our British staff, none of them accustomed to work of this sort. Specially, perhaps, was it wonderful how the two nurses, and the cook, and the honorary secretary, held out, for physically they were not as strong as the rest of us. They did not lead ponies, but they were always at hand, to help with the packs or to prepare food, light fires, and make others generally as comfortable as possible. If they had grumbled, or grown weary, they could have made unpleasant, conditions which were only difficult.

As the day wore on, the way became steeper, and more and more slippery, both up and down the mountain sides. In the afternoon, when we were half-way up a steep hill, which was covered with snow—a foot, and sometimes two or three feet deep—we reached a space which was a solid block of oxen, men and horses, all jumbled together in chaotic confusion. Evidently there was only a narrow outlet into the thick forest of pines and beeches, which covered the valley to which we must descend. To avoid the block, some columns were climbing higher up the mountain, in order to make the descent at a farther point. The majority were trying to join a track which entered the wood on the south side, and, like sheep through a gate, they were all tumbling over each other, in the scramble for places in the narrow line. We had not heard close-range guns of late, and we were now surprised to hear again loud, continuous, and near firing. We were soon told, in explanation, that a party of Arnauts, or Albanians, had entrapped, for loot, some convoys which were close behind us, in a narrow gorge, and that they were now murdering the members of the convoy. I have since heard that the wife and eight children of the Commissariat Major, including the two boys in uniform, who had walked with me one night, were all murdered that day, with many others, by these Arnauts.

We should have had to wait for hours, perhaps all night, before our turn came to get into the main line of entrance to the wood, therefore, as the further climb up the mountain, must be avoided if possible, an alternative route into the wood must be found. "Vooitch! come here." "Yes, madame." "How deep is that snow? Try it with your stick." "Two feet, madame." "Oh! That's all right. Tell the others to follow at once." And we plunged down the snow slope, on a track of our own, and forced an entrance of our own into the wood.

But the wood was as bad as anything we had yet met—steep, slippery, with rocks, and stones, tree trunks across the track, and low branches overhead hitting you in the face. It was enough to make even a woman swear, and no woman would have been human if she had not said, just now and then, a quiet "damn." The wood was interminable, and it seemed as if we should never reach the end, and touch the valley bottom, but we must get out of it before night. Besides, we could not stop; we were in the narrow line of columns. To my surprise, just before dusk, the sergeant, who always stayed with the oxen party, as there was less work to do, came up and asked if he should lead my horse for a while. It was nice of him, and, in order not to discourage him, I gave him the reins and walked ahead, selecting, as usual, the route to be followed by the others. Soon we came to a point from which the descent, for a couple of hundred yards, was sheer, and slippery with snow and ice, to the end of the track and of the valley, and the temporary end, as we believed, of trouble. For though no road was visible, and the hill rose abruptly on the other side of a small river-bed, now dry, we heard that the river-bed ended in a road, a little further on to the left. The sergeant, during his brief spell of work, was troubled by the constant slipping of the saddle, and this with other difficulties at the end of an exhausting day, was too much for his temper. When he saw this steep descent in front of us, he stopped; on our right there was a precipice. "Come along, Narednik" (sergeant), "only another two hundred yards, and our troubles are over for the day." But he refused to move, and he was holding up the rest of our column, and all the thousands who were pressing on our heels. He said the ponies couldn't do it. "But they must; they can't fly. Look! Only that tiny distance. Quick! We can't spend the rest of our lives here, and remember the Arnauts; give me the pony." I took the reins. To my horror, the man gave the pony a shove, and it fell on the edge of the precipice. I dragged at the reins, and saved the pony from falling over. I have never felt so angry, and "Damn!" saved me from bursting. I needed no interpreter. I swore, the one word I knew, and was not ashamed. I repeated it in loud tones all the way down the hill, and it took me and the pony safely to the bottom. If I had not been so angry, I couldn't have done so well. The sergeant was afterwards penitent, but I never let him lead the pony again.

It was now dark, and we must wait for stragglers who had got cut off in the wood. I stood on a rock, blowing the whistle continuously. But it was more dangerous waiting than moving. I heard a shout from one of our men, and I jumped aside, as two oxen and a horse, rolled down the hill on to the spot where I had stood. I sent some of the party a few yards up the river gully, to light a fire and make tea, whilst Vooitch and I waited for those who had been cut off. Then, when these had collected, we went on another two or three miles up the river-bed of mud and rocks, which opened into a narrow road of mud, with a thick wood on either side. With thousands of others, we bivouacked for the night, at eleven o'clock, sleeping on the ground, round a fire, amongst the trees, near the road. The snow was deep, and the ground sloping. I left my overcoat for a minute in the place where I had been sitting at supper, and when I came back, I found that it had rolled into the fire, and was making a cheerful blaze, but we fished it out, and, though full of holes, it was still wearable.

RESCUING FALLEN PACK PONY IN BRIDGELESS RIVER NEAR JABUKA

ALBANIAN MOUNTAIN TRACK OF ROCKS AND MUD HOLES
Dead Horse in foreground

CHAPTER XXXVII

Next morning at daybreak, we were about to sit round the fire, for breakfast, when old Marco, the gaolbird, strolled into camp. He had lost himself yesterday, and we had been anxious about him, for he had with him the strongest horse, which was carrying, amongst other things, our precious tea-pail and our frying-pan, the only kitchen implements now left, also some much-prized foodstuffs. We were welcoming him, when an excited officer rushed up and shouted to us to get away at once, as the Arnauts were close behind us. No one grumbled at having to go without breakfast: nobody minds going without necessaries; we only grumble when we are deprived of luxuries; and it was not necessary to hustle the few preparations for departure, and indeed these grew fewer every day. As we moved off, daylight revealed dead men, unnoticed last night, lying close beside our camp, and as we plunged into the muddy road, we saw that dead horses, and oxen, by the hundred, were lying on the track.

We welcomed mud as an improvement on the slippery ice and snow of previous days. We now realised that if worse weather had befallen, the larger portion of the Army must have perished in the snows. There was truly much cause for thankfulness.

This day the travelling was comparatively easy. At one place where there were two tracks, the road was even being controlled by officers, who, to hasten the escape from the Arnauts, and the pursuing enemies, divided horse from oxen convoys, and sent horses up the higher, and oxen along the lower mountain road. The roads joined a little later, but our convoy was allowed to keep together along the lower road.

Under normal circumstances we should have thought ourselves lucky to see such scenery—of snow, mountains, and pine woods; now we felt our luck lay in leaving it, yard by yard, behind us. But this day we stumbled upon a flowing river of real water! This was indeed lucky; the first drink, except from snow, that we, or our poor animals had enjoyed for three days. We had hoped to reach Roshai and, perhaps, house-shelter that night; but darkness came, and with it a recrudescence of track atrocities, boulders and holes, and mud above our knees. We had no more oil for our hurricane lamps, and it was unprocurable. At seven p.m. I saw that further progress, till daylight, was impossible, and the animals were exhausted. We turned aside, and with no light but the camp fires, we bivouacked in a dryish field above the town.

Every day the numbers of our oxen and of our horses were reduced, and for the last two days the poor beasts had starved on dead beech leaves; but now we were near a town, and we hoped for hay. But Sandford and Merton came back complacently with their dreadful "Nema" (there is none). There is something inexpressibly exasperating about this word "Nema." It doesn't mean, in a polite, apologetic way, "Very sorry, but there is none to be had," or "Very sorry, but I have done the best I could, and failed." It means, "Can't; shan't; won't; couldn't if I would; wouldn't if I could"; it epitomises all the obstructive negatives capable of expression in any language. It is the obverse of "Dobro," which means "All right, I will do what I can." "Nema" means "There was difficulty, and I gave it up." You can't fight against "nema"; it hits you below the belt; it represents inaction, inanity, indolence and indifference; a fourfold disease, for which there is no remedy. And "Nema nishta Bogami" ("There is none, by God"), the Montenegrin form of "Nema," was even worse; it invoked deific corroboration for assertions that you knew to be untrue.

Sandford could get no hay, so Vooitch and I must waste much precious time by searching for it. In the morning early we all trekked into the town. In ordinary times this picturesque place would have been a delight to us: the houses were of wood with grey shingle roofs; wooden ladders led from outside to the living rooms; under the living rooms were the stables in which the cattle lived. But now the houses were all shuttered and deserted; all shops were evacuated. There were no foodstuffs; nothing was obtainable. "Nema nishta Bogami" stalked triumphant, up and down the street. But hay we must have, or our animals could go no farther. The column waited in a yard, whilst Vooitch and I explored. Some regiments were quartered in the town; they had horses, and these, presumably, must be fed. We ascertained the names of the regiments, but it was not easy to find the address of their headquarters, as everyone was a stranger in the place, and no one knew anything except that he himself was looking for food and hay, and was not keen for others to find it first. Eventually we ran a regiment to earth, but the officer in command, who was in a room upstairs, must, I think, have seen me, and afraid, no doubt, that he might be asked to yield something which he could not spare, he sent word that he was not there; and in his supposed absence, the under-officer said he could do nothing. We found a mill, and gained entrance. Mealies were there, but not for us. We tried everything and everybody—in vain. Were we after all to be beaten by that beastly "Nema"? It was time now for the miracle, and at that moment two officers came riding down the street. I boldly stopped them, and found that we knew each other. We had met on the trek. They said that no hay was procurable anywhere, but that they had more than they needed, and they would—bless them!—give us twenty kilos—enough for a feed, to take us on to the next military station. We returned to the convoy, the hay was fetched, and the horses and oxen were fed. We had lost a pony, which had strayed during the night, and the others might drop down any moment, and we were lucky therefore to be able to buy two ponies, each still with four legs.

It was noon when we started; prospects were now wonderfully cheerful; the mountains by which we were surrounded, looked less forbidding, and we crossed the swiftly flowing river by a bridge. We outspanned at dusk at 4.30, a short day for once, and, for a wonder, we were offered, by an Arnaut, shelter in two rooms of his house (against payment). This was, in normal times, a roadside inn, near what was called the village of Kalatchi, though, as usual, no village was visible. The eagerness with which the offer of house shelter was accepted by our British staff surprised me; it was a fine night; the views were glorious, and I didn't want to miss seeing the dawn break over the mountains. Also, I would rather have slept out, than risk the dirt. But the desire to enjoy the comfort of having a roof overhead, was understandable, and, in case our Albanian host was not dependable, we must keep together. We had bought a sheep in Roshai, and we pretended to enjoy mightily, the toughest mutton ever chewed, as we sat round the fire in the big open chimney-place. Our host came and stared at us, and we made friends, and gave him some tea, which he much appreciated. He was not an Arnaut proper, but a Serbian Mohammedan; he was very tall and handsome; his dress, stagelike; a white turban, a short black and yellow striped coat, over a soft white shirt, tucked into white frieze trousers, which had a stripe of black braid down the leg—the dress of the Albanians, and very beautiful. But I was much worried by the trousers, for, instead of fastening nice and safely, like Christian trousers, round the waist, these fastened below the hip. This fashion was not peculiar to our friend: it was common to all Albanian "nuts," and until I learned from experience that my fears were groundless, the trousers of the Albanian gentlemen gave me much anxiety. I was possessed by a shy curiosity, which was never gratified, to know how they kept up; but an accident never occurred in my presence.

Our host, as he watched us eating, was equally surprised at our customs, and, finally, he could not restrain his curiosity. "Why on earth," he asked at last, "are you all eating separately?" (instead of all together out of a common bowl) and no one knew the answer.

We were up next morning at five (Thursday, December 9th). I saw the dawn break, and I saw the sun rise, ushered over the mountains by the usual proclamation, in pink and mauve, that here was another day, another chance of discovering some of the great truths, which we ignore, as we crawl, cramped, within our three dimensions. Everything in Nature points to the sky except man, who keeps his eyes upon the ground. I stood for a precious moment of uplifting, then I returned to crawl, and creep, and stumble, during that day, in mud worse than any yet encountered. But I wanted to take a photograph of the starting of the column. The group of men, women, and pack ponies, all in flight—emblems of this transient life—outlined, in the frail light, against the dark mountains—emblems of eternity. I placed my whip, and gloves, upon the ground whilst I took the photo. In the meantime, a passing soldier picked them up, and walked off with them. One of our men saw this, and shouted threateningly, and the soldier, in response, aimed his rifle at us. Hunger, fatigue, and misery, made men short-tempered and desperate in these days. The soldier's thumb was already on the trigger, and, quick, as lightning, one of our men put up his gun; both were on the point of firing, in "self-defence." The thunder of Austrian guns, rapidly approaching, was in our ears, so I walked briskly up to the soldier, beckoning with one hand, behind my back, to our men to keep quiet, and, as I pointed to the mountains in the north, I said, in my best Serbian, "Plenty of shooting going on over there; not wanted here; gloves and whip mine; no use to you, Molim (please)." I held out my hand for them; he gave them to me, and walked off quietly.

The loud firing near us all day, and news that a stiff battle was pending, put spurs into weary feet. The strain and effort of wading through mud, sometimes above the knees, during hour after hour of a twelve-hour day, made such a spur sometimes useful for safety. Along, and up, and down, mountain sides, and in woods, through mud lanes which never saw the sun, we scrambled till dusk. Then we outspanned on a grass slope, at the edge of a wood of firs and beech trees.

During the night, all the stars of heaven, especially Orion, and the Pleiades, blinked at us, with superior unconcern; but I told them, as I fell asleep, that it was easy for them to look pure and bright; they hadn't been wading, knee deep, all day in Balkan mud. It put me in my place, as an earthworm, that they took no notice of our troubles, but I excused them, for, if the sun, moon, stars, and all the furniture of heaven, had tumbled, in sympathy, at our feet, they would only have been buried in the mud.

CHAPTER XXXVIII

On Friday, December 10th, we were up at dawn as usual, and we trekked along a better road to Berani. When we were outside the town, halting for a few minutes, I found the men talking excitedly, and I discovered that they were very angry with Sandford and Merton. This couple, on the pretext of going on ahead, to procure bread and hay, had left us on the morning of the Arnaut scare, had taken with them the Government money, and had not returned. We had elected another commissaire, and J. G. was acting as treasurer, and using our own money. The men knew that many soldiers from other columns had deserted. To avoid evils of which they knew—hunger, weariness, discomfort and home-sickness—they had flown to others of which they knew nothing, and I guessed that our men might argue, that if now the superior Sandford and Merton had also thought it wise to desert— —. But I reminded them that there would be no Serbian homes to go to, unless the Serbian Army was preserved. The longest way round was the shortest way home. "For the sake of your own people, and your own land, you must," I told them, "march bravely forward now." "Your own people, your own land!" The words came glibly enough, though I knew that they would hack, like a sword with jagged edges, at the hearts of those dead living men. But it was my duty to keep them with us to the end, wherever and whatever that end might be.

And then, by a coincidence, Sandford and Merton at that moment reappeared. I asked them sternly where they had been, and they replied with a naïve frankness which disarmed me: "We were afraid of the Arnauts, and we ran away, to get quickly to Berani; we thought we should be safer there." Comment was useless: we are not all born heroes. But had they, I asked, at least, during their time in Berani, secured bread and hay for men and cattle? I braced myself for the inevitable answer, but when the poisonous words exuded, dropping soft and pulpy into the mud in which the men stood, "Hleba nema" (bread, none), "Ceno nema" (hay, none), "Y Berani, nema nishta" (in Berani, nothing at all), I wished I had been born in Whitechapel. Piety was out of place. But I was pious, and I told them to go back to the town and try again; Vooitch and I should also go there to secure what they would try for.

The column waited for Vooitch and me on the far side of the town. A few shops were still open, and maize bread, at exorbitant prices, was being carried by triumphant buyers through the streets. This made our mouths water, and presently gaolbird met a Montenegrin friend (from the United States) who had an official position in the town, and he generously made us a present of a huge loaf of corn bread, and sent a gens-d'arme with us across the bridge (over the river Leem) to the other side of the town, to direct us to the houses of the Prefect and of the Governor, from whom I hoped to get bread rations, now very much overdue. I felt sure from the look of things that we should get them. But I was told that the Governor was ill in bed. All the better, I thought; he won't be able to get away from me. Starving people don't stand on ceremony. I went to his bedroom, knocked at the door, for form's sake, and walked in. He didn't seem very ill. Perhaps the shock of seeing me revived him. I expressed sympathy with his illness at such an inopportune moment. Could we help him in any way? No? Very well, but he could help us. Military rations were overdue, and somewhat difficult to get. Would he very kindly write a note for us to the Prefect? This was done. The Prefect was away lunching, but after a little trouble we unearthed him, and we obtained 25 kilos of bread for the men and for ourselves. Thanks to a little searching-eye business, short-weight of loaves was discovered, and finally the glad-eye business secured an extra couple of loaves. We also obtained the hay for the cattle. I hoped that Sandford and Merton would be ashamed, but they were not.

It was three o'clock before we rejoined the others, and were able to give the ponies and the oxen food. Roshai was already in the hands of the Schwabes, and we must not dally, so we trekked till dark, bivouacked partly in a paddock, and partly in two rooms of a house belonging to an Arnaut and his wife. The latter could not read, and had never been beyond her village of Vootsche.

On Saturday, December 11th, the usual routine. Over mountains, and through mud which had been churned into jelly, by countless hoofs of oxen and horses. Towards the end of the day we were in a narrow lane, which was bounded on one side by a high hill, and on the other by a deep precipice over the river. The mud was three feet deep, and when I looked round to see if all were following, I saw one of our ponies lying, half-drowned, in the mud, and our indomitable cook was sitting on its head, to prevent the pony rolling over the edge, whilst one of the men was loosening the pack.

We were now near Andreavitza; our road led near to, but not through the town, and we cherished hopes of oil, and candles, meat and bread. We arrived at 4 (dusk) at the cross-roads, and placed the column in a convenient field, amongst trees, on the eastern side of the bridge. A blustering sergeant came up and ordered us to move; no one was allowed, he said, to camp on this side of the bridge; the officer on the bridge had given this order. I didn't believe it; our sergeant wanted to give in and meekly to move on, but as there was no other good site near, I rode on to the bridge, and saw the officer, who, of course, allowed us to stay. I would have given much that evening not to have been obliged to sally forth to look for bread and hay, but if I had not gone, the result would have been "nema nishta." The shopping party set forth full of high hopes for the town. "Buy me this, that, and the other thing," cried optimistically those who were left in camp, as if we were in Piccadilly.

But, as usual, in the town it was "Nema! nema!" everywhere. The only triumph was a tiny bunch of tallow candles, and a promise from the Prefect of bread for to-morrow. Always bread to-morrow; never bread to-day. But we met an officer who knew us, and he kindly insisted on treating us to cups of coffee, at a café which had open doors for the last time. No food was procurable. We were on our way back to camp, when in the street, a man came towards us carrying—we couldn't believe our eyes—three shining silver fish upon a string. They were not trout, but memories of happy fishing days in Norway, Sweden, Finland, gave this fish an added glory. We stopped him and asked if he would sell them. The sight of them made us fastidious towards thoughts of bully beef awaiting us in camp, and we would have given almost anything he asked. He would not sell them, but to our surprise he said: "I will give you this as a present," and he put the largest fish into my hands, and at that moment I thought Andreavitza, with its mountain setting, and its picturesque church, the most lovely townlet in the world. In camp we slept round the fire as usual, under the espionage of the highest mountains of Montenegro.

Next morning, Sunday December 12th, we were late in starting, as we had to wait for the return of the men sent to fetch the bread from the military station in Andreavitza. When the sergeant saw the fifty loaves (25 kilos), he brought with him to the distribution, an admonitory rod, to ensure that no man should take more than his due share. As long as bread was procurable, the men need not starve, as trek ox could always be sacrificed, and I frequently had the melancholy task of deciding that the weariness of death was coming over such and such an ox; he had been lovely and pleasant in his life, and now in his death, he must be divided. And for ourselves, our supply of mealie meal, and rice, and beans, still held out. We saw too much of the inward ways of oxen, along the road, to be keen to eat the roast beef of

Montenegro. We had said good-bye to butter, jam, milk, sugar, and biscuits, long ago, but we were, of course, in luxury compared with many thousands, and we had long outgrown the absurd habit of thinking that it is necessary to take nourishment every two or three hours.

And now, on this Sunday, to our surprise, we found ourselves upon a road which was more like a Corsican, than a Montenegrin road. Steep, very steep, all day long, but with excellent surface and excellently graded. We were grateful, as it allowed us to be more polite than we had been of late, to the wondrous scenery. But even now, only in a distant fashion. The beauty of Nature depends, for each one of us, upon what the mind reads into it, and the mountains of Montenegro, reflected from every stone, the hungry hearts of an exiled people.

By the evening we were amongst the hill-tops; the mountains of Montenegro and Albania were all around us, naked, precipitious, and inhospitable rocks, with occasional gloomy forests of beech, and fir trees, interspersed. Majestic, magnificent, and the magnitude of outlook, wonderful, no doubt, but my heart refused to praise this sarcophagus of hope. How could mountains be beautiful which enclosed such sorrow? How could their air invigorate, when it carried, not the scent of flowers, or the breath of the sea, but the stench of the unburied dead? As empty shells, upon the hills, reveal the presence in the past, of the waters of the sea, so the bones of men upon these mountains, will, in the future, betray the wave of human life, which flowed westwards to the coast.

The river at Andreavitza had been, when we saw it, green, of a colour which no painter could ever hope to mix; but I found myself comparing it to a green satin ribbon, which is a detestable thing. The river fell in fine cascades, and should, to a sympathetic ear, have sounded the arpeggio of the common chord of Nature; but I only heard the thumping of a child's fists upon the piano. And now the sunset hues amongst the hill-tops were, to me, the funeral colours of the dying sun, and the crimson gleam slowly spreading over the dead white snow, was bloodstain which would never melt.

Moist clouds, and mist, came down from heaven to try and veil the harshness of the mountains, in gossamers of mauve and purple, dragged from the setting sun, but they could not veil the memory of the suffering they enclosed; suffering of battle-fields and suffering worse than that of battle-fields.

We turned our eyes impatiently again to the road scenes. We were much interested in trying to induce a pony, which had been abandoned on the road, and was now recovering, to come with us: we needed all the four-legged help we could get. Colson and Jordan cheered it on with bundles of hay, and a touch of stick, and brought it into our night's camp. This latter was in a thick beech wood. The ground was our bed, and the dead beech leaves were our mattresses. During the night we had a scare of Arnauts, when a number of men rushed past us, shouting excitedly, but they were only in pursuit of a thief. If he was caught, he would be shot; if he was not caught, he would die of starvation. Death! Death! everywhere. Always Life fleeing from Death, and always Life overtaken in the end.

CHAPTER XXXIX

Next morning, Monday, December 13th, we were off early, and after half an hour's further climb, we began, to our joy, to descend. The road was tolerable, but it rained all day, and our adventures were with swift and bridgeless rivers. Ponies, with their packs, stumbled in mid-stream, and everyone, wet to the waist, must go to the rescue. We were now carrying the minimum of food and blankets, and could not afford further losses. But the ponies were so weak that, if they fell, it was unlikely that they would rise again, and then both pony and pack must be abandoned.

We wanted to reach Yabuka that night, as there was, we were told, a military station there, and bread might be obtainable. It was dark when we arrived, and rain was falling in torrents. We couldn't find the military station, for the good reason that it had already been evacuated: therefore, no bread. There were only three cottages in the place, and they were packed with soldiers and prisoners. Before turning them out into the wet, I went with Vooitch another mile, as we saw a long wooden shed ahead of us, and hoped that it might be available; the column halted by the cottages. The shed was inhabited by some officers, who said that half a mile further on there was—an hotel! and that the landlord would be sure to make room for us; some officers also were there, and if I addressed myself to them they would make things easy, etc. I was a little incredulous about the hotel, and the readiness to welcome us, but Vooitch and I rode on, only to find "nema nishta Bogami." The so-called hotel was crammed, there was not standing room; the officer of whom we had been told, was in a house opposite. We went to this, and found that one tiny room had been given to him and to his wife and family for the night. I asked him if my family might share the room with his family. He began demurring, but I suggested that it was not an ideal night for picnicking outside. He shrugged his shoulders, then pointed to the corner of the room farthest from his family; in this many soldiers, and odds and ends were crouched, and sleeping, but at the first shrug, I sent Vooitch off to fetch the others. We boldly brought in, not only ourselves, but our packs. After eating our supper, we lay down on the dirty floor on our rugs, luxuriating in having a roof over our heads. The soldiers found shelter in sheds and stables.

Amongst the fellow-inhabitants of our room, was a priest. In the game of musical chairs, for possession of the only chair in the room, he had triumphed, and he sat tight on this chair, all through the evening, and all night long. He was evidently particular about proprieties, and liked things to be done in order. Bedtime was bedtime, wherever you met it, and it must be scrupulously regarded. At ten o'clock he looked at his watch, replaced it, then, with the calm deliberation of a man who, in a well-appointed bedroom, performs the same act in the same way regularly every night of the 365 nights of the year, he removed his trousers. For a moment I was in trepidation; what was coming next? I looked round to see if the girls were asleep. Their eyes were shut. I couldn't take mine off the priest; he never looked round, he took no notice of anyone, and when the trousers were off, he sat down again on the precious chair, folded his trousers, placed them on his lap, went to sleep, sitting bolt upright, and snored vigorously all night long. I understood the trouser action; the removal was a danger signal, to keep off talkative people, or people who might want his chair. By this simple act, he established all around that chair, a Brunhilde ring of fire, through which no one dared to break. It was original and effective, and I was so grateful to him for giving me something to laugh at, that I could have—but the trousers prevented me.

Next day, Tuesday, December 14th, the weather gave us a variety. Rain, and hail, and sleet, and bitter cold all day. We had found hay for the animals last night, but none for the morning's feed, and we were still fifty-four kilometres—a two days' journey—distant from Podgoritza. No wonder that animals were lying dead in hundreds by the roadside. Bread, too, became more and more difficult to get. We had to-day seen a woman coming out of a cottage, with a loaf of corn bread in her hand. We flew at her and bought it for thirty dinars (18s.). Was it a wonder that men also were lying dead, and dying, in hundreds by the roadside? But I never grew callous to the things I saw. On the contrary, my heart grew softer, and I became more and more angry at a system of world government which permits those second-class angels to bluff mankind, and keep him from the Tree of Life, by the flourishing of a flaming sword.

After trekking for three hours, we heard that there was hay to be bought some way up a mountain on our left. So we halted at a cottage by the roadside, while the men climbed the hill to fetch the hay. Some of the drivers at first wanted to shirk the climb; I did not blame them, though I told them they must go; but one of our Englishmen commented scornfully on the laziness of the Serbian soldier, so I reminded him that yesterday, when he was in trouble with his pony, owing to mud and rain, he had lost his temper for a moment, and I now asked him if he would like his character to be judged by his behaviour at that time of only a slight trouble? The Serbian soldier, in addition to such slight troubles, was suffering from troubles which we British islanders can scarcely imagine. The Englishman had for the moment forgotten all this, and he agreed with me that the behaviour of the Serbian soldiers was, under all the circumstances, marvellous.

The road ran in hairpin curves between huge mountains of grey, bare, rugged rock. You might as well expect milk from stones, as food amongst such mountains. It was a terrible land, and I felt, as I trudged through it, that I should never want to see another mountain. But at dusk (4 p.m.) we reached the military station of Levorcka. Would this also be deserted? I sent gaolbird on to try and find rooms. He found one room and a kitchen in which we could cook food, in the house of an Arnaut woman. When I went into the living room to ask her to let us boil a kettle on her fire, a pretty little girl of eight was fastening the dress of her little sister, six years old. I said something about the children in my best Serbian, and the woman who was, at first, very curt with us, told me that she had no children; these were two lost refugees; an officer had picked them up on the road, and had left them here. The woman was very kind to them, and had grown to love them. She said that it was possible that the mother might come past this way. But the elder girl was already useful, and I wondered if the childless woman would keep a very vigorous look-out for that lost mother?

After much trouble we housed the ponies in cattle stables, and the men slept with them to prevent their being stolen. We had lost two more ponies to-day; left on the road too weak to rise, and it was doubtful whether my horse could go much further. But the men found a fine strong pony on the mountains, when they went for hay, and this was a great help.

We were, alas, too late to get bread that evening, but we were told to come again in the morning. That looked hopeful; but when, on the morning of Wednesday, December 15th, we arrived at the military station, the officer said that no bread had come, and that he had just received a telegram saying that all bread, when it came, was to be sent to the soldiers at the front—an effective silencer.

On that day we saw epitomised, the barbarous beauty of the land of Montenegro. Our route lay in narrow valleys between steep mountains of grey rock; bare of vegetation, bare of life, bare of everything but inhospitable jagged peaks which dared you to come near them. The rocks were grey, the sky was grey, and yet, suddenly, at a sharp turn of the grey road, a grey precipice pointed grimly all the way down, three thousand feet, to a tiny ribbon of the most brilliant green water that ever flowed in fairyland. In such drab surroundings, where did it get that colour? Prosaic people would say "melted snow water," but Hans Andersen would have known better than that. And so did I. But as it (the river) was quite inaccessible, it was, like everything else in the country, a forbidding sight.

But there was that day another moment of stolen joy, when, before beginning the descent towards the plain in which lay Podgoritza, the grey prison walls slid open, and revealed vast stretches of open country, distant mountains, valleys, and, in the middle of a grey mist of mountain ranges, glinting in the midday sun, a line of gold—could it be—yes, it was the Lake of Scutari. Ah! that was beautiful indeed! We had never seen anything so refreshing as that.

Old gaolbird and Sandford and Merton went on to try and get rooms, and bread and hay, in the village of Vilatz. After winding round and round the mountain side, on a narrow road, we arrived, and found Sandford and Merton sitting calmly on a rock this side of the village, "nema nishta" written in capitals all over their faces. So Vooitch and I went on into the village, and the first man to whom we spoke said, "Oh, yes," he could give us hay, and bread, and a house in which to spend the night. It was too good to be true, but we told him to wait while we went on to see the officer at the military station, to ask for bread for the men. But the officer said "nema nishta" to bread and to everything, so we went out to see what our first friend could do for us. We found the local Prefect standing outside; a tall, fine-looking man, dressed in dark blue uniform, with a revolver hanging conspicuously from his waist-belt. To our surprise, he accosted us aggressively, and said we must not buy hay or bread from the man who had offered it. The man remonstrated, and said it was his hay and his bread, and he could do what he liked with it. I was inclined to agree with him, but the Prefect then stormed and shouted, and brought out his revolver, and threatened to shoot the man if we went with him. He did not realise who we were, and that, though I was in woman's dress, I had majorly authority. We mentioned this. Then I took his name and told him that I should tell the English newspapers how a Montenegrin Prefect treated his English allies. That was a great success. At once it appeared that we had misunderstood him. He had only spoken for our good, fearing that we might be disappointed of the promised hay and bread; but, by all means, if we wished to go to the man's house, we could go. But I now guessed that, as food was scarce in the village, our friend might get into trouble if we took his stuff. The house was out of our way, so I expressed cold thanks for the permission, and we trekked to the next village (Klopot), which was said to contain hay.

The village consisted of half a dozen one-storied houses, amongst the barren rocks. Only here and there, like plums in a school pudding, were patches of green winter corn, amongst the grey boulders. To carry on the usual farce, Sandford and Merton had gone on ahead to procure hay, and we found them sitting comfortably in a cottage. "Hullo! Here you are! How much hay have you found?" "Nema nishta." "How much bread?" "Nema nishta." This form having been gone through, Vooitch and I went, as usual, to search. At the end of a long trek, I sometimes wished I was not obliged to start out to do the work of another man who had nothing else to do. But I always remembered that I was not enduring the misery of leaving my country in enemies' hands; I must not judge them till I had been similarly tried. These men were probably jewels at their own jobs in normal times. Sandford had been employed in a bank and had perhaps there learned to say "nema nishta" to his customers. The other man's job had been commercial.

But it was a little unlucky for them that on this occasion, the first man in the street whom Vooitch and I approached for hay, replied promptly, "Oh, yes," he could sell us a thousand kilos; and it was still more unlucky for them that, when we followed this man to his house, to complete the bargain, he took us straight to the house in which Sandford and Merton were at that moment comfortably settled; a proof that they had not even troubled to ask for hay. We did not want a thousand kilos, and at first our friend said we must buy all or nothing; but that was only a preamble, and he gave us 200 kilos at half a dinar a kilo. At the last village they had asked two grosch.[1] Our poor tired pony- and oxen-leaders now had a two-miles' climb over boulders, and up steep hills, to fetch hay. No bread or food for the men had been obtained or sought, and as Sandford and Merton were now quite helpless and did nothing for the men, I decided that the latter should, in future, be given money wherewith to procure food for themselves. This was at first resisted by S. and M., but I insisted, and forced them to make a list of the men's names, and to start giving the money immediately. And the men were well content, and I knew now that if there was food to be had, they would find it.

[1] A grosch equals about three half-pence.

We were in luck's way that night, for it was bitterly cold, with sleet and snow, and a Montenegrin policeman allowed us to sleep on the mud floor of his room. Going to bed was, in these days, a delightfully simple operation. Men one end of the room, women the other. No undressing, no washing; one rag on the ground to lie on, and another to cover you, and you had gone to bed, and were generally asleep in a few minutes. The unshaved men looked like elongated hedgehogs, and I was humbly thankful that Nature hadn't given me cheeks that were liable to sprout with stiff and bristly hairs at the slightest provocation.

The ponies and oxen found shelter under some rocks in a field next to our house. Our host had some rakiya, and, for a wonder, he sold us a little, so we called in the pony leaders and gave them each a small glassful. They expressed themselves, both then and on other occasions, freely, concerning the Montenegrins. They were all, of course, desperately keen to get back to Serbia one day, but never, they said, vehemently, through Montenegro. "Nema nishta Bogami" had been too severe a trial for their overstrung nerves.

The Montenegrin people seemed, to our men, selfish and unfriendly, and almost, like their country, hostile. But I reminded our soldiers that Montenegro was a poor and barren land; there was probably not more than enough food for the Montenegrin people, and now the Serbian Army and a portion of the Serbian nation had been billeted on them, and they could not afford to be generous. But, in my heart, I sympathised with our men's sentiments. I gathered, during my passage through the country, the impression that Montenegro desires above all an extension of commerce; that good roads are of first importance for this, and that Montenegrin hearts would warm most to the nation which was most likely to give them the best roads.

I was not surprised that a stouter resistance was not offered to the Austrian enemy.

CHAPTER XL

Thursday, December 16th, the last day in the mountains of Montenegro, consummated the impressions that had been stamped upon our minds of the gaunt, desolate nature of this country. Rain fell all day, as we trekked through valleys which were only wide enough for the narrow road, and for that bright green ribbon river which, below us, ran between mountains of bare, precipitous rock. Occasionally there was an interlude of basaltic formation. That was a relief, for it spoke of kinship with our Giant's Causeway, and the Caves of Staffa. By a further stretch of the imagination, it was just possible sometimes, when relenting boulders hung less threateningly over the river bank, to be reminded of the cliffs of Cornwall, but, as a rule, nothing reminded you of anything you had ever seen, or ever wished to see again.

On all sides grey prison walls, and mist and rain, shutting out earth and heaven; only the track visible, and on the track, dead oxen, inside out, surrounded by their entrails (I never knew before how multitudinous and how disgusting the internal arrangements of a simple ox could be); hungry men, slashing with knives, the still warm carcases, and marching off with hunks of bleeding flesh in their bloody hands; dead horses; dying horses who understood, and forebore to harass you with the appealing eye; and now, too, dead men at every turn—men dead from hunger, cold, fatigue and sorrow. With the dead men the pathos lay, not in their deadness—we shall all be dead some day—but in the thought that these simple, ignorant, peasant soldiers had, in these desolate mountains, laid down their lives, away from military glory and renown, for an idea which must, for many, have been blurred and indistinct, almost sub-conscious. The idea was the same as that for which Serbian soldiers had laid down their lives at Kossovo, an idea which had nothing in it of vulgar conquest or aggression, the idea that the soul of Serbia must be free, to work out its own salvation. Home, family, even country, count for nothing, if the soul of Serbia is not free. Home, family, even country must be sacrificed, if needs be, to ensure that the soul of Serbia shall be free.

At two o'clock that day we could scarcely believe our eyes. In front of us, was a break in the imprisoning rocks, and we saw an open plain, and on the far side of the plain, a town—the town of Podgoritza. Could we dare to think, for the first time, of rest from cold and hunger, treks and columns? Could we dare to think of home, and of those we loved, from whom, during three long months, we had had no tidings? No! No! Not yet.

We descended, and emerged into the open country. Our backs were now turned to the mountains; and whatever might happen in the future—and we had a notion, alas! mistaken, that the road from Podgoritza to Scutari would be more normal—whatever might be before us, the mountains of Montenegro were behind us, and we uttered a Sbogom (good-bye) of intense relief.

The mountains ended with characteristic harshness, abruptly on the plain, and soon, along a good road, we outdistanced them; but between their folds, the octopus of death was still busy, clutching with tentacles of hunger, cold, and sorrow, victims who had escaped the battlefield. I wanted to forget the past, and I would not at first look back on Sodom and Gomorrah—I remembered Lot's wife. But I had prayed, often enough, in vigorous determination, for strength to bring the column through; should I not now look back, with equally vigorous prayer and thankfulness for their deliverance? I looked back; the high mountains were closing ranks behind us, as though to guard their horrors; there was now no sign of passage-way. Yes, I looked back, and I saw a vision which would, in olden days, have been called supernatural. For, across the black mountains, from peak to base, a rainbow shone, and hid the hideousness of bare rocks, beneath its lustrous colours. It spanned earth and sky, and formed a highway from heaven, even to this cruel land. And in it I saw the token of the Covenant, which, of old, God made between Him and all flesh, that He would not destroy the living creatures that are on the earth. I saw and understood. God's Covenant still holds good. Hope guarded the entrance even to that purgatory. Therefore, we must not forget the past that was enshrined in these mountains; the memory of that past must be carried with us as a fire, wherefrom to kindle counter-fire, against the flaming sword which now destroys the living creatures which are on the earth, and keeps them from the Tree of Life.

We were soon in Podgoritza. Leaving the column in a side-street, V. and I went, according to custom, first to the military station, to ask for bread and hay. The captain in command was extremely genial and kind. But he said that no bread was available till to-morrow. I knew it was not his fault, and I said "Thank you," and was leaving; but he then broke into a eulogy of our nation; he seemed pleased because we had not grumbled at not getting bread, and he compared us with some other nations, who were not, he said, so adaptable to circumstances. Then he tried to persuade me to go to Scutari, more or less comfortably, by boat, across the lake, and to leave the soldiers to come by themselves, with the ponies and the remaining oxen by road—only ten oxen were now left. The road was, he said, execrable, and we couldn't make the journey in less than three days. But as long as there was one man and one ox left, I couldn't desert the column: I must carry on.

**MORNING MIST ABOVE THE BRIGHT
GREEN RIVER IN MONTENEGRO**

**TRACKLESS MOUNTAINS IN
MONTENEGRO, BEYOND ROSHAI**

There seemed no reason, however, why the British staff should not take advantage of the offer; they could meet me at the other end of the lake, and save themselves from days of discomfort; the Captain would make all arrangements for them. But the suggestion was met with scorn. Having gone through so much together, they loyally insisted on sharing with their chief, the fate of the column.

I then asked the officer if he could help us to find rooms, as we should be glad to get out of the rain, and he gave us an address; but every room in the town was occupied a hundred times over, and I decided that we must commandeer a room in the big school building. There must be a few spare corners left there. But "nema nishta" greeted us in every room, and no one would let us share their corner. One big class-room was being guarded by an officer's servant, for his master alone. We couldn't let that be, and eventually, as the result of a combination of fierce-eye and melting-eye business, we British staff all shared that room with the Major and his servant.

And then a charming incident occurred, typical of Serbian chivalry. The floor was filthy, but I was about to go to bed upon it, like the rest of the unit, when the Major very politely came up to me, and invited me to share the tiny platform on which his mattress was laid; the floor was there less dirty than elsewhere, as it was raised, and away from the traffic; there was just room for two people if they lay quietly. Serbian majors don't snore, so I accepted, and, raised regally above the others, the Major and I slept side by side; but it all seemed so natural that we didn't even smile. I should like to meet that Major again. We could laugh at it now. The soldiers were housed in a room downstairs, with many others, and when night came, the stairs, and the landing, were blocked with snoring soldiers.

In Serbia, sanitary arrangements had been a little difficult, but in Montenegro they gave no trouble, for they were non-existent. It was not the custom to include lavatories in the building scheme, and in that huge school-house there were none.

The town was, as usual, on the point of being evacuated, and no stores of any kind could be bought; we were told that no restaurants were open, and that no food was obtainable, but we discovered one restaurant which was that evening serving the last meal before evacuating, and we partook of that meal with some zest.

We parted here from gaolbird. He wanted to come to London with us, and I thought that the nearer we were to the coast, the more difficult it would be to prevent his coming on board, so we gave him enough money to enable him to communicate with his well-to-do friends in America, and parted. Next morning, Friday, December 17th, we did not leave till noon, as we had to wait for the bread, and for the shoeing of some ponies. Fifty-four loaves came, and these had to last us and our sixty men, till we reached the next military station, wherever that might be. We only had four loaves for ourselves.

CHAPTER XLI

The first few miles of the road were passable, over an uncultivated plain, but as the mountains of Montenegro closed sulkily behind us, the mountains of Albania opened threateningly before us. The grass plain became a swamp, and soon we were playing the same old game, wading and splashing through mud and water, no road traceable. The Albanian mountains were evidently twin brothers to the Montenegrin fiends, and after we had crossed a river, with a bridge broken off at both ends, our route lay across an expanse of basaltic rock, which looked impossible for horses and oxen.

By that time it was dark, and it seemed wise to wait till daylight to attack the new enemy, so we bivouacked in a tiny grass enclosure, near an old ruined chapel. The field belonged to an Albanian, who promptly told us to be off, but the sight of money, five dinars, and a promise of five dinars for wood, mollified him, and he became friendly, and he even said he would sell us a sheep for the men's supper. The time went on, and the sheep never arrived. I kept asking Sandford and Merton about it, and they kept saying it would come soon. Then, finally, they confessed that they had not bought it because it was too expensive. Of course, it was more expensive than it would have been in normal times, but if it kept men from starving, it was cheap at any price, and I insisted that it should be fetched. They went away as though to buy it, and came back saying that the Albanian owner had gone to bed, and couldn't bring the sheep in from the hills in the dark. Flaming-eye business; I would not be defeated, so I discovered where the Albanian lived, and went with Vooitch to his house, over stone walls and boulders and through the usual bogs.

It was a one-roomed cabin built of stone, and without windows. We knocked at the door, opened it and walked in, before there was time for anyone to deny us entrance, and in the dark, we stumbled over—the sheep! This made V. and me laugh so much, we couldn't talk for a minute. We couldn't see if the Albanian had been in bed, but he came quickly to us. We told him that we had come to fetch the sheep for supper. "But would we pay for it?" "Why, of course. How much did he want?" "20 dinars" (about 11s. 8d.). "All right. Here's the money. Now please help us to carry the sheep to the camp." It was a tiny creature, and he and V. carried it, bleating, in their arms. When we had climbed the last stone wall, and the men, who were sitting round their empty fires, saw the sheep, they shouted with joy and excitement, "Dobro, Maika; dobro, dobro." In a marvellously few minutes that poor little beast was in joints, cooking on the various fires, round which the different little groups of men sat, and, later, slept. Were Sandford and Merton really so unadaptable that they couldn't bring their consciences to pay 20 dinars for an article which, in normal times should only have cost 12? Or was there another alternative? I later reported my suspicions at Headquarters, and, in the meantime, I watched that the men did not suffer.

On Saturday, December 18th, we saw at once that it was good-bye to our hopes of a better road between Podgoritza and Scutari. Our route this day was, if possible, worse than anything we had yet encountered. Huge boulders, with deep mud-holes between, dead oxen, dead horses, dead men, every few yards. Sometimes thick scrub, with spiky thorn bushes, and with slippery foothold, was interlarded with the mud and boulders; then came basaltic rocks, superimposed in fantastic fashion, and mountainous boulders, with beech scrub, and berberis, and juniper between; but always, whatever else there might or might not be, there was mud, two and sometimes three feet deep. To-day this was of a rich red colour.

In one wood there were many dead men. In a patch of grass near one poor fellow, who was lying, where he had fallen, in the snow, green buds of young snowdrops were bravely peeping through the dead leaves, as though to adorn his grave. Beside him was his tin mug, from which he had been drinking his last drink of melted snow. For him no roll of honour; for his family no news of "killed in action." But when the war is over, and other men return, his place in the home, and the places of thousands of his comrades, will be empty. We picked bunches of snowdrops in that wood whilst waiting, during moments of a congestion of oxen, men and horses, which was now worse than ever. In another wood a long halt had to be made, whilst convoys ahead of us, took precedence at the narrow exit. One convoy which said it had been waiting there for two days, had with it hundreds of oxen, and was on the point of pushing past us, but, at the critical moment, a friendly officer came to the rescue, claiming that our horses should have precedence of oxen, and he shouted and insisted and bluffed and pushed, both our column and his own, which was even smaller now than ours, into the line. He came with us, and we bivouacked together for the night, in a tiny walled paddock, a couple of miles (over rocks and mud) above the end of the Lake of Scutari, and outside the hut of an Albanian.

The latter, as usual, at first refused us the hospitality even of his field, but he eventually yielded to the money bribe. The captain and his lieutenant supped with us. We gave them hashed and warmed tinned Serbian meats, of which we still had a few, with white beans, and a second course of boiled rice, which was one of our mainstays. We were a quaint-looking group as we sat round the fire, all smothered to the waists in thick red mud. We were obliged to let it dry upon us, as there was no water to wash it off. We had no change of clothes; we had left the last relics of such superfluities behind, when the carts were burned.

We could see, from the convergence of columns from all directions, that we should have trouble to-morrow in getting into the line of the narrow track along which we must travel. So we were up at 4.30 on Sunday, December 19th, and as the result of combined tactics, our two columns eventually pushed into the narrow track of mud and rock.

Some distance below us, was the north end of the Lake of Scutari, and it was cheering to see the beginning of the lake upon which stood—at the other end—Scutari, our goal. We hoped that our route would be beside the lake, as that would at least mean certainty of water, but we never touched it at any point.

After standing blocked during four hours in the mud, we advanced four yards. There was evidently some extra bad place causing the crush ahead of us; the horses had had no food, either last night or this morning, except from nibblings on the nearly bare paddock, and the delay might prevent us from reaching hay to-day. A slow move, a yard at a time, brought us eventually to a wood, and we understood the cause of the delay. I think nothing but the knowledge that the enemy—four enemies—were close behind, could have heartened the thousands of weary, hungry, dispirited soldiers, to urge their skeleton animals forward over the difficulties and obstructions which now met us.

Owing to the size, and number of the trees, there was only one narrow track, and progress was only possible in single file; the descent to the level of the lake, was steep and slippery, over a jumble of huge boulders, half-covered with melting snow, and ice, fallen tree trunks, deep mud-holes, and dead bodies. In one hole, we had to trample over the bodies of three horses, one on the top of the other, the top one not yet dead. Bodies of men who were dead were lifted to the side of the track; the oxen and horses had to be left where they fell.

But bad and treacherous as the track was, there was never time for hesitation; thousands of animals, and of soldiers, were pushing into you from behind, and if, leading your pony, you fell, you would be trampled on, and your pony would never rise again.

The most imaginative dreamer, after a supper of lobster and port wine, could scarcely dream a more complete nightmare. But our staff came through, as usual, with flying colours, smothered from head to foot with the aggressive red mud, but without loss of an ox or pony.

After some hours of horrors in this wood, we eventually emerged on to a narrow lane which was a sea of gelatinous and slippery mud; two steps forward, and one back. In places it was so deeply sticky that Vooitch had to haul my legs out, one after the other, as if they were things apart from me, whilst I looked on. This was refreshing, as it made us laugh at Vooitch's opportunity of pulling the chief's leg. We must continue till we reached the military station, or some place where hay could be found. Sandford and Merton had been sent on to find hay and bread, and they greeted us with the familiar "Nema." But our captain of last night had also gone ahead, and to our joy, in the evening, when it was dark, and there were symptoms of fatigue amongst the staff, and rain was falling, as it had fallen, in heavy showers all day, he appeared on the road, and said that he had found some kukurus, both for his, and for our animals, and a good camping-place for us near him. In return we gave him some of his favourite rice for supper, and porridge of mealie meal, before we started in the morning.

It was his "Slava" day, and in celebration of the event, he killed an ox, and gave us some beef, which we cooked almost before it was dead; we were very hungry, and we tried to pretend that it wasn't tough. But in the meantime another column, which was camping near us, also had a "Slava" day, and they celebrated it by killing one of our oxen. Our man, to whom the ox belonged, hadn't a sense of humour, so I had to see the officer in command of the offending column and get compensation.

We had been in luck's way here, with plenty of wood, and that, to a Serbian, is almost of as much importance as bread. I think that perhaps one of the reasons why Serbian soldiers disliked Montenegro, was the universal lack of firewood. War brings men back to primitive ideas, or lack of ideas, about things. For those engaged in war, a tree is never an oak, a beech, a willow, a fir, the marvellous result of growth and decay, birth and death, in mysterious process, during hundreds of years—a thing of beauty to be admired—it is firewood. Likewise, man, the evolutionary keystone in a process of marvels which we can only dimly divine, is not a human body, the shrine of an immortal soul: he is a soldier, reared like a pheasant, to be shot. And yet the Churches, which should lead the evolutionary movement of progress, adopt the attitude of the lamb before the shearers, and raise no protest. The human race flatters itself that it is advancing in civilisation: it mistakes the movement of the merry-go-round for progress.

CHAPTER XLII

We were early on the move on Monday, December 20th, and hoped to reach the military station within an hour or two. The route began with its usual ferocity of mud, and the continuous effort, during hour after hour, of dragging the feet out at every step, was wearisome; leg-pulling that morning became a common form of entertainment, and rain fell in torrents all day.

We reached the military station at Ritzik at 11 o'clock a.m. The office was in an old monastery, and we waited for our turn to be served with bread, in an upper room. There our hosts were two Albanian (Franciscan) monks. The ponies and oxen had to wait in the pelting rain. There was, after all, no bread, but mealies were given instead, both for the men and for ourselves. We were disappointed, but made no comment, and, as we were leaving, the officer in charge whispered to me to say nothing about it, but he gave me quietly two large corn loaves of his own, in addition to the mealies, so we gave the extra mealies to the men.

The weather grew worse all day, and at dusk a heavy thunderstorm, with drenching rain, made shelter desirable. We had fortunately reached a village, and we went up to a house and knocked at the door. The occupants were women (Albanians), and we asked for shelter; this was refused, and we tried two other houses, with the same result. But the first house had a large shed which was only open on two sides, so I insisted on putting the ponies, and men, and ourselves, under the partial shelter during the storm, but it was already crowded with soldiers, and there was not standing room for us all. The women of the house came out, and we pleaded with them, asking them to allow us to go into one of their rooms, but in reply they burst into tears. This turned the tables on us; we could not all cry, and they had thought of it first. So we had to comfort them; a horrid waste of time in the deluging rain. They said that their neighbour's house had been pillaged by soldiers, and they were afraid of our soldiers. Finally, when we dried their eyes with money, they said that they would take in the women, but that all the men must move on at once. We would not, of course, agree to this, and as we were already wet to the skin, we thought we had better get warm by walking, and try and reach the next military station, which was, we were told, only two hours distant.

The night was now pitch dark, though there should have been a moon, and as we moved away from the slight shelter of some haystacks, into the road, the heavens shook, and thunder, lightning, wind, and hailstones, hurled themselves in unrestrained fury on us from the folds of night, and progress on the invisible road, which was full of mud-holes, was difficult. After we had been walking for an hour, a flash of lightning suddenly revealed that the road had disappeared, and that we were on the edge of a broad expanse of lake. Had we missed the road in the dark, and were we about to stumble into the Lake of Scutari? Another lightning flash showed us that there was no way round the water, unless we climbed steep hedges, impossible for the pack ponies. But it could not be Scutari Lake; it must be flood, and there was nothing to be done but to plunge into the water.

It was, of course, my job to go first; so I jumped on my pony, and told the others to wait and see what happened. There was nothing to guide you as to the depth of the water, and you couldn't see a yard ahead, except when the lightning flashed capriciously; but the worst that could happen would be a ducking. I plunged; the water was up to the saddle girths, and there were holes and boulders every few yards; but we all crossed safely. We were now doubly wet, from rain above and from water below, but this was a useful encouragement to everyone to continue in spite of fatigue.

And at this point we decided that we would be bold, and push on to Scutari, as no earlier military station seemed likely. A hot drink might save some of them from catching cold, but we couldn't light fires, or stop in the pouring rain, and we had no brandy or whisky, so I concentrated thoughts on obtaining some refreshment. The miracle always happens, if you will it to happen, and look out for it. We were trudging along silently, no sign of life anywhere. All the other columns had mysteriously disappeared, and we had the dark road to ourselves, when I noticed a house, a hundred yards back from the road, on our right. I told Vooitch to go up to it, and knock, and to ask the inhabitants to give us something hot to drink; he said the house was uninhabited. "Never mind; do as I ask you." He went and knocked, and, behold, the door was promptly but charily opened. I rode quickly up, and went in, before they could shut the door, and I saw that the house had been a wine and spirit shop. Round the walls were shelves on which stood bottles. A fire was lighted in the middle of the floor, and three or four men were seated round it, on the floor, smoking and drinking. The owner said he had no wine and no rakiya in the place. He had closed his shop and had sent away his wares. But he couldn't get away from the fact that the men round the fire were drinking cognac. "Yes; very well." He would give us what he had, but he was nervous lest we should let it be known to others that his shop was open. We reassured him on this point, and within a few minutes, we were all inside that room, drinking cognac out of tiny glasses, and every man and woman of the column had his or her share. We then divided amongst us all, the two cornbread loaves given us in the morning, and we all felt much refreshed.

And at 10 p.m. we reached Scutari—Military Headquarters. It seemed too good to be true. We had reached our goal, and the human portion of the column was intact. *Nunc dimittis.* The town was deserted for the night; the streets were empty; everyone in bed. The column halted in a side street, while V. and I went to find quarters. It was too late to bother the Commandant at Headquarters. I came to the conclusion that he would not have expected men to arouse him out of his slumber, and we mustn't take advantage of sex. But we must wake somebody. People are impersonal till you know them, and you can be callous with impersonals; so I fixed on the Prefect.

He was guarded by a sentry, who was clothed in impenetrable armour of stupidity, obstinacy, and ignorance; but before he closed the door in our faces, he suggested that we should go to the headquarters of the gens-d'armerie.

We went. And after various adventures in a huge rabbit-warren building, an officer who was on duty, sent a man to take us to our own Commandant, who would, he said, probably have made arrangements for us. For an hour, whilst the others were waiting in the rain, we wandered up and down the streets with this soldier, who pretended he couldn't find the Commandant's house. Finally, when I grew fiercely angry, the man at last discovered the house, and we went in, only to find that the soldier on guard would not awaken the Commandant. I told him how angry the Colonel would be when he learned how we had been treated, and that the Commandant need not even turn in his bed, to tell the soldier where we were to go; and, in truth, as I heard next day, rooms and a good dinner had been prepared for us. But I was then desperate, and decided to go boldly to the British Consulate. We had found quarters for the men and ponies in the barracks. We, V. and I, marched to the big door in the high walls which enclosed the British Consul's house, and rang the bell. An old Italian servitor answered it. I asked him, as it was now too late to see the Consul, to let us have the use, for the night, of the Consul's kitchen, in which to dry our clothes. He said, "No; impossible." But another, older man, appeared and he was softer hearted, and said we might have a room; not the kitchen, but an empty room next to the kitchen, which was, at this time, kept for tramps. I completed the heart-softening process, with a little palm oil, and Vooitch went back to fetch the staff.

When they arrived, at 1 a.m., I was able to usher them proudly into a room which contained—a rare luxury in Scutari—a fireplace. The grate was tiny, but wood—very scarce in this town—soon made a hospitable blaze, and we crowded round that tiny fireplace, trying to dry wet clothes. Our old Italian friend brought us a kettle of boiling water for some tea, dragged out some mattresses from a corner of the room, and we laid ourselves down to sleep. We could have cried for joy at being inside a friendly house once more.

Next morning, Tuesday, December 21st, no early trek! Breakfast at the grotesquely late hour of eight o'clock; almost the first time that I had been up later than 4.30 since we left London. I was up in time to write a line to the Consul, for him to receive with his seven o'clock cup of tea, telling him of the increase of his family during the night. We didn't know that though the British Consul lived here, the owner of the house was Major Paget, an old inhabitant of Scutari. The Major came to see us at eight o'clock, and most hospitably said we might stay as long as we were in Scutari, and he told his man, Parkes, to make tea for us and to do all that he could to make us comfortable. Parkes did not need to be told twice. He was an Englishman and glad to see other English people, and he was very kind to us.

At nine o'clock, Major Paget took me to see the British Consul, Mr. F. W. Monaghan, who was also very kind. And all day long, the scene at the door of our little ground-floor-back was like a scene in the last act of a play, in which every sort of unlikely person unexpectedly turns up. We had just indexed Major Paget, and Mr. Monaghan, when the kindly countenance of Sir Charles Des Graz, British Minister, whom I had met at Nish, appeared in the doorway. He asked me to have tea with him, in the afternoon, upstairs; he also was living in the house! After that, we were not surprised when Colonel Phillips, British Military Attaché, also arrived. He had often dined with us at Kragujevatz, and he and I had never agreed upon the subject of Balkan politics.

CHAPTER XLIII

But my main business was to report myself to Colonel Guentchitch, the head of the Army Medical Service, and at eleven o'clock I went to Headquarters. There, to my great pleasure, I found, not only Colonel Guentchitch, and our P.M.O. (Major Popovitch), and Colonel Michaelovitch, and various other old friends, whom it was a joy to see again, but also our beloved Divisional Commandant, Colonel Terzitch. He had, this morning, been promoted to be Minister of War, and I was proud to be amongst the first to congratulate him on an appointment which gave everybody great satisfaction. I am not a military expert, but I cannot help believing that the retreat of our Division, as well as that of the whole Army, had been, from beginning to end, marvellously handled. To retreat, during nearly three months, fighting rearguard actions all the time, under circumstances which could scarcely have been more difficult, and to have saved the Army and its morale, was a great performance.

The new War Minister was, as he always had been, very kind to me, and he said things about the work which we had done which made me very happy. He, and our P.M.O. and Colonel Guentchitch all seemed especially pleased with us, because ours was, they said, the only column which had come in intact, without deserters, after a trek which, from first to last, had totalled a distance of about eight hundred miles. They did not, I was humbly thankful to find, regret the experiment of having given to a woman, the command of a Field Hospital Column with the active Army. I felt happy to think that we had, in an infinitesimal way, been able to give proof of British sympathy with the brave Serbian people, in the cause of freedom and idealism; and I was also glad to think that we had perhaps shown that women need not be excluded from taking a recognised share in national defence, on account of supposed inability to suffer hardships incidental to campaigns.

But credit for any success which may have been achieved, is, of course, mostly due to the loyalty and excellence of the staff who worked under my command. The doctors and the nurses never spared themselves, night or day, during times of stress of work, and adapted themselves admirably to unusual and difficult conditions. If the army had been advancing instead of retreating, they—the doctors and nurses—would have had more patients, but their work was of great value, when, and where, it was much needed. The cook was a marvel of good temper and adaptability. There was no need of a Daylight Saving Bill with her. It was never too late, or too early, for her to prepare food, when there was any to prepare, or to go without it cheerfully, when there was none.

The chauffeurs (five men and one woman) performed miracles with the cars, and showed pluck and endurance such as is not often exacted from ambulance drivers. To have brought those Ford cars over those unique roads, from Barchinatz, in the north of Serbia, to Petch, near the Montenegrin frontier, with only one accident to one car, was a wonderful feat, and their work of evacuating wounded from our own, and from other field hospitals, was of inestimable value.

The interpreter, George, did his best, but for practical purposes he knew no language but his own, and he could only read that in Croat characters.

But Vooitch, a young Bosnian Serb, spoke French, German, English, and Italian, besides his own Serbian. His position was, for various reasons, not an easy one, but I never saw him out of temper, and by unfailing service to me, night and day, he did much to strengthen weak places elsewhere in the Serbian staff. He was invaluable.

Our secretary, John Greenhalgh, had, owing to the circumstances of our prolonged retreat, not much secretarial work to do; but he acted as honorary treasurer to the British members of the unit, and, in a thousand ways, he was of service to us all. His hobby, in ordinary life, is to help others; in our field hospital he was, therefore, in his element, helping both the wounded and the staff, with kindly, unostentatious, and unsolicited services. I owe him much, for his loyalty to the command of a woman, was a fine example of unselfishness.

The sergeant was not a soldier born; he was, by constitution, weak and lazy, but he meant well. The men had at once summed him up, and they had told me, with charming *naïveté*, after the first few days of our trek, that he had no influence over them, but that they liked him because he was amiable.

Sandford and Merton were fish out of water; they were not adaptable, but they were invariably courteous and loyal.

Of the Serbian soldiers, drivers, and ambulance men, I cannot speak too highly. I loved them, and I recommended that their services should be given official recognition. They were not perfect; none of us is. While we are waiting for our wings to grow, we must fly by machinery, which is liable to defects. But these men, who had been brought up under Turkish traditions as to the position of women in the world, yielded to their woman commander, a willing obedience and a loyalty which never failed during three months. There was no physical force to back up the commands, and it was conceivable that, under the demoralising conditions of retreat, continuous flight, and privations, discipline might almost excusably have weakened, or even failed. But these men were whole-heartedly loyal from the first day to the last. It should also be remembered that every step these soldiers took, was taking them farther from their families, their homes, their country, but—and this applies also to the thousands of soldiers whom I saw during the three months of retreat—I never heard, or saw, a soldier say, or do, anything that could have given offence to the most fastidious girl, and I am proud if I have been able to render to this Serbian Army, and to the Serbian people, whom I love and respect, even the smallest service.

All, both Serbians and British, performed excellent work under difficult conditions, but the behaviour of the gallant little band who stuck bravely to the column and followed their chief over the mountains at a time when the fate of that column, and of the Army, was uncertain, deserves special recognition.

CHAPTER XLIV

But now at Scutari there was no further work in prospect, and there seemed to be no object in remaining as an embarrassment to a behungered town. If we could have been of use, we should have stayed. But the Army, at that time, intended to remain at Scutari, and there recuperate itself after its exhausting labours; it was, therefore, best for our British staff to return to England and await there subsequent events.

The British Minister and the Consul were anxious that we should leave next day for Medua, as it was uncertain how many more boats would be available to Brindisi. But we felt that we must, if possible, have one day for rest before starting on another country walk.

Colonel Guentchitch kindly arranged for us to have meals at the Hotel de la Ville, otherwise reserved for Serbian officers. In the evening J. G. and I were invited to dine, as the Colonel's guests, at the officers' mess at Staff Headquarters. About one hundred officers of the Serbian Army were dining, and I shall never forget my feelings as I took my place amongst these brave men. Of their bravery in the field, I and all the world had known, but here, now, was a more difficult bravery, most admirably shown. The hearts of these Serbian officers were brimful of the knowledge that everything which they prized on earth was lost. Their wives and children were in enemies' hands; their homes were desolate; strangers devoured their land; the imperative of a cruel suffering was upon them; yet, if you had sat and thought, for a year, of the demeanour which should be shown, under the circumstances, by officers of a defeated army, met together in exile, at the end of three months of retreat, no finer ideal of quiet dignity and courage could have been conceived.

I had seen them in the heyday of success, when, during the spring and summer of 1915, they enjoyed the knowledge that they had been the conquerors of the Austrian Army, whom they had driven from the land. They had then shown no arrogance, no vain-glory, no petty conceit of their wonderful achievement. They were modest, as conquerors, and now they were equally modest in defeat. They had been outnumbered, and attacked simultaneously on three fronts, but they had never lost heart or hope, because, though the men who fought the physical battles might be killed, the ideal for which they fought would never die; the spirit of Serbia was unconquered; the Serbian Army was saved, and in the Serbian Army, whether conquered or defeated, the Serbian spirit lived, immortal.

There were no repinings at the non-arrival of the French and English, who might have saved Serbia. There was, the officers still said, probably some good reason why the Allies had not arrived. And even if this sentiment was only expressed to spare our feelings as British subjects, it showed good taste and a refinement worthy of an advanced civilisation.

The Serbian people whom I had met during the first six months had appealed strongly to me. Lovers of poetry and of peaceful arts; intelligent and imaginative; impressionable to new ideas; warm-hearted, gay, with a keen sense of humour; brave as soldiers, courageous as citizens; responsive to the best within reach, whilst aiming at ideals possibly beyond reach: how could they fail to awaken a sympathetic response? Is there any other of the Balkan nations which could more safely be entrusted with responsibility for the evolution of culture in the Near East, than our youngest ally? I had felt this strongly during their time of triumph, but I felt it more strongly in their time of trouble. Adversity, like X-rays, reveals the bones, and the marrow, too, within the bones; and if adversity reveals no weakness, the constitution may be reckoned sound.

My old friend, Captain Doctor Yovan Yovannovitch, from whom I had received many kindnesses, was present at the dinner, and he told me that His Royal Highness the Crown Prince, had, in the morning, expressed a wish to see me. Accordingly, after dinner, I went, with the Captain, to the house in which the Prince was staying, and the Captain sent a messenger to ask if H.R.H. would like to see me now? Some important general was, at the moment, having audience, but the general was dismissed, and I was graciously asked to come in and have a talk. The Prince was in his study, sitting at his writing table, and we talked, in French, about Serbia, not as though she were dead, but as though she were a bride preparing in an ante-room of the world's cathedral, for union with the great ideal. Serbia is fortunate in possessing as heir-apparent, this intelligent, brave, and modest prince.

On Thursday, December 23rd, we must, without fail, start for Medua, or we might miss the last steamer, and we should then have to walk to

Durazzo, over tracks, which, from all accounts, were, if possible, more difficult than those we had already met. Most of our ponies were now unfit for work till they had had rest and food, and we gave them to Headquarters, and kept six.

But the road to Medua was said to be possible for ox-carts; we, therefore, ordered four, with Albanian drivers, to be at the Consul's house at 7.30 a.m. to carry our food and bedding. The girls would not ride, and I thought they might accept a lift on the carts when tired.

But the carts did not arrive. Colonel Michaelovitch, who came from Headquarters to see us off, inquired, and found that they had been kidnapped on the way. He very kindly, with much difficulty, commandeered other carts, oxen and drivers. But, in the meantime, German aeroplanes arrived, and dropped their little souvenirs all over the town. Sir Charles and J. G. and I climbed up the tower to get a view of the Taubes, and of the country around; the Lake of Scutari and the fortified rocks beyond; and the mountains—God forgive them—over which we had come, and which we had overcome. And now one of these Taube bombs elected to fall in the barracks yard, in which our men were lodged, and some of our oxen were killed as they were starting to come to us; this so scared the Albanian drivers that it was difficult to re-collect them, and it was one o'clock when they finally arrived.

Albanian carts are two-wheeled (this looked of bad omen for the road conditions), and the wheels tower above the oxen, which are very small. The cart looks as if it was composed of wheels only, the rest of it consisting of a few planks loosely nailed together. Our own Serbian soldiers now remained in Scutari, with the exception of half a dozen, whom we took with us as pony leaders. They were to return to Scutari from Medua. The Albanian drivers seemed sulky, but we hoped it was only because we didn't understand their language. The road was fairly good, and near Scutari bazaar town, which was extremely picturesque, we crossed a swift river on a real iron bridge. The lake, with its setting of high mountains, was magnificent. It was such a relief to be no longer officially responsible for a column, that there was temptation to dally. But Sir Charles had told us to hurry; he was nervous about that last boat; so we jogged on till 7.30 p.m., when we reached the village of Bashat. For a wonder, the Albanian host of the first house in which we asked for shelter, welcomed us warmly to his room, which was, as usual, up a step-ladder. He sold us hay for the horses and the oxen, also he gave us the use of his wood fire. There was no fireplace; the fire was at one end of the room, on the dried mud floor. There was no chimney, but there was no smoke in the room, because the roof was full of holes, and the plank floor also had many gapes, so there were plenty of smoke exits, both above and below. I put my whip on the floor beside me, and it disappeared into the stable below.

Our host was a widower with four sons. These sat all round the fire with their father, and gazed at us as we tried to eat our tough trek-ox steak, with some fried onions. When bedtime came, we all lay down on the floor, on our packs. I was on one side of the fire, and our host fetched his mattress and quilted bed-cover, and spread the mattress on the floor, on the other side of the fire. I wondered if he was going to undress, and I began to wish I was not quite so near. The next minute he alarmed me, for he came over to my side of the fire with his bed quilt in his hands. Good heavens! "No! No! Indeed! Many thanks. I can manage all right by myself," I answered hurriedly, in broad English, as I tucked my rug tightly round me; but he persisted in offering me his bed quilt, and as I found it was not necessary to take the owner with the quilt, I accepted the latter with gratitude, much touched at his fatherly care. But I wished with all my heart that he had not been so kind, for now I was nervous lest I might, after all, have to share that quilt with other smaller undesirable companions; it seemed highly probable from the look of the room. But it would have hurt my friend if I had refused the quilt, or had not made use of it, so I risked everything, put it over me, and—spent the night alone. I expect the cold had killed them.

I had told the ox-drivers that they were to be up at four in the morning for an early start; we must reach Medua that night. No one at Scutari had any certain knowledge about boats; but Sir Charles had said, as plainly as he could, that haste was desirable. At 4 a.m. therefore, I went out to see if the men were up, and I was greeted by our own men with the news that the Albanians had bolted, and had taken their oxen with them. They had left the carts, but these were useless without oxen. Our biggest and best horse (gaolbird's) had lain itself down to die directly we arrived last night; and unless we could procure other oxen or ponies, we must leave all our remaining food and blankets behind, and, not knowing what might still be before us, this was risky. Vooitch and I rode into the village, a couple of miles away, and saw the Prefect, but it was "Nema nishta Bogami." He could, or would, do nothing. No ponies or oxen were available, and there was no telephone or other communication with Scutari. But there were other columns encamped near. Perhaps they could lend us animals. We waited until 7 a.m., as the officers would not have liked to be disturbed before, and then Vooitch and I climbed over walls, and waded through streams, until we reached the nearest likely camp.

The captain was in bed. Seeing people in bed had lost all its terrors in these days, for no one ever undressed. He came out on being awoke by his servant, but the answer was "Nema nishta." He had no animals to spare, but he was very kind, and gave us a note to an artillery officer stationed three miles away. This time I spared Vooitch, and took our old "narednik" (sergeant) from Kragujevatz, who had joined us at Scutari. Colonel Guentchitch had wished, and had even ordered, him to accompany me from Kragujevatz, and I should have been thankful to have him, but he was so serviceable to the Kragujevatz Hospital, that I would not obey orders. On our worn and weary ponies, we crawled to the camp, and to our joy and gratitude it was "Dobro! dobro!" and we were given half a dozen ponies and half a dozen men to lead them, and with these, added to our own, we had enough. The men would bring the ponies back when we had done with them.

LEADING THE COLUMN ON FOOT OVER THE MOUNTAINS
Other columns following down the slope (to the left) behind us

LEAVING OUR NIGHT'S BIVOUAC
(between Petch and Roshai)

We eventually started with thirteen ponies at 11 o'clock. Another of our horses fell within the next quarter of an hour, and had to be left at the artillery camp as we passed. We trekked hard till 4 p.m., then halted for half an hour, to make tea in a field near Barbalucci. The main road after that was impassable, with three feet of mud, and we were warned to take to the fields. Here great caution had to be exercised, as every now and then, stretches of bog had already engulfed other unwary wayfarers, and wreckage of carts and of fiacres was plentiful. We grew more and more thankful that our drivers had run away, and had saved us from having our stuff left in a bog. Also we were able to move much quicker without oxen, and time was, as instinct told me, of importance. I am glad I did not then know of how much importance it was.

There were still mountains—mountains everywhere, but they had lost their sting. We no longer formed part of a suffering nation in flight from an invading enemy. Whatever sufferings we might meet, they would only be our own, and—we were on our way home. Home! We had not allowed ourselves to think of home till now; and now—no, it was still too early for the luxury of personal hopes.

We reached the cross-roads, near Alessio, at 6 p.m., and much regretted that the darkness hid from us the ideally beautiful little town, built picturesquely on the mountain-side by the swift River Drin. The town was only distinguishable by the lights in the houses, and by the eternal camp fires on the mountain, on the other side of the bridge. The girls, and the men too, were exhausted, and would have liked to halt for the night, but the possibility of that walk to Durazzo, gave me courage to be hard, and we pressed on, leaving Alessio on our left. Once or twice, murmurs of "Can't go any further" were audible, but I pretended not to hear; we could not be beaten on the last lap. Would the lights of San Giovanni de Medua never come in view, and what should we find when we arrived?

The last stretch of road seemed interminable. On our right were the usual bare and rocky mountains, and caves, and between them and our road, a narrow belt of grass, on which soldiers and refugees were camped. And then, at last, we saw ahead of us, lights—of Medua? And to the left of this, apart, a collection of lights like those from the cabins of a big vessel, and above, were those the mast-head signal lights? Then, thank God, this was the harbour, and this was a boat to take us home. But look! Was it only we who were moving? Or—no—there was no doubt, the huge vessel was slowly gliding out of the harbour, and making for the open sea. We were just too late.

CHAPTER XLV

It was 8.30 p.m. when we marched into Medua. We were not allowed to take the ponies through the village, which was crowded with soldiers and refugees, and amongst these we had to jostle our way. I left the party, and the ponies, and went to find Admiral Trowbridge, who was in charge of the port. I found him sitting at a table in a tiny room, about five feet square, in a cottage on the quay. I sent in my name, and when I entered the room he said: "Good God! Mrs. Stobart, why are you so late? I have been expecting you all day. The last British boat has just gone." I explained that the Germans had a trick of dropping bombs on parties who were starting to catch boats, and that Albanian peasants didn't always play the game, etc. But here we were now, and what should we do? "Well," he said, "there is a small Italian boat, already overcrowded, leaving to-night, in half an hour's time, and I have been spending a very uncomfortable day telling 3,000 people that I can't find them room on a boat which only holds 300. But, of course, you shall have places." He then amused me, for he warned me that travelling by this boat involved grave risks; to-day, all day long, submarines from below, and bombs from Taubes above, had been trying to destroy her, and had fallen within five yards of her. Medua had also been attacked, and all the Admiral's windows were smashed. The sea outside the harbour was thick with submarines, and — —. "But is there any alternative way of getting home?" "No. This is probably the last chance, except by that terrible march to Durazzo. And by that route, the rivers are swift, deep, and bridgeless, and can only be crossed by swimming. It would be almost better to fall into the hands of the Austrians than to face all that." "Very well, then," I answered, "do not let us waste time." He then sent for Commander Kerr, and told him to see us on board at once. The latter was an old friend, for he had visited our Kragujevatz camp, and we had also met him on the trek, two days out from Petch, when he had, like most people, grown his beard, and I did not at first recognise him. But I recognised him now, and shall always be grateful to him, and to the Admiral, for the successful exertions they made during that next half hour, to get us on board. My only regret was that I had not time to send a line of thanks by the returning soldiers, to the officer who had lent the ponies, and enabled us to catch this steamer. We bade a hurried farewell to our own soldiers, who cried, although we gave them our little stock of beans, and rice, and mealie meal. We had no tinned foods left.

We were hustled into a little boat, which was hailed with difficulty, to take us to the steamer, and we had no time to drink the coffee which the commander's men had kindly prepared for us. But though we were hungry, when we stepped on board, and heard that no food, not even tea or coffee, was available on the boat, none of these trifles could trouble us now, for now we were on our way home; home—a word that had during three months been banished from our minds.

There were no berths or places downstairs; the boat was crowded with refugees, and with Serbian wounded officers, and some families, on their way to France and Switzerland; but the night was fine, and the sea smooth, and we sat on deck all night, in life-belts. We were accompanied by two torpedo boats, and we reached Brindisi without adventure, at noon on Christmas Day.

We had promised ourselves a Christmas dinner at a good restaurant or hotel, but we were greeted, in the harbour, with the news that the Brindisians were afraid of typhus, and that we should not be allowed to land, until just before the train left for Rome in the evening. We had had no food since the night before last, and we spent Christmas Day, close to the first town we had seen for three months which was not in process of evacuation, gazing at the big houses, in which greedy people were probably overeating themselves with good things. The British Consul could not come on board. He had sprained his ankle—a Christmas Day sprain with which we had every sympathy. I sent him a message, and the Vice-Consul arrived, full of abstract kindness, but the non-landing rule was inexorable. He stayed with us to take me and our treasurer, at 6 p.m., to see the Consul and to make money arrangements for the journey to London. The rest of the party must wait at the station. In the station restaurant the most tempting-looking food was flauntingly displayed. Might the staff not enter this Land of Promise while I saw the Consul? No; admission was forbidden to all who had come from overseas; but a kindly English resident in Brindisi, who made it his work to look after refugees, undertook to bring food, from the restaurant, to our starving ones on the station platform, and, bless him, he worked nobly for them whilst I went to see the Consul.

There were no cabs, and we three walked to the Consul's house. I thought we should never get there. On the way we passed a shop, the most glorious shop I had ever seen. I couldn't believe my eyes. It was full of real hams, and tongues, and sausages. "Oh! I must go in here and buy some food for the unit for the journey," I cried to the Vice-Consul, overcome by the desire to see and touch and make sure of real food. "Better not now; it will do on the way back," he answered indifferently, and we left the shop behind. I turned round to locate it in my memory, for even though it was closed, I should not leave Brindisi till I had secured some of those good things.

We reached the Consul's house at seven o'clock, and went into the drawing-room with the Vice-Consul. The door of the dining-room was partly open, and I saw the sprained ankle laid out all over the side-board. I have never felt so hungry in my life. The Consul greeted us kindly. He was walking about; the ankle only confined him to the house. "How do you do, Mrs. Stobart? Would you like a biscuit?" I hoped at first that he was joking, but he was not. "Oh, yes," I answered, ready to cry with disappointment, "we're starving." Then he brought a tin of biscuits and some port wine. That was better. He gave us the biscuit tin to take with us, and he very kindly told the Vice-Consul to arrange for supper for us all in the train. As to money, we could have as much as we wanted; he had plenty. He gave us the sum for which we asked, sealed in an envelope; it was not worth while, he said, for us to count it. He was sure it was all right. I knew I ought to have counted it, but there was not much time to spare to catch our train; and when we opened the envelope, later, we found he had given us a thousand lire too much. Had it been a thousand lire too little, I should not have liked to write and tell him.

My anxiety now was to obtain a railway pass. As it was Christmas Day, the Consul said he couldn't get an official pass. The Prefect couldn't be found; his ankle was more seriously sprained; we should have to take our chance. We should get to Bari, two hours distant, safely, and if we had trouble there, we must telegraph to the Consulate. Not a very encouraging prospect, especially as the Vice-Consul told us that another party had been kept for two days at Bari.

But now for that sausage shop. The V.-C. came with us, in a cab, and we found the shop. It was crammed full of things we had not seen for nine months. On the counter was a lovely-looking Italian sausage. I asked the shopman to cut a slice, and to let me taste it. It was an absurdly thin slice, and I soon asked for another; and then I looked for J. G. He was busy browsing all round the shop, on bits of cheese, and figs, and dates, but he gave immediate attention to the slice of sausage I offered him. I don't know what the V.-C. must have thought of us, but my thought was that everybody ought to be made to starve sometimes, just to know what it feels like; they wouldn't then ask starving people to look in at sausage shops on their way back. But the V.-C. was delaying his own Christmas dinner for our sakes, and he nobly insisted on coming with us to the station. He saw us into the train, which left at 8.37 p.m., and he gave us lovely parcels of supper for the journey; supper number two for the others, who had now eaten well, and drunk red Italian wine, and were very happy. We reached Bari three hours later. I went to see the Station Commandant; he was charming, and made no trouble about the railway passport, and he gave us, free of cost, compartments to ourselves in the train leaving at 11.30 for Rome, through Central Italy. We reached Rome at 6 p.m. on Sunday, December 26th, and at the Station Hotel Restaurant, we had our first good sit-down, hot meal. We shall never forget that dinner.

At Rome station, and everywhere on the journey, we were stared at, as though we were a menagerie. People crowded round us in quaintest fashion. We did not realise it, but perhaps our clothes looked weather-worn.

From Rome we were, at last, able to send telegrams home to our friends, who had heard no news of us for three months. At this station again, directly we arrived, I went to see the Station Commandant, and asked him to expedite us farther. "Yes, by all means; first or second class?" "First, of course." And we reached Pisa at 6 a.m. on Monday, December 27th; Spezzia at 8. At Culoz we changed, at 11 p.m., for Paris, and arrived there at 8.30 a.m., December 28th. Here I had a little difficulty, and was sent from one department, in one end of Paris, to another department, at the other end of the town, all the morning, to obtain the railway pass. Amongst other offices to which I was directed, was that of the "Intelligence Anglaise." But when I arrived there, I found neither the one nor the other. Finally, I went to the War Office, and I saw the Minister of War, who was very courteous, and, though I had to wait a long time, I eventually took away the necessary papers. We all drove from the Gare de Lyons to the Gare du Nord, for Boulogne, only to be told that the boats from Boulogne had been discontinued three weeks ago, and that we had better make for some other port. That was a blow; but as the pass had just been made out by the War Office, for Boulogne, I assumed that a military boat would take us across, and that we had better risk it.

We left for Boulogne at 1.15 on Tuesday, December 28th. The train was horribly slow, and we did not reach Boulogne till 11 p.m. I thought we might possibly have trouble here, about the pass, as we were nearing the land of white chalk and red tape. I inquired at once, as usual, at the station, for the Commandant, found his office, and, to my surprise and joy, was greeted by "Hulloa! Mrs. Stobart, I *am* glad to see you." An old friend, of whom I had lost sight for some years. He was in charge of the Transport Service, and I knew that the way would now be smooth. He gave us supper in the excellent Red Cross restaurant; found rooms for us at a good hotel (no easy job, as the town was crowded), and facilitated in every way our departure for London, next day, by military boat. We reached Charing Cross on the evening of Wednesday, December 29th, after an absence in the Balkans of nine months—having travelled free of railway cost, through Serbia, Montenegro, Albania, Italy, France and England.

Our telegrams from Rome must have misfired. There was no one at the station to meet us. Were they all dead? Or—but evidently London had not yet been evacuated. Indeed, as we drove through the streets, we wondered if peace had been declared. What a contrast! Here, thousands of sleek and well-dressed people, jostling each other for places in the music-halls; and out there, thousands of people, hungry, thirsty, and in rags, jostling each other to escape every conceivable form of horror. But we were, thank God, at home again. We had done nothing wonderful—women are not allowed to do wonderful things—but we were content to feel that we had contributed our tiny share towards the relief of suffering, and we had, perhaps, made it easier for other women to do more in future times.

PART IV

But this story will have failed in its purpose if it has not served as a demonstration of three facts. It should show, without need of further proof, that women can be of service, not only in base hospitals of war, both in subsidiary positions, and in positions of command—that had already been shown—but in flying field hospitals at the front. Thus men can be set free for the fighting line. Much work at present done by the Royal Army Medical Corps could safely be entrusted to women. The proof given of the capacity of women to endure hardships and privations incidental to campaigns, also points to the possibility of the employment of women along the lines of communication, in various forms of war work now performed by men. Much valuable fighting material could thus be liberated.

The story should also show, if only, alas! in a small way, something of the courage, dignity, and spirit of the Serbian people. It is difficult for those who have not had first-hand evidence, to realise the heroism of the Serbian nation, not only during their defeat and their retreat, October to December, 1915, but also during the summer of political temptation in 1915. At that time Serbia understood, only too well, the intentions of the Bulgarians, and if she had acted as her political instinct prompted her, the inevitable clash would have occurred, not at the moment of Bulgaria's choice, but at a time favourable to Serbia. It is useless now to conjecture the effect of this "might-have-been" on the history of the war. But in the summer of 1915, the temptation for Serbia to strike at her own convenience, must have been great. And whether the Allies, in urging Serbia to abstain, were right, or wrong, successful or unsuccessful, they owe much to Serbia for her loyal adherence to their policy. Serbia was justified in expecting from them, in return, the help which never came.

But another, and perhaps a greater, temptation must have presented itself to Serbia. Why should not the Serbians have acted as the Bulgarians had acted? Why should they not save their country from further invasion, avoid further conflict, and come to terms with Austria? Their nation and their Army were impoverished by previous efforts; would it not now be wise to save their country from further devastations? Their performances against the Austrians, in the autumn of 1914, had shown the latter that they were worthy of respect, and no one in Europe could accuse them of cowardice. Why, and for whose benefit, should their beautiful land and their heroic people be further sacrificed? As Serbian politicians looked from the heights of their Serbian mountains, upon the glories of their fertile land, a land of corn and bread, a land of wine and vineyards, they must have heard the Tempter's words, whispering as of old, "All these things will I give you if—if—you will fall down and worship militarism and the Central Powers." But with one voice, the Serbian people answered, "Get thee behind me, Satan. It is written in our hearts, 'Thou shalt worship Freedom: her only shalt thou serve.'" Thus Serbia, the latest evolved of the European nations, perceived, with an insight at which history will one day marvel, the inner, the true interpretation of the word "nation." She perceived that the life force of a nation is a spiritual force, and is not dependent on material conditions for existence. Serbia had existed during 500 years of material annihilation under Turkish rule. Through all that wilderness of time, the ideal of freedom had been her pillar of cloud by day, and of fire by night, pointing to the Promised Land. Serbia is again in the wilderness, and the same light guides and cheers her. She is full of courageous faith, because she understands that a nation means, primarily, not physical country (mountains, rivers, valleys), not State, not Government, but a free and united spirit. That is the only definition which allows of the indefinite expansion which will some day include all human kind in one united nation. Serbia is full of faith and hope, because she knows that she is not, and never will be, deprived of nationhood.

In some minor ways, Serbia may, in her civilisation, have been behind other nations in the west of Europe, but she was ahead of Western Europe in that one thing, which is of real importance, that one thing which cannot be copied or learned from other nations, and which is, therefore, either innate or unachieveable: Serbia is ahead of other nations, in her power of sacrificing herself for ideals. All nations are ready to sacrifice life for nationhood. Serbia made first this common sacrifice, but when that did not avail, she voluntarily, for the sake of an abstract and spiritual ideal, made the supreme sacrifice, the sacrifice of country, the sacrifice for which other nations make the penultimate sacrifice of life. The Serbian people sacrificed their country, rather than bow the knee to militarism and foreign tyranny; they sacrificed their country, in Utopian quest for the right, both for themselves and for other Slav brethren, to work out their own salvation, in spiritual freedom. A people with such ideals, and with such power of sacrifice, must be worthy of a great future.

CHAPTER XLVI

Finally, the story will have failed in its purpose, if it has not shown something of what women feel towards war; if it has not shown that militarism is likely to find in woman, its most vigorous opponent, not because woman lacks courage to face death, but because she is awake to the duty of facing life; life as the basis, the evolutionary basis, of a higher life.

Until woman had obtained some experience of war, she could only express sentiments concerning war; but now she is at liberty to give opinions as to the meaning of war. And in the opinion of woman—at least, of one woman, who is, presumably, representative of some other women—war means—the failure of society.

Society has failed to protect its members from its own more savage elements; it has failed to overcome the tendency to atavism, latent in all living creatures; it has failed in its primary function of preserving life. In all its dealings with life, society shows cynicism and inconsistency. It punishes the taking of life, called "murder," by a further taking of life, which it calls the "death penalty." Again, society holds that no motive justifies murder when it is retail, and concerns individuals; but that when murder is wholesale, and concerns nations, no motive justifies abstention from the murder-fields.

Society thus teaches that the taking of life, though it is regarded as the biggest crime, and receives the biggest punishment, is not, in itself, wrong. It is only, on some occasions, and for some social purposes, inexpedient. Society is not yet awake to the idea that, for spiritual purposes, the taking of human life is always inexpedient, because human life is not an end in itself, but a stepping-stone to further life, which may possibly be forfeited by blundering mankind.

In the eyes of woman, war also means the negation of civilisation and of progress. Of what use the care and labour spent in science, art, culture, education, if, at the command of militarism, these and their votaries are to be periodically blotted out.

Civilisation, as we were taught, meant the progress of the human race in ideals, spiritual and moral. Civilisation, as our children are being taught, means progress in the invention of machines for destroying life—the one thing on earth which can't be made by machines. (The word "artillery," with its present murderous meaning, derived from Latin "ars," "artis," art!)

War means that all the finest intellects, of the finest of God's creatures, are set to vie one with the other—on what false track of evolution are we rushing?—to vie, one with the other, how best to destroy life and to precipitate death! Death is sacred, but not life.

War means blood, slaughter, brutality, deformities, and always death, death, death. Is man jealous of God, that he destroys God's handiwork, and spares his own, when he runs amok? When the Germans destroyed, at Louvain, the works of man, a howl of horror rose from every voice and newspaper throughout the civilised world. But during this European war, thousands of unique specimens of the works of God, Europe's finest manhood, are every day being destroyed, and we are still waiting for the howl of horror.

The other day I was told by one who witnessed it, that, from one trench, 800 men were killed within three minutes. Now it takes women years and years of infinite love, and patience, of sacrifice, and devotion, to mould their sons—their creations—after the image of God, in body, soul and mind. They fashion, with infinite pains, these precious lives for God, and the end is—to be blown to pieces, 800 in three minutes. To this end has the wisdom of Man brought Man. Could the wisdom of Woman bring us to a worse abyss than this? However desperate the remedy, must not the help of woman be hailed, to save life from the abyss?

This thought came to me vividly one summer night in Serbia. It was during the typhus epidemic, and I stumbled unawares upon an open grave. It was three-quarters full of naked corpses. They were typhus victims. They had been prisoners of war, and the grave would not be closed until there were enough dead to fill it. Heavy rain had fallen, and the bodies were half-submerged in water; but I saw one man above the others. His body, long and strong-limbed, was all uncovered, but his face, fine featured, proudly ignorant of the ignominy, his face was covered with—flies; filthy, bloodsucking flies. Round his finely-cut nostrils, his mouth, his half-opened eyes, squatting, buzzing, sucking, shunting one another for best place—flies, flies, flies, and no one to beat them off. Flies in thousands, squabbling for his blood, and no one to beat them off. Only flies knew where he was. His mother was, perhaps, at this moment, picturing him as a hero, and he was—food for flies.

The night, in old parlance, would have been called glorious. But is there glory on this bloodstained earth? The stars of heaven were shining; but could stars be of heaven, and blink, and blink, and blink complacently, and nothing else, when they might have set the heavens ablaze, in a million fiery points of indignation, at the bloody sights which they were seeing on the earth?

And the moon—cold, cruel, heartless moon, hidden at first, behind a thunder cloud—emerged suddenly, with revengeful triumph, to illumine the grave, lest I might miss the horror; turned on full candle-power to show me, a woman, to show me *that*, and other things unspeakable. I walked away quickly, tears burning in my eyes; angry, cursing in my heart, the ways of men who bring these things to pass. But I remembered that he was unmourned—alone—and for her sake, his mother's sake, I came back, and knelt beside that charnel pit, to spread round him, as she would have done, thoughts of love, and, oh, God! how difficult, of Faith and Hope. "You're not alone!" I cried aloud, that the stars and moon, and God, if He were near, should hear, and understand. "You are not alone, for the hearts of all the mothers on the earth are with you—in your open grave—and will one day rescue you and all their sons from—flies."

The glamour, the adventure, the chivalry, which of old gilded the horrors of war, have vanished. War is now a bloody business; a business for butchers, not for high-souled gentlemen. Modern militarism involves tortures and extermination, not only of the fighting, but of the non-fighting portion of the population, in a manner which would have shocked even the heroes of the Old Testament.

War is not merely an encounter between rival armies of men. War is, in these days, an encounter between equipped armies, and unequipped women and children, with results that are bestial and humiliating; between equipped armies and unequipped civilisation, with results that are destructive of civilisation.

War, with brutal butchery, destroys millions of human lives for paltry purposes: to avenge the death of an Archduke or to gain commercial profits. But if life is a thing of meaning, a divine gift, to be divinely handled, for divine purposes; if life is, as mankind generally professes, the chain upon which the evolution towards super-conscious man is strung, the chain upon which the pearl of immortality is hung; if life, as an abstract possession of the human race, is all this, and more besides, then war, which aims at the destruction of this priceless gift, is a cosmic blunder, which only devils bent upon the annihilation of the human race, could have conceived.

Militarism has, in one country at least, reached a climax, and I believe it is because we women feel in our souls, that life has a meaning, and a value, which are in danger of being lost in militarism, that we are, at this moment, instinctively asking society to give us a share in safeguarding the destinies of those human lives, for which Nature has made us specially responsible.

The idea of votes for women, or justice for women, is not here my concern; the idea, which, as a result of my small experiences, engulfs all others, is the necessity of votes for life, justice for humankind. This can only be achieved by the suppression of war, and wars will never be suppressed by men alone. Man, says Bacon, loves danger better than travail; man, says Nietzsche, loves danger better than play. Men still regard battles as magnified football scrums; war is still for many men a glorified sport, as letters from the soldiers at the front daily testify. "The spirit of our boys was splendid. They simply loved the fun." "He simply turned from right to left, and fired as if he was in a shooting saloon. It was the best bit of fancy shooting I have seen," etc. (*Daily News*, Saturday, July 8th, 1916). The courage required for facing battlefields is superb, but that same courage, channelled for moral, social, and spiritual purposes, might create a new heaven and earth. The more "natural" it seems for man to fight his fellow-man, in order to acquire supremacy, the more urgent is it for society to intervene; for the progress of man is secured, not by yielding to natural environment, but by resistance to environment.

Society has failed in its primary function of preserving life. But society has hitherto been controlled by men only, and men have always been more interested in producing death, than in preserving life. Bergson shows that man, who is so knowing when he deals with the tangible dead life of machines, is quite unseeing when confronted with the intangible life of humans. We have yet to see whether Bergson's "man" should also include woman. Had one-tenth part of the money spent by society in producing death—and we, in this country, are spending five million pounds sterling for that purpose every day—been spent on investigations as to the best methods of preserving life, the world might have reached a higher stage of evolution than its present phase of militarism. But Nature, in her beneficence, generally arranges that side by side with the poisonous plant, the antidote shall grow, and thus, side by side with the growth of militarism, has also grown the woman's movement.

The care of life, before and after birth, has been given by God, and by man, to woman. Woman has hitherto protected the concrete life of individuals; must she not now, in an enlarged sphere, also protect the abstract life of humankind?

Democracy, in which pacifists had placed high hopes, has failed as a protective social force; but democracy is not yet democracy, for it consists of men only, and democratic men do not differ from other men in instinct.

The Scriptures say that it was a woman who first had courage to taste the Tree of Knowledge of Good and Evil (symbol of the dawn of human consciousness). That woman was, at the time, blamed by both God and man; but man certainly would not, if he could, go back to the state of subconscious life from which she delivered him, and God, if He is all-powerful, permitted the deliverance.

And now the Tree of Life, of spiritual life, or super-consciousness, still stands in the unwalled garden, waiting for some daring soul to force an entrance, to taste of its fruit, and live for ever. With prophetic insight, the poets of Genesis predicted the order of salvation: first, the Tree of Knowledge, material knowledge, and then the Tree of Life, spiritual life. But they tell us, that the way to the Tree of Life, is past the flaming sword, which turns north, south, east, and west; and we, in these days, can well believe it. Now man, with his physical force, has failed to extinguish the flame, which flames at this moment more forbiddingly than ever. Man has failed, but may not this be because the force required for the extinction of the flame, is not physical, but spiritual? And now woman, who has not her own interests, but the interests of human kind, at heart, suggests, with all humbleness, that if human kind is ever to reach the Tree of Life, the spiritual power of woman must be added to the physical force of man, in a determined effort to extinguish that flaming sword—for ever and ever. Amen.

PART V

Letter from Colonel Dr. Lazar Guentchitch, Head of the Serbian Army Medical Service, to the Chief of the English Medical Mission, Madame St. Clair Stobart.

"Knowing your hospital as one of the best arranged amongst foreign hospitals, thoroughly organised for the work nearer the front and supplied with all up-to-date necessary material and utensils, I have the honour to inform you that your hospital is on that account selected to keep in touch with our Army—in case it moves or comes into contact with the enemy—keeping always behind the Army and close thereto, and thus be enabled to do the work of a real Field Hospital.

"Since your arrival in Serbia, Madame, you have succeeded in giving to your hospital—first intended for military purposes only—a further function of wider importance, by extending the same in a form of Ambulance sections solely for civilian needs. This meant a greater boon still, as our nation was almost left without doctors, all having been engaged with the Army. The huge number of ambulance patients who call on your Roadside Dispensary, situated close to the hospital of your Mission in Kragujevatz, is the best proof how good the idea was of forming such ambulances.

"Therefore it will quite meet the situation that your hospital—during this lull until the Army operations begin—be extended by adding a few sections for the treatment of civilians in the nearer districts.

"With the personnel and material now at your disposal you will be able to establish some other small dispensaries in a few places in the vicinity, besides the hospital in Kragujevatz, and thus work right up to the re-commencement of war operations, when all the various sections will quickly join into one big sanitary organisation, prepared to meet every requirement near the front.

"I have the honour, therefore, to request you to kindly inform the Committee, by whose help you have organised and brought your Mission to Serbia, as well as your personnel, which is assisting you most heartily in your continuous aims to help the Serbian nation, and to make clear to them how urgent is the necessity for your hospital to continue its work in Serbia for a further period.

"Colonel Dr. Guentchitch,
"*Chief of Sanitary Section.*

"*June 26th (July 9th), 1915.*
"Kragujevatz."

Letter from the Chief of the Serbian Army Medical Service (translated at the Serbian Legation, London):

"General Headquarters.

"S.D. No. 29273.

"On the occasion of the suspension of the combined Anglo-Serbian Field Hospital, over which you had command during the last fighting and retreat of the Serbian Army, from the first half of September until the 9th December, 1915, I have the honour to address the following letter to you:

"Soon after your arrival in Serbia, at the head of the Mission whose chief you were, you organised, by the middle of April, 1915, a hospital at Kragujevatz, where the Serbian Headquarters were—a hospital, including tents for the Serbian wounded and sick soldiers, and provided with all the necessary things, and a trained medical staff. Your hospital began with our wounded work at once, and was an example for all, with its inner organisation.

"Everybody who took an interest in the sanitary organisation, and visited Kragujevatz at the time, considered it as his duty to visit your hospital, and everybody has observed its work and order with pleasure; and thus your hospital has become one of the most popular organisations in Serbia.

"It did not take long before your hospital at Kragujevatz enlarged its work for the civilians and female population, and so became a combined hospital for the Serbian wounded and civil and female population.

"At the very beginning of your work you conceived the idea of starting an ambulance not far from the hospital, and close to the road, where the Serbian peasants had to pass going to Kragujevatz, free of charge to these peasants, for medical consultation and the distribution of medicine, and providing the sick with tea and food.

"The success of your first Road Ambulance was so quick that nearly 150 persons a day from the town and villages came for consultation and medicine. It was quite natural, for just at that time the population remained without medical help, as our doctors were very busy with the difficult task of suppressing the contagious diseases in the Serbian Army.

"The unexpected success and popularity attained by your first ambulance, in so short a time, suggested to you a plan to organise such ambulances outside Kragujevatz, in outlying districts. Your persistent work, and the reception given to your useful idea by the Serbian Relief Fund in London, and other people, who helped you with their contributions and personal participation, made it possible to have in a short time, in the very heart of Serbia—in Shumadia— quite a number of such useful and humane ambulances, provided with all the necessary things to give medical help to the population and, indeed, those ambulances during the time of their existence, have done invaluable service to our country, and population, and have become popular, and attracted always increasing numbers of sick people. For the short time in these ambulances which you erected in Kragujevatz, Lapovo, Natalintsi, Rudnik and Ovcarska Banja, Vitanovatz, and Rekovatz, there were more than 20,000 medical consultations and successful injections of serum, for diphtheria and typhoid, on children and grown-up people, and much medicine has been distributed free of charge, and not only all the possible help, but consolation too.

"The sick people who required hospital attendance were sent from these ambulances to your Base Hospital at Kragujevatz, there to undergo operations, to be bandaged and examined with the X-rays, and poor soldiers provided with clothing, underwear, and other necessities.

"With the erection of the road and village ambulances was satisfied a great necessity to fight the contagious diseases of our people, because in that way medical help was given there where it was not easy to be found. Respected Madame,

"In Petch they were ordered to take as much hospital material as could be conveyed by the bullock carts, which are specially arranged for such purposes, and the personnel were instructed to call upon the English Military Attaché for further instructions regarding the evacuation.

"The Chief of the Hospital, Mrs. St. Clair Stobart, with her Secretary and the other Serbian Nurses, left Petch for Podgoritza, Kastrati, until Scutari, she traversing almost impassable roads. The remainder of the English personnel were directed previously to go to Scutari.

"During all the warfare, as well as during the retirement, the Chief of the Hospital, Mrs. St. Clair Stobart, was riding continuously (on her horse) at the head of her unit, as a splendid example to all, keeping the discipline at the most critical moments.

"For her strenuous and successful work in her hospital, besides grateful thanks, Mrs. St. Clair Stobart (Chief of the Hospital) deserves the highest merits and decorations for her unceasing and untiring work.

"Bozidar Terzic.
"*Commandant Colonel.*"

The Serbian Legation certifies that this
Document is a true translation from the Serbian.
By order of the Serbian Minister,
(seal)

Georges V. Tadorovic,
Secretary.

Traduction and Certifying free of charge, No. 1489.
London, January 5th, 1916.

you can be satisfied with the result you and your helpers attained, and believe that your action, and the work of the Serbian Relief Fund in London, will be remembered deeply by the Serbians, who have suffered much, and you have earned their eternal gratitude.

"In the sanitary history of the Serbo-Austrian War 1914-15, and the history of fighting with epidemics and diseases amongst the Serbian population, the village and road ambulances of Mrs. Stobart took the first place at that time.

"When, at the beginning of September, to every Serbian it was clear that there were new enemy attacks to be expected on all sides, the invasion of Austro-German troops on one side, and the Bulgarians on the other, you did not stop in carrying your original idea into practice, and during the military operations you followed the troops. At once there was organised the First Combined Anglo-Serbian Hospital, which consisted of your medical staff from Kragujevatz Military Hospital, and a certain number of the Serbian additional staff. The inspector of the Serbian Headquarters appointed you Chief of the Hospital in appreciation of your services. It is the first case in our military history that a lady has been given the appointment of Commander of an operating unit during the war. Your First Combined Anglo-Serbian Field Hospital, together with the automobiles and other material for transports, has been attached to one of our best divisions, the Shumadia Division, which, during the last campaign has had the most important and most difficult task. You have been in command with the Division on the Bulgarian front (Second Army), and afterwards you were transported with the same Division to the Northern Front (Third Army), where your Division had to fight against three German Divisions.

"The Commander of the Shumadia Division, Col. B. Terzitch, who is the Serbian War Minister at present, has expressed his best praise for the First Combined Anglo-Serbian Field Hospital, and your cleverness and endurance in commanding that hospital. With your automobiles for the wounded, you have transported during the fighting with the Germans, about 650 wounded officers and men, and all who have seen you work, agreed with the favourable opinion about you. And when the Serbian Army started the first difficult retreat through Montenegro and Albania, you did not abandon your hospital and Division, but, riding on horseback and at the head of your Hospital Unit, you remained as part of the Division till the arrival in Scutari, going through all difficulties.

"You brought successfully, with your energy and splendid behaviour, all your staff to Scutari. It was a tremendous task to achieve, on account of the many difficulties and inconveniences through which the Serbians had to pass. Your hospital was the only one that knew how to save the staff and bring same to Scutari. That can be explained by the fact that you did not give up your command for one moment, and shared all the war difficulties and inconveniences. You have made everybody believe that a woman can overcome and endure all the war difficulties, and as a Commander of a Medical Unit, can save all the staff, and at the same time doing useful work whilst going back to your great Motherland. You can be sure, esteemed Madame, that you have won the sympathies of the whole of Serbia through your useful work, and that you have left the best impressions. The Serbian Army feels a very deep gratitude for the work you have done.

"By order of the Chief of the Staff at the Headquarters.

"Colonel Dr. Lazar Guentchitch.

"*Scutari, December 9th, 1915.*"

The Serbian Legation certifies that the above is a translation from the Serbian.

By order of the Serbian Minister.

(seal)
Georges V. Todorovic,
Secretary.

London, January 21st, 1916.

LEGATION ROYALE DE SERBIE.

Who is writing: Commandant of the 1st Schumadia Division, Scutari.
To whom: The Chief of the Headquarters of the Army Medical Service.
No. 25201. 9-xii-1915.

"By order of the Chief of the Headquarters of the Serbian Sanitary Department, the Anglo-Serbian Field Hospital has been added to this Division, under the name of the First Combined Anglo-Serbian Hospital. For the Chief of this Hospital has been nominated Mrs. St. Clair Stobart, and for the Secretary Mr. J. H. Greenhalgh. In addition, this hospital had two Lady Physicians, Nurses and other English personnel, altogether a total of 17 people.

"This hospital had 30 bullock-carts, 7 horse-carts, 6 light automobiles, a great store of sanitary material, medicines and other sanitary necessities, with a sufficient number of large tents. The above hospital has the capacity for receiving up to 150 military patients. For the work in the hospital 50 orderlies have been engaged, also one chemist, an accountant and the other necessary personnel.

"This hospital, with the personnel, had been transported from Kragujevatz to Pirot by railway, and they started their work in the village of Suvodol, on August 20th of last year. Since that date, during all the warfare, this hospital has done the principal work as the second firing line Field Hospital, because this division had always a very long fighting line.

"This hospital, in this capacity, has always been on the spot, according to their official orders, and even near the firing line, where they have done stoically their work until they received further orders to move.

"According to the hospital's Register it has received and attended to 596 wounded soldiers and 52 patients. Notwithstanding these figures, the number is even greater, for on certain occasions the wounded were not entered, so many were there and so little time to enter their names.

"The wounded soldiers have been excellently attended to and very well dressed.

"The evacuation of patients and wounded, not only from this hospital, but also from the central firing line Field Hospital, as well as from other hospitals, has been greatly facilitated—taking into consideration the terrible weather—by the loan of the light automobiles of this hospital. The hospital retired, acting according to official orders, together with the troops of this Division, beginning from the place in front of Smederevo to Petch.